The Concept of
Schizophrenia:
Historical Perspectives

The Concept of Schizophrenia: Historical Perspectives

Edited by
John G. Howells, M.D.

American Psychiatric Press, Inc.

Washington, DC
London, England

Copyright © 1991 American Psychiatric Press, Inc.

ALL RIGHTS RESERVED
Manufactured in the United States of America on acid-free paper.
First Edition

94 93 92 91 4 3 2 1

American Psychiatric Press, Inc.
1400 K Street, N.W., Washington, DC 20005

Library of Congress Cataloging-in-Publication Data

The concept of schizophrenia / edited by John G. Howells. — 1st ed.
    p.   cm.
    Includes bibliographical references.
    ISBN 0-88048-108-0 (alk. paper)
    1. Schizophrenia—History.   I. Howells, John G.
    [DNLM: 1. Psychological Theory. 2. Schizophrenia—history. WW 11.1 C744]
RC514.C587   1991
616.89′82′009—dc20
DNLM/DLC
for Library of Congress   90-529
                                                 CIP

British Library Cataloguing in Publication Data

A CIP record is available from the British Library.

Contents

Contributors

LAURETTA BENDER, M.D.
Formerly Clinical Professor of Psychiatry, University of Maryland
School of Medicine, Baltimore, Maryland

JOHN HOENIG, M.D.
Professor of Psychiatry, Clarke Institute of Psychiatry, University of
Toronto, Toronto, Ontario, Canada

JOHN G. HOWELLS, M.D.
Formerly Director, Institute of Family Psychiatry, Ipswich, United
Kingdom

DORIS B. NAGEL, M.D.
Clinical Assistant Professor of Psychiatry, History of Psychiatry Section,
New York Hospital-Cornell Medical Center, Ithaca, New York

CHARLES P. PETERS, M.D., F.R.C.P., F.R.C.Psych, F.R.C.P.(C.)
Chief of Service, Personality Disorder Treatment Program, Sheppard and
Enoch Pratt Hospital, Baltimore, Maryland

U. H. PETERS, M.D.
Director, Universitas-Nervenklinik, University of Cologne, Cologne,
West Germany

GIUSEPPE ROCCATAGLIATA, M.D.
Associate Professor of Psychiatry, University of Genoa School of
Medicine, Genoa, Italy

MARK J. SEDLER, M.D.
Department of Psychiatry and Behavioral Sciences, State University of
New York at Stony Brook, Stony Brook, New York, and the Section
on the History of Psychiatry, Cornell University Medical College,
Ithaca, New York

MICHAEL H. STONE, M.D.
Professor of Clinical Psychiatry, Cornell University Medical College,
Ithaca, New York, and Unit Chief, The New York Hospital-Westchester
Division, White Plains, New York

Introduction

John G. Howells, M.D.

The statesman, Winston Churchill, had a vivid saying: "The farther back you look, the farther forward you can see." This phrase contains the main justification for historical research: past knowledge can be of value to present practice. The subject of this volume, the concept of schizophrenia through past history, is a prime example of this justification at work. From the effort of an international group of historical researchers—Italian, German, Canadian, American, and British—we are able to draw conclusions of fundamental importance to contemporary psychiatry, both research and practice. A reward of such a magnitude was unexpected.

The volume is divided into two areas of research. In the first, the concept of schizophrenia is traced from the classical period up to the present; an additional related chapter describes the history of the concept of childhood schizophrenia. We wish to know whether the condition we term *schizophrenia* today existed in former times. We are interested in any views held on etiology, nosology, symptomatology, and treatment. Of special interest are any clinical or research insights highlighted by a consideration of a time span of approximately 4,000 years.

In the second area, the history of the psychodynamics of schizophrenia is explored as to its possible etiology in adult or family psychopathology; a brief chapter also considers the attempts at psychotherapy of schizophrenia by a distinguished group of early psychotherapists. We are concerned to know whether there is a psychodynamics of schizophrenia and what insights spring from this field of inquiry.

Historical research on schizophrenia will meet the same methodological problems as in different types of research (e.g., biochemical, epidemiologic, histologic) as well as problems particular to historical research. Before a discussion of methodological problems, attention must be addressed to a recent controversy.

Is Schizophrenia of Recent Origin?

Some would argue that to search the centuries for schizophrenia is a valueless task because schizophrenia is of recent origin. Torrey (1) stated that schizophrenia is associated with modern civilization and is possibly of viral origin. He asserted that there are no descriptions of schizophrenia as we know it before the early 19th century, when Halsem (2) in England and Pinel (3) in France gave clear descriptions. Hare (4a, 4b) supported Torrey's viewpoint. He pointed to the sudden increase in the mental hospital population in the second half of the 19th century and argued that much of this was due to an epidemic of schizophrenia, suggesting again a viral hypothesis in etiology.

Jablensky (5), however, reported that only 9.1% of the men and 7.3% of the women first admitted to the University Psychiatric Clinic at Munich in 1908 were diagnosed as suffering from dementia praecox, and this was at the time of the expansion of mental hospitals in Europe. Hare (4a, 4b) conceded that there may be sociological factors at work to explain the sudden increase in the hospital population. We know that the decrease in recent times is not due to a reduction in identified cases of schizophrenia, or a specific treatment. It is due to an increase in the psychiatric work in the outpatient departments of general hospitals and the planned program for moving patients from the hospital to community resources. The same explosion in the provision for the physically ill also occurred at the end of the 19th century.

Others have argued strongly in the opposite direction, claiming clear accounts of schizophrenia through history. Wilson (6) claimed that there are verbatim utterances of schizophrenic patients in Babylonian documents of the second millenium B.C. and gives instances. (There would be more conviction if hallucinations were not invariably of the visual kind.) Moss (7) quoted the Satires of Horace (65–08 B.C.), which are said to teem with terms referable to mental illness. He wrote of a man of Argos in Horace, Epistles 2.2, who was clearly deluded. Moss also pointed to a description given by Caelius Aurelianus in the fifth century A.D. and Alexander of Tralles (A.D. 525–605). In addition to the cases quoted by Wilson and Moss, Jeste et al. (8) also quoted descriptions from ancient Indian medicine from as far back as the 14th century B.C. and that of Herodotus (480–425 B.C.) with his description of the mad king Cleomenes, king of Sparta. Jeste et al. quoted from Celsus (9) (25 B.C.–A.D. 50), who noted three types of insanity. The first two were phrenitis and melancholia. The third type of insanity was described as follows:

There is a third kind of madness, the longest of all so that it does not injure life itself, and which is accustomed to be a disease of a strong body. But there are two kinds of this; for some are deceived by false images, not in their judgment: such as poets report the raving Ajax or Orestes to have perceived. Some are disordered in their judgment. (p. 242)

Jeste et al. (8) also mentioned some of the material on the medieval period covered elsewhere (Howells, Chapter 2, this volume).

Diethelm (10) maintained that Felix Platter (1536–1614) presented "clear observations of schizophrenic illness" but under the term *mania*. He also quoted André Du Laurens (1560?–1609), who gives account of vivid delusions under the term *melancholia*.

Jeste et al. (8) also quoted two cases of the 17th century. The first case is of an English minister, George Trosse, plagued by auditory hallucinations. However, Hare (11) convincingly showed that the minister was suffering from alcoholic hallucinosis. The second case was that of a diary kept by a patient Christoph Haizmann, which was later published (12).

Ellard (13) analyzed 2,039 mentally disordered patients of a country general practice in England between 1597 and 1634 (37 years). It seems that there is one clear-cut description of schizophrenia, four possible cases, and a number of suggestive cases. Ellard concluded: "if what we are seeking [schizophrenia] existed in G. K. Napier's time it was probably not a common disorder" (p. 306). Warner (14) estimated that Napier saw no more than a dozen patients a year in the category of "mad," "lunatic," "distracted," or "mopish" (but not necessarily schizophrenic). The prevalence of schizophrenia seems to be low in general practice, which deals with a representative sample of people, as indicated by John Hall in the early 17th century (discussed by Howells and Osborn [15]) and by Kessel (16) in the 20th century.

In the 17th century also came Thomas Willis's (1621–1675) notions on "foolishness," which appears to resemble descriptions of simple schizophrenia.

Ellard (13) considered a collection of cases reported by Perfect, the keeper of a private madhouse. The cases, drawn from the last quarter of the 18th century, consisted of inmates of a private madhouse. Of the 108 recorded cases, 4 may approximate schizophrenia. This does not suggest that private mental hospitals then were full of schizophrenic patients.

After the 18th century came descriptions by Haslem (2) and others of dementia in the young.

Jeste et al. (8) discussed a number of reasons why descriptions of schizophrenia are rare in history. First, many physical conditions recognized today were not recorded in previous centuries either. Schizophrenia has to be recognized in written sources and not in mummies, statues, and photographs, which makes recognition more difficult. Second, a syndrome-orientated approach is recent; in previous centuries, the concentration was on symptoms and their description. This helps to explain why only partial glimpses of schizophrenia are seen in patients classified by their symptoms. Third, given that schizophrenia is a chronic, intractable condition, it was not likely to attract the attention of physicians whose success depended on effective treatment. Fourth, there was confusion over terminology in the past, as there is today. Fifth, due to their condition, schizophrenics were unlikely to take the initiative to seek help and to make their plight known. Finally, Jeste et al. pointed to the possibility that schizophrenia may have changed with time; catalepsy was described frequently over the centuries but is a rare manifestation of schizophrenia today.

Some see the manifestations of schizophrenia having changed over the last 50 years, not the condition itself. Ellard (13) is convinced of this; he sees a less florid condition today. This view is supported by Zubin et al. (17), Romano (18), and Hare (19).

If schizophrenia has not changed, then conditions confused with it may well have changed. Toxic states set up by dietary deficiency in early history may be replaced by industrial toxins later (e.g., the mercuric nitrate of "The Mad Hatter") and by drug addiction today. Treatment by herbs was replaced by mercury, later by bromide, and today by powerful drugs; all could confuse the clinical picture by their side effects.

Again, as will be shown later, the occurrence of cases of schizophrenia under the terms *dementia* and *amentia* rather than the term insanity may have been neglected in historical research.

Finally, to the above can be added the argument that schizophrenia is known to exist widely in the world today and in preindustrialized countries (20). However, there is much to suggest that its prevalence is low, then and now.

Methodological Problems

Diagnosis

An essential component of the methodology of a research project is to define the nature of the object under study. Immediately, in the case of schizophrenia, there are difficulties. The name itself is unsatisfactory. The term *schizophrenia* was first employed by Eugen Bleuler (1857–1939), a Swiss psychiatrist and, for a time, a collaborator of Sigmund Freud (1856–1939), who saw the condition as a split in psychic functioning due to unknown causes, some primary, or physiogenic, and some secondary, or psychogenic. The term, derived from the Greek words for "to split" and "mind," replaced the term *dementia praecox* first used by Benedict A. Morel (1809–1873), a French psychiatrist; *praecox* for Morel denoted "a rapid mental impairment" and not "dementia at an early age" as is often supposed. Early age, however, is a feature of the condition and is found in one of the first modern descriptions of the disease—that by J. Haslem (2) below, the English apothecary of Bethlem Hospital.

Early descriptions of schizophrenia were made by Willis, Haslem (1764–1844), and Pinel (1745–1826); all are reported here.

Cranefield (21) claimed that Willis gave the first description of schizophrenia when discussing dementia under the term *foolishness*. He quoted from a chapter of Willis's De Anima Brutorum (Chapter 13, Section S) as follows:

> for those affected with this latter, apprehend simple things well enough, destrously and swiftly, and retain them firm in their memory, but by reason of a defect of judgment, they compose or divide their notions evilly, and very badly inferr one thing from another; moreover, by their folly, and acting sinistrously (awkwardly) and ridiculously, they move laughter in the by standers.

Herewith Haslem's (2) detailed account:

> Connected with loss of memory, there is a form of insanity which occurs in young persons; and, as far as these cases have been the subject of my observation, they have been more frequently noticed in females. Those whom I have seen, have been distinguished by prompt capacity and lively disposition: and in general have become the favourites of parents and tutors, by their facility in acquiring knowledge, and by a prematurity of attainment. This disorder commences, about, or shortly after, the period of menstruation, and in many instances has been unconnected with hereditary taint; as far as could be ascertained by minute enquiry. The attack is almost imperceptible; some months usually elapse, before it becomes the subject of particular notice; and fond relatives are frequently deceived by the hope that it is only an abatement of excessive vivacity, conducing to a prudent reserve, and steadiness of character. A degree of apparent thoughtfulness and inactivity precede, together with a diminution of the ordinary curiosity, concerning that which is passing before them; and they therefore neglect those objects and pursuits which formerly proved sources of delight and instruction. Their sensibility appears to be considerably blunted; they do not bear the same affection towards their parents and relations; they become unfeeling to kindness, and careless of reproof. To their companions they show a cold civility, but take no interest whatever in their concerns. If they read a book, they are unable to give any account of its contents; sometimes, with steadfast eyes, they will dwell for an hour on one page, and then turn over a number in a few minutes. It is very difficult to persuade them to write, which most readily develops their state of mind: much time is consumed and little produced. The subject is repeatedly begun, but they seldom advance beyond a sentence or two: the orthography becomes puzzling, and by endeavouring to adjust the spelling, the subject vanishes. As their apathy increases they are negligent of their dress, and inattentive to personal cleanliness. Frequently they seem to experience transient impulses of passion, but these have no source in sentiment; the tears which trickle down at one time, are as unmeaning as the loud laugh which succeeds them; and it often happens that a momentary gust of anger, with its attendant invectives, ceases before the threat can be concluded. As the disorder increases, the urine and faeces are passed without restraint, and from the indolence which accom-

panies it, they generally become corpulent. Thus in the interval between puberty and manhood, I have painfully witnessed this hopeless and degrading change, which in a short time has transformed the most promising and vigorous intellect into a slavering and bloated ideot. (p. 64)

For Pinel (22), *dementia* was characterized by

a rapid succession or uninterrupted alteration of insulated ideas, and evanescent and unconnected emotions. Continually repeated acts of extravagence: complete forgetfulness of every previous state: diminished sensibility to external impressions: abolition of the faculty of judgement: perpetual activity.

It might be expected that since there have been descriptions of the illness since Haslem, a period of 180 years as I write, there would be agreement by contemporary writers on the symptomatology of schizophrenia. This is not the case. The criteria adopted by Kurt Schneider for diagnosing schizophrenia (discussed by Mellor [23]) are so different from those by Feighner et al. (24) as almost to suggest that there are two separate conditions under the term *schizophrenia*. Torrey (1) asserted that the Russian description of schizophrenia differs so much from the American DSM-III (25) criteria as to cause one to ask whether they are the same condition. Seven systems for the diagnosis of schizophrenia (26) were compared for their agreement for the diagnosis of schizophrenia. They varied eightfold on their rates of the diagnosis of schizophrenia. Nor did any of the systems (27) predict strongly the short-term outcome of the management of schizophrenia at follow-up. International researchers are not in agreement on the criteria for schizophrenia (28, 29). It has been estimated that about 16 papers per week are published on schizophrenia (30). Faced with this confusion, researchers might be expected to be particularly careful to publish their notions of schizophrenia in their reports. Fischer (31) surveyed 26 papers in a reputable psychiatric journal, *The Archives of General Psychiatry*, and found that only one included the investigator's definition of schizophrenia. Fischer concluded that the prevailing concept of schizophrenia "does not comply with the criteria of a scientific law."

Much weight is given to Kraepelin's (1855–1926) description of dementia praecox. From where did Kraepelin get his cases? Altschule (32) pointed out that "in those days about half the patients in the mental hospitals had syphilis and perhaps another large group had different kinds of degenerative brain diseases and tumours. Some of the cases that Kraepelin and others reported at the time were really cases of syphilis." In states of early dementia, was he describing juvenile syphilis? Kraepelin was aware of the marked variability of the psychiatric manifestations of general paralysis (33); he speculated that this occurred because "the destructive process acts on individuals with different types of constitutional predisposition." The "marked variability" could be responsible for his different groupings of schizophrenics. The standards Kraepelin established for differential diagnosis were highly unsatisfactory (34).

There is, however, some general consensus concerning the important features of schizophrenia. First, it is a disorder of younger age groups. Second, there is disordered thinking, which may be manifest in abnormalities of speech and action. Third, there is emotional flattening. Fourth, delusions are common. Fifth, auditory hallucinations are much more common than are visual hallucinations.

Differential diagnosis is not always easy. Kroll and Bachrach (35) pointed to the difficulties of diagnosis in the present upsurge of drug addiction. Of 23 subjects in a research project on hallucinations, they found that 11 (48%) used street drugs to a significant extent. This fact "is a major source of contamination in diagnostic studies of young adult psychotics." Could this suggest that insidious types of schizophrenia are early dementias on Feighner criteria, whereas the florid types of schizophrenia are being confused with toxic states?

Prevalence

In searching sources for traces of schizophrenia in the past, a key issue is how common a condition is this disorder? Should we find it intruding everywhere as common as the common cold or is it a rarity? The answer depends on what you call schizophrenia. If the definition is so wide as almost to embrace all mental disorder, then the rate of prevalence is high. Some say that schizophrenia affects 1% of the population, with an estimated two million new cases occurring in the world every year (36). However, in a general medical practice of approximately 3,000 patients, Kessel (16) could find only 3 schizophrenic patients—a prevalence rate of 0.1%. One estimate is 10 times the other. It seems that another factor is the country in which the estimate is made. The Cooper et al. (28) study showed that schizophrenia is commonly diagnosed in the United States and depression is commonly diagnosed in the United Kingdom. It may well be that the rarity with which schizophrenia appears in the literature before 1900 is due as much to stricter criteria as to paucity of data. The flood gates had yet to be opened by Bleuler.

This brief overview of the present state of our understanding of schizophrenia throws light on some of the inevitable difficulties to be met in tracing through history an unclear, and probably rare, entity. The problems are so great as even to raise the question: "does schizophrenia exist today?" However, this attempt at historical research may throw light on the true nature of the condition itself and offer some commentary on our present difficulties.

Problems of Historical Research

Research is dependent on data. In some periods of history, the data are scant. Greek and Roman sources are remarkably rich in material, and there are many scholars expert in these languages. The study of the post-Roman period in Europe, on the other hand, often reveals little material. Linguistic experts in this period are few. Only after the 16th century in England, for instance, are scholars able to read material unless they are expert in Old English and Middle English or are fortunate to work on translations. This difficulty leads to this period of history being dubbed the "Dark Ages," a derogation dependent on a particular lacuna of expertise by scholars.

Some of the material is poor in quality from all periods. Usually it lacks sufficient content and descriptive quality to make its interpretation possible with certainty. Again, the interpretation of data on schizophrenia depends on the researcher's notion of schizophrenia. Paradoxically, the widening of the definition of schizophrenia in this century adds to the difficulties. Again, related but peripheral clinical data are taken for the substance of the condition. The ideal situation—a detailed, systematic, case history that would be acknowledged by a diversity of clinicians as indubitably schizophrenia—is not forthcoming.

Established schizophrenia, by its nature, does not allow the subject the initiative to record his or her mental experiences. In the 17th century, the writings by Trosse (37) appeared to be an exception; however, as has been said, Hare's (11) careful analysis of the autobiography explodes any notion that it might be schizophrenia. In the 19th century, Perceval endured a number of admissions to private madhouses (38). There are vivid descriptions of his experiences in his well-documented account. However, the acute nature of the episodes and the presence of visual hallucinations taken together with the subsequent course (he married and fathered four children) create some doubt about the diagnosis of schizophrenia.

A real difficulty in historical research on mental disorders is to find that a great number of terms can be used for the same condition. For *insanity*, we have *insania* (first used by Cicero [106–43 B.C.] in his *Tusculanae Disputationes), furiosus, furor, frenetics, paranoia* (Hippocrates 460–377 B.C.), *demes, de non sain memoire, madness, possession, catalepsy,* and *non sans mentis.* For *mental retardation*, we have *amentia, fatuitas, witless,* and *amens et extra sensum.*

To this must be added that tendency by authorities to use a term to cover different entities. The Greeks used the term *frenzy* for what the Romans called *melancholia. Mania* in the classical period was reserved for states of great excitement, but in the 19th century it was used as a generic term for insanity; today it covers a specific syndrome indicating elation. *Paranoia* in the classical period was used to cover mental disorders, but later in the 19th century and today it covers states of abnormal suspicion. *Amentia* was used by Cullen (1710–1790) to cover dementia. *Hebephrenia* was employed by

Hecker (1843–1909) to cover "youthful insanity," but by the 20th century it was employed to cover "florid" schizophrenia. A term might also be employed to cover more than one condition; *melancholie* in the medieval period covered the condition of depression and a less common one manifesting delusion (akin to schizophrenia?).

Schizophrenia had a clear description as an early form of dementia in the 19th century. Before the 19th century, however, its different symptoms would appear under different terms. In the medieval period, for example, "disorders of thought" and "withdrawal" would be features of melancholie. Schizophrenic excitement would be covered by mania. Delusions, with ideas of reference or influence, would appear under "possession." Visual hallucinations would be classified under "visions."

Too little attention has been given to the possibility that schizophrenia was classified as "dementia" in early history rather than under "insanity." The history of dementia is traced by Berrios (39). The term *dementia* was probably first used by Celsus (Book III) but covered states of severe delirium (phrenesis). Berrios recorded that dementia has been known as *démence* in the French literature since 1381. In the 19th century schizophrenia was seen as a form of dementia occurring in the young. Quain's (40) *Dictionary of Medicine*, for example, described acute primary dementia as occurring in young people under 20 years of age; the description has many of the features of schizophrenia but is classified under "dementia" rather than under "insanity."

In searching sources for traces of schizophrenia as early dementia, Zelmanowits (41) cited accounts by Esquirol (1838), Rousseau (1857), Moreau (1859), Morel (1860), Falret (1876), Saury (1886), Langdon Down (1887), Clouston (1888), Spratling (1889), Charpentier (1890), Svetlin (1891), and Pick (1891). There were also descriptions by Burrows (1820), Gauthier (1883), and Kraft Ebbing (1904). In 1896 came Kraepelin's first description of the condition of dementia praecox. The description taken from the 5th edition of his *Psychiatrie* is happily now available in translation (34). He regarded dementia praecox as a disease of young people, "usually" accompanied by physical signs, and accounting for 5–6% of admissions to his clinic. In addition, he postulated a morbid process in the brain to account for it. His account of differential diagnosis is most inadequate. Kraepelin maintained that the first precise description of dementia praecox was given by Hecker (42) in 1871. Hecker's term *hebephrenia* was his term for "youthful insanity"—the "hebe" is derived from Hebe, the Greek goddess of youth (43).

Again, schizophrenia in the past may have been classified under mental retardation. Cullen used the term *amentia* for the condition termed *dementia* by others. Willis, as quoted in Cranefield (21) earlier, described a condition akin to schizophrenia under the term *foolishness*; we are reminded of *stolidus* (foolish) used in Roman nosology. Had others in history recorded their cases of schizophrenia under "mental retardation" rather than "mental disorder" or "insanity"? Schizophrenic patients, even today, can be found in hospitals for the mentally retarded.

Findings

That throughout history, abnormal states of mind, "madness," have been recognized is proven. This behavior was deemed outside normal limits, outside understanding, and outside the individual's control. States of abnormal rationality; strange, inexplicable, irresponsible behavior, and an inability to organize one's affairs led to the protection of the individual, of others, and of the individual's property. Treatment was offered within the capacity of the times. Sometimes management involved confinement.

"Madness" was also differentiated from "idiocy." Legislation from the Roman period made a distinction between the mad and the foolish, as reviewed in Chapter 2 (Howells, this volume). Shakespeare stated it clearly: "Fools are not mad folks" (Cymbeline). John Locke, as quoted in Howells and Osborn (43), expressed it succinctly as follows: "Madmen put wrong ideas together, and so make wrong propositions, but argue and reason right from them: but idiots make very few or no propositions, and reason scarce at all." These attempted differentiations, however, would not prevent states of amentia and states of dementia being sometimes confused, nor schizophrenia being considered as either.

Whether "mad people" contained schizophrenics within their numbers, however, is a main consideration of this volume. Despite the methodological difficulties mentioned earlier, it would seem that since the early 19th century there was a form of dementia in young people that has been recognized by a number of clinicians. In addition, the core of the descriptions tally with one another and with what is regarded as a form of schizophrenia today—the simple type, conforming to Feighner et al.'s (24) criteria and approximating Crow's (44) type II schizophrenia. Perhaps the more florid types of schizophrenia—Crow's type I schizophrenia—should be separately studied in future studies. It has been suggested (45), but not proved, that simple schizophrenia may always start in childhood and that the more florid form starts later in life.

Whether schizophrenia as we know it today existed before the 19th century is a more open question. However, it is possible that from the classical period to the 19th century there is a continuum of core descriptions of schizophrenia. The "stupiditas," "stultitia," and "hebetudo" of Hippocrates (460–377 B.C) may link with the "mental alienation" of Celsus and the "fatuitas" of Posidonius of the 4th century A.D. and Aëtius of Amida of the 6th century A.D, as described elsewhere (Roccatagliata, Chapter 1, this volume). Posidonius observed a disease typical of "adolescents whose rational minds had been intact" who developed a regression that led to "dementia." Aëtius said "those affected by 'fatuitas' " are "young people with a modest but intact mind, who after the disease appear as though demented." These in turn may link with the "stolidatas" of Bernard de Gordon of the early 14th century, the illnesses of Charles VI and Henry VI of the 15th century, Platter's descriptions in the 16th century, Willis's description in the 17th century, and the many descriptions in the 19th century. A number of difficulties, already discussed, make recognition less sure. Bearing these difficulties in mind, it would be rash to say that schizophrenia could not have been recognized before the 19th century.

Childhood schizophrenia was also recognized in the 19th century. There are reports by Haslem (2) in 1809, Morel (46) in 1860, and Dickson (47) in 1874. These children as adults were found by Howells and Guirguis (45) to conform to a form of simple schizophrenia as described by Kraepelin in Kendler (33) and all were schizophrenics on the criteria of Feighner et al. (24); they were also close to the "residual schizophrenia" as described in DSM-III.

Two further linked major findings emerge from the study of Chapters 1–7 and Chapters 8–11 in this volume. From the former chapters it can be seen how the definition of schizophrenia has been widened to the point of imprecision, thus hampering contemporary research. The latter chapters consider individual psychopathology and family psychopathology in relation to schizophrenia and the efforts in the psychotherapy of schizophrenia by distinguished major figures in the early 20th century. From these chapters it can be seen that a psychogenesis for schizophrenia is doubtful. The supposed psychopathology is hard to demonstrate. That treatment is effective based on such notions is hard to prove.

Matters went wrong at the start of the 20th century, as is so clearly demonstrated in Chapter 6 (Peters, this volume). Kraepelin's concept was based on descriptive symptomatology and a supposed organic pathology. As is reported in Chapter 4 (Peters, this volume), Kraepelin was close to defining the essential dysfunction of schizophrenia with his statement that the schizophrenic was "not using his mental apparatus in an appropriate way." He is not able to do so because of some insidious organic process. He was followed by Bleuler, whose departure from Kraepelin can be seen in the title of his work: *Dementia Praecox or the Group of Schizophrenias* (48). The second half of his title makes it clear that his thinking was of a group of conditions. He envisaged a physical etiology for some, but accepted also that psychological stress could be responsible for others; for the latter he would accept psychoanalytical concepts. As is stated in Chapter 6, anyone with associational thought disorder was schizophrenic for Bleuler. Thus he widened Kraepelin's notion of a disorder of physical origin that ended in a state of dementia—nuclear, core, process.

Although some clinicians followed Kraepelin, many followed Bleuler. Supposing a psychopathology, the concept of schizophrenia was steadily widened to the point of imprecision, diffusion, and overinclusion. Indeed, in many circles, schizophrenia became an extension of emotional disorder with the same psychopathology.

Yet in the past, even nonclinicians could see that neurosis (emotional illness) was not madness. For example, in his *Tusculanae Disputationes*, Cicero reviewed nosologic topics and found he could not agree that the mind was influenced by black bile only. Rather, he believed that in many instances it was influenced by the strong power of wrath, fear, or pain; he thus defined the nature of emotional illness (neurosis). In the Saxon miscellany of the 14th century is found the following couplet, which defines the same entity:

Oft do we burn in rage
And become as if we were mad.

This puts the situation very clearly—"as if." The composer Verdi also made this clear differentiation. He sent his librettist a prescription for the personality of Azucena in *Il Trovatore*. He stated, "Do not make Azucena mad. Exhausted with fatigue, with sorrow, terror, and lack of sleep, she is unable to speak rationally. Her senses are overwrought, but she is not mad." He saw clearly that states of emotional illness (neuroses) are qualitatively different from madness and insanity (psychoses). Furthermore, all the above-quoted authors saw that emotional disorder is a severe disorder.

Parkin (49) studied the development of ideas on neurosis and schizophrenia from the 18th century onward. He pointed to the works of Greisinger (1817–1868), Kahlbaum (1828–1899), Hecker, and Kraepelin, who regarded neurosis and schizophrenia as fundamentally distinct. Thus they saw a qualitative difference. He quoted adherents of the opposite point of view, which saw neurosis and schizophrenia as having a common basis, with one being able to transform itself into the other. Those who believed this include Conolly (1794–1866), Feuchtersleben (1806–1849), Maudsley (1835–1918), Meyer (1866–1950), and Mapother (1881–1940). Thus they saw only a quantitative difference. To these may be added Bleuler, whose attempt to marry physiologic and psychological concepts was particularly unfortunate. Meyer labeled the neuroses as "the minor psychoses," increasing the confusion. Parkin pointed to the unsatisfactory nature of such concepts as early schizophrenia, nonpsychotic schizophrenia, prepsychotic schizophrenia, neuroses-like schizophrenia, incipient schizophrenia, ambulatory schizophrenia, pseudo-neurotic schizophrenia, pseudo-schizophrenic neurosis, attenuated schizophrenia, diluted schizophrenia, latent schizophrenia, atypical schizophrenia, mitigated schizophrenia, borderline schizophrenia, prodromal schizophrenia, and larval schizophrenia. No such disorganization would be acceptable in the diagnosis of any other medical condition. A disorder exists or it does not.

Neurosis (emotional disorder) is a major disorder in terms of the number of people suffering from it; a collective estimate of emotional disorder in general practice put the figure as 30% of attending patients (50). The estimation of schizophrenia in general practice, as has been said earlier, is that of 0.1%; thus emotional disorder is a 300 times more common condition. Emotional disorder is a major disorder in terms of the severity of its symptoms; these are, as expressed in psychosomatic conditions, often life threatening. Schizophrenia is not a common cause of morbidity.

Confusion may be increased by many factors. The two conditions can coexist; if one-third of the population are neurotic then by chance alone a number of these will also suffer from schizophrenia. In the early stages of schizophrenia, there may be some emotional reaction as a schizophrenic becomes aware of his or her failing mental powers. Some symptoms are in common with schizophrenia; for example, withdrawal in neurosis, suspicion in anxiety states, stupor in reactive depression, and mannerisms in neurosis. Drugs administered in emotional states may lead to a toxic reaction, with symptoms simulating schizophrenia. Neurotic alcoholics may, in severe states, pass into alcoholic hallucinosis, which may be confused with schizophrenia. Neurotic drug addicts may suffer hallucinosis and again become confused with schizophrenics. Psychiatrists trained in emotional disorder may not readily identify psychosis; equally, clinicians trained in psychosis may not readily identify emotional disorder. A severe neurotic condition may be equated with schizophrenia because the severity of neurotic states is often underestimated. Finally, an emotional state of advanced degree, as in panic states, can produce a hormonal and biochemical state that temporarily simulates schizophrenia.

Neurosis (emotional disorder) and schizophrenia are qualitatively different. Schizophrenia would seem to be a form of organic dementia. The organic nature of schizophrenia is a thread running through its history—from hormonal physiology, to Kraepelin and his adherents, to contemporary research. This area is the subject of a massive research effort today; it is outside the range of this volume.

It follows from the material of this volume that the definition of schizophrenia must be narrowed to the point where clinicians with great clinical experience of schizophrenia worldwide can find an acceptable definition consistent with their immediate knowledge of the disease. That the DSM-III nosologic system is veering back to a more inclusive, precise, description of schizophrenia is to be welcomed and encouraged.

We must also free ourselves from the notion of two schizophrenias: 1) a pseudo-schizophrenia based on a misconception of severe emotional states, and 2) a true, nuclear, process, core schizophrenia. Only the second can stand as schizophrenia. Great care must be exercised in including as a subject in research any person who cannot be a proven schizophrenic acceptable to international expert opinion. It must be demonstrated that there has been a careful exclusion of any related organic state that could simulate schizophrenia. It must also be demonstrated that there has been an exclusion of those severe emotional states that can simulate schizophrenia. A case history with data on its presenting symptomatology, the course of the disorder, and the results of a mental examination must be published. This information is essential in any research protocol on schizophrenia.

Clarity will be helped by a more operationally effective term to cover the condition. The *Haslem-Pinel syndrome* is not to be advocated because it tells nothing of the condition. A return to *dementia praecox* is a possibility. We need to describe a form of schizophrenia that occurs in the young but that does not lead to complete, but near, incapacity. *Praecox*, used in Krae-pelin's meaning to denote "occurrence in youth," would be apposite, but not in Morel's meaning of "a rapid deterioration." Should an organic basis sited in the brain be accepted, then the term *encephalo* could be employed; a supposed brain pathology would be established in the term. The main effect of pathology is disorganization, mental confusion, mental disorder, or dysfunction of the mental apparatus (in Kraepelin's sense). This is covered by the term *ataxia*, which is defined as "want of order, irregularity, con-fusion, disorderliness" (51). Thus we have a blend of pathology and symp-tomatology to make *encephalo-ataxia* (52). This may savor of etymological exactitude; the essential need is to find a precise, acceptable term.

The lessons of history as seen in this volume are cogent to today's psy-chiatry. Indeed, the volume clearly points the way to the future. A clear concept of schizophrenia based on organic pathology is the basis for valuable hypotheses, and a springboard for successful research efforts. This could lead to the sure diagnosis of schizophrenia and effective treatment based on proven etiology.

The initiative to prepare this volume came from a meeting of the His-torical Section of the World Psychiatric Association at a regional meeting held in New York in 1981. It is a pleasure to record thanks to its Organizing Committee and to the officers and Executive Committee of the World Psychiatric Association. The volume is in keeping with the avowed aims of the Historical Section of the World Psychiatric Association to promote historical study that will be of value to clinical practice today.

References

1. Torrey EF: Schizophrenia and Civilisation. Northvale, NJ, Jason Aronson, 1980
2. Haslem J: Observations on Madness and Melancholy. London, G. Hayden, 1809
3. Pinel PA: A Treatise on Insanity. New York, Hofner Press, 1962
4a. Hare E: Was insanity on the increase? Br J Psychiatry 142:439–455, 1983
4b. Hare E: Schizophrenia as a recent disease. Br J Psychiatry 153:521–531, 1988
5. Jablensky A: Epidemiology of Schizophrenia. Schizophr Bull 12:52–73, 1986
6. Wilson JUK: Organic diseases of ancient Mesopotamia, in Diseases in Antiquity. Edited by Brothwell D, Sandison AT. Springfield, IL, Charles C Thomas, 1967

7. Moss GC: Mental disorders in antiquity, in Diseases in Antiquity. Edited by Brothwell D, Sandison AT. Springfield, IL, Charles C Thomas, 1967

8. Jeste DV, Del Carmen R, Lohr JB, et al: Did schizophrenia occur before the 18th century? Compr Psychiatry 26:493–503, 1985

9. Celsus AC: The First Four Books of De Re Medica. Translated by Steggall J. London, Churchill, 1853

10. Diethelm O: Medical Dissertations of Psychiatric Interest. Basel, Karger, 1971

11. Hare E: Schizophrenia before 1800? The case of the Rev'd George Trosse. Psychol Med 18:279–285, 1988

12. Macalpine I, Hunter RA: Schizophrenia 1677. London, Dawson, 1956

13. Ellard J: Did schizophrenia exist before the eighteenth century. Aust N Z J Psychiatry 21:306, 1987

14. Warner R: Commentary two. Aust N Z J Psychiatry 21:317–318, 1987

15. Howells JG, Osborn ML: The incidence of emotional disorder in a seventeenth century medieval practice. Med Hist 14:192–198, 1970

16. Kessel WIN: Psychiatric morbidity in a London general practice. British Journal Prev Soc Medicine 14:16, 1960

17. Zubin J, Magaziner J, Steinhauer SR: The metamorphosis of schizophrenia from chronicity to vulnerability. Psychol Med 13:551–571, 1983

18. Romano J: On the nature of schizophrenic changes in the observer as well as the observed. Schizophr Bull 4:532, 1977

19. Hare E: Commentary one. Aust N Z J Psychiatry 21:315–316, 1987

20. Sartorius M, Jublensky A, Korton A, et al: Early manifestations and first-contact incidence of schizophrenia in different cultures. Psychol Med 16:909–928, 1986

21. Cranefield PF: A seventeenth century view of mental deficiency and schizophrenia. Bull Hist Med 35:291–316, 1961

22. Pinel PH: Traite Medico-Philosophique sur l'alienation mentale. Paris, Chez J Ant Brosson, 1809

23. Mellor CS: First rank symptoms of schizophrenia. Br J Psychiatry 117:15–23, 1970

24. Feighner JP, Robins E, Guze SB, et al: Diagnostic criteria for use in psychiatric research. Arch Gen Psychiatry 26:57–63, 1972

25. American Psychiatric Association: Diagnostic and Statistical Manual of Mental Disorders, 3rd Edition. Washington, DC, American Psychiatric Association, 1980

26. Endicott J, Nee J, Cohen J, et al: Diagnostic criteria for schizophrenia. Arch Gen Psychiatry 39:884–889, 1982

27. Endicott J, Nee J, Cohen J, et al: Diagnosis of schizophrenia and prediction of short term outcome. Arch Gen Psychiatry 43:13–19, 1986

28. Cooper JE, Kendall RE, Gurland RE, et al: Psychiatric Diagnosis in New York and London. London, Oxford University Press, 1972

29. World Health Organization: The International Pilot Study of Schizophrenia, Vol 1. Geneva, World Health Organization, 1973

30. Howells JG, Guirguis WR: Schizophrenia and family psychopathology. International Journal of Family Psychiatry 1:113–126, 1980

31. Fischer AA: About concept formation in relation to treatment in schizophrenia, in Studies of Schizophrenia. Edited by Lader MH. Ashford, United Kingdom, Headley, 1975

32. Altschule MD: Historical perspective: evolution of the concept of schizophrenia, in Advances in Behavioral Biology, Vol 19: The Biology of the Schizophrenic Process. Edited by Wolf S, Bishop B. New York, Plenum, 1976
33. Kendler KS: Kraepelin and the differential diagnosis of dementia praecox and manic-depressive insanity. Compr Psychiatry 27:549–558, 1986
34. Cutting J, Shepherd M (eds): The Clinical Roots of the Schizophrenia Concept. Cambridge, United Kingdom, Cambridge University Press, 1987
35. Kroll J, Bachrach B: Medieval visions and contemporary hallucinations. Psychol Med 12:709–721, 1982
36. Lehman HE: Psychotic disorders: schizophrenia, in Comprehensive Textbook of Psychiatry, 3rd Edition. Edited by Kaplan HI, Freedman AM, Sadock BJ. Baltimore, MD, Williams & Wilkins, 1980
37. Trosse G: The Life of the Rev. George Trosse . . . Written by Himself. Exeter, White, 1714
38. Bateson G: Perceval's Narrative: A Patient's Account of His Psychosis. Stanford, CA, Stanford University Press, 1961
39. Berrios GE: Dementia during the seventeenth and eighteenth centuries: a conceptual history. Psychol Med 17:829–837, 1987
40. Quain R: A Dictionary of Medicine, Vols 1 and 2. London, Longman Green, 1894
41. Zelmanowits J: A historical note on the simple dementing form of schizophrenia. Proceedings of the Royal Society of Medicine 46:931–933, 1953
42. Hecker E: Die Hebephrenie. Virchows Archiv Fur Pathologische Anatomie 52:392–449, 1871
43. Howells JG, Osborn ML: A Reference Companion to the History of Abnormal Psychology. Westport CT, Greenwood Press, 1984
44. Crow TJ: Molecular pathology of schizophrenia: more than one disease process? Br Med J 280:66–68, 1980
45. Howells JG, Guirguis WR: Childhood schizophrenia 20 years later. Arch Gen Psychiatry 41:123–128, 1984
46. Morel BA: Traite des maladies mentales. Paris, V Masson, 1860
47. Dickson JT: The Science and Practice of Medicine in Relation to Mind. New York, Appleton, 1874
48. Bleuler E: Dementia Praecox or the Group of Schizophrenias. New York, International Universities Press, 1961
49. Parkin A: Neurosis and schizophrenia, I and II. Psychiatr 40:203–235, 1966
50. Council of the College of General Practitioners: Working Party report. Br Med J 2:585, 1958
51. The Oxford English Dictionary. Oxford, Clarendon Press, 1933
52. Howells JG: Classification of psychiatric disorders, in Modern Perspectives in Adolescent Psychiatry. Edited by Howells JG. New York, Brunner/Mazel, 1971, p 209

CHAPTER ONE

Classical Concepts of Schizophrenia

Giuseppe Roccatagliata, M.D.

Indolence makes one obtuse
and causes precocious senility;
work strengthens and promotes
abiding youth.
Aulus Cornelius Celsus

In the history of humanity and of the development of science, each day draws inspiration from the previous day, and each century from the previous century. Each scientific phase is related to the previous one, even though the links are not always obvious or are neglected or not stressed. It is therefore important to study the history of psychiatry, since the common ground from which both modern and ancient psychiatry were born was clinical experience.

Within this framework, the purpose of this chapter is to trace the history of the concept of schizophrenia during the Graeco-Roman-Byzantine-Arab period—that is, between the 7th century B.C. and the 11th century A.D.—by means of a critical and philological study of the original sources. The deep and strong interest that classical psychiatry shows in this form of mental disease gradually diminished during the 11th century, when the clinical picture of schizophrenia was based on a stereotypic and uncritical reproduction of ancient texts.

Interest in schizophrenic psychoses increased with the work of B. A.

Morel toward the middle of the 19th century, and it grew even stronger with the work of Emil Kraepelin (1). This scholar identified the typical symptoms of the disease as "emotional blunting . . . or foolish dementia" and the loss "of the unity of higher psychic life." The result of the psychosis is based on such symptoms; it is characterized by "a particular state of psychic weakness." Kraepelin deemed that at the basis of dementia praecox there was "an alteration of the cerebral cortex . . . which brings about a slow deterioration in a constitutionally weak psychic state . . . similar to a tree whose roots can find no nourishment."

Eugen Bleuler coined a new word for Morel's dementia praecox, as described and interpreted by Kraepelin: schizophrenia. In his opinion, at the origin of this psychosis there is "a weakness of the associative psychic acts," which brings about "a loosening of the mental links between mental contents" (2). According to Bleuler, who was influenced by Wundt, the loss of unity in mental life is related to "a weakness of the psychic tone"; all the other symptoms derive from this "primary" one (2–4).

The study of classical medical texts reveals that the concept of dementia praecox or schizophrenia was well known to the physicians of that period, who considered it a precise clinical entity. It held a precise place in nosology, its limits being defined with respect to other psychoses, which were identified as "catatony," "paraphrosyniae," "fanaticism," and "furor."

Dementia praecox—or schizophrenia, as it is called in modern psychiatry—has been given different names (although they all pertain to the same semantic field): *fatuitas, hebetudo, morositas, stupiditas,* and *stultitia* (5–7). We shall see that due to a series of semiological and etiopathogenic reasons, however, a distinction was maintained between hebephreny and other psychoses (insanities or mental alienations) that modern psychiatry considers to be identical to hebephreny. This clinical picture, which was usually interpreted as a synthesis between a mild form of oligophrenia and a constitutional weakening of the vital tone—considered a "stupid oligophrenia"—was, in fact, differentiated from other mental disturbances, which are equivalent to what we now call schizophrenia.

The paranoia called "fanaticism," the paranoid psychoses called "paraphrosyniae," the catatonia called "cathoco," the acute schizophrenia-denominated "furious mania," and the cycloid psychoses called "extasis and explesis" were, in fact, all considered individual psychomorbid pictures because of their semiological aspects, their course and outcome, and, above all, their etiopathogenic mechanisms. The interpretive model for all these psychoses in classical psychiatry, however, remained anchored in an organistic approach: that is, a biochemical, neurophysiologic, and neurohumoral approach. It was primarily and substantially naturalistic philosophical thinking that determined the interpretive paradigm of these psychoses.

The biophysical and biohumoral schools of thought of the pre-Socratics, the atomism of Leucippus and Democritus, the vitalism of Aristotle, and the neurophysiology of the Alexandrian school furnished the clinical psychiatrist with appropriate aid in elaborating an interpretive model for those mental disturbances now defined as schizophrenia.

The Philosophers of Nature (7th–6th Centuries B.C.)

Classical psychiatry has its scientific basis in the biochemical model of mental life, elaborated between the 7th and the 6th centuries B.C. by the "philosophers of nature"—the school of Miletus, the Eleatics, Heraclitus of Ephesus, Empedocles of Agrigentum (493–433 B.C.), Democritus of Abdera, and Melissus of Samo.

According to these thinkers, psychic life in its totality—emotional, affective, instinctive, and intellectual—is the epiphenomenon of underlying physiochemical mechanisms, the expression of a basic "metabolism" of the original matter that constitutes the soul. The mind is therefore subject to the physiologic or pathologic variations that appear in the organic base. According to the philosophers of nature, the soul is the principle of life and it consists in a force similar to "a spark of life." This fire is intelligent and has the capacity to make one wise by rendering the brain tissue lively and active. From this perspective, any process that alters the physical composition of the soul may give rise to a psychiatric symptomatology. It is especially the "humors"—yellow bile, black bile, blood, and pituita (or phlegm)—that can, when they are "unbalanced," modify the qualities of the soul. Because of the excessive "power" of one humor, the brain and soul undergo a change in their physiologic "temperament," which is transformed because it is influenced by the physical characteristics of the prevailing humor.

The igneous nature of the soul can thus be modified through the action of a somatic factor with certain physical characteristics. Yellow bile, which is "dry and hot," increases the energy of the fire of the soul, thus causing acute psychosis, a state of excitement and delirium. On the other hand, a humor with a "cold and moist" temperament—such as the pituita—makes the soul weak, slow, and lifeless because the soul becomes "cold and moist" under its influence. When the primary fire is extinguished through the action of a pathogenic factor, all neuropsychological functions are also altered, and they take on certain forms that reflect the characteristics assumed, in a physiopathologic way, by the soul (8–13).

A watery, cold, and moist substance pollutes the purity of the primary fire, which is an energy designed to carry out the higher psychic emotions and functions. As a consequence, the soul is "moistened" and loses its typical characteristics while assuming those of the pituitous humor. The psychic symptomatology of dementia praecox is the reflection of this underlying phenomenon of denaturation of the specific composition of the soul. In dementia praecox, the soul changes from hot and dry to cold and moist, thus acquiring both the characteristics of an old person's soul ("cold") and those of a child's soul ("moist"). As a consequence of the moistening and cooling of the fire of the soul, the patient suffering from dementia praecox manifests an overall mental life that is like a synthesis between the psycho-physiology of a child and that of an aged person.

This implies that the individual makes no progress, but rather regresses, lacking a hot and dry soul, which would support an adequate intelligence and energetic vital emotions, capable of facing the difficulties of life. For the philosophers of nature, the fire of the soul represents a general factor of intelligence, and it is the tone of this fire that sustains a full emotional and affective life suitable for objective relationships.

The psychopathology of dementia praecox has its origin in a primary process affecting the fire of the soul; the symptoms are but an epipheno-menon thereof. According to this naturalistic paradigm, all psychological mechanisms derive directly from an underlying thermodynamic biochem-ical metabolism that has been "corrupted" by the action of a humoral factor. The material and primary factor of the soul is the fulcrum of classical psychopathology. This science defines the symptoms that reflect an alter-ation in the original energetic source (14–16).

Hellenic naturalism is based on a synopsis justified, from a pathologic point of view, by the fact that the term *pituita* has both a physical meaning (indicating a watery, dense, and mucous humor) and a psychic one (defining a slow and idle personality).

This way of seeing the psychopathologic world as the direct expression of the action of a certain physis of the soul determined by a pathologic factor, and not dichotomously, as a disharmony between the physical and the psychological worlds, is typical of classical thought.

It is therefore the nature of the soul that gives the psychic world its shape, whether it be normal or pathologic. The configuration of the symbol, the psychopathologic form, the mode of being of the "foolish" psychotic derive from an impoverishment of the vital tone of the soul; the sign is merely the expression of the chemical mutation that has taken place endogenously in the physis of the soul.

The psychotic manifestation is a sign of the nature of the soul, which presides over the psychic life. Heat, fire, and vital physical energy (i.e., the sphere that contains the cosmic gift of life) become contaminated by a watery substance that is the cause of a new physiochemical existence, transforming the organism. According to the naturalistic paradigm, it is substantially an endogenous, somatic modification that determines the onset of a specific psychosis. It is therefore possible, because of an innate excess of pituita, to have psychotic disturbances in which a delirious hallucinatory symptom-atology prevails, accompanied by "foolish laughter" and, above all, by "apathetic indolence." This happens because the pituita alters the brain; it corrupts it and as a consequence brings about "mental alienation" (17–19).

During this historical phase, the scientific presuppositions were laid down for the creation of a clinical psychiatry that one century later was to break every tie with religion and myth, thanks to the work of Hippocrates. A physician, Hippocrates combined the centuries-old psychiatric experience of the medical-sacerdotal class of the Aesculapian temples with the naturalistic interpretive models. Classical psychiatry sees the total life of the soul in its rational, emotional, and instinctive factors as regulated by humoral mechanisms because it adopts the organistic biological approach of the philosophers of nature (20–23).

The brain is considered as an organ that is the target of several pathogenic factors, among which the humors are the most influential. It is only an "intemperies cerebri"—that is, the alteration of the physical and chemical constants of the brain (due to the action of a pathogenic factor)—that is the basis of psychopathology. A humoral imbalance or the denaturation of certain bioelements cause a "corruptio cerebri" and, as a consequence, psychotic symptomatology. Phrenitis and mania originate from an excessively "dry and hot" brain tissue through the action of fever and yellow bile. Melancholy arises from the action of black bile, which transforms the physical state of the brain into a "cold and dry" one. The symptomatology of dementia praecox, or "desipientia stupida," has its origin in the action of an inhibitory humor, the pituita, physiologically "moist and cold"; increasing its concentration in the central nervous system leads to this psychotic process (5, 18).

According to the philosophers of nature, psychic life is determined by the soul. By the soul they refer to the primary energy that drives the body and carries out neuropsychological operations. The soul includes the intellect, the affective and emotional life, and the instincts. The soul as a whole is divided into strata and is fused with the body below and the brain above. It is formed by a guiding structure, the self, which is hegemonic and substantially autonomous. The soul is seen as an entity compared to "fire" or, as Thales thought, "to the energy of a magnet" (15, 22, 24).

The work of the philosophers of nature, between the 7th and 6th centuries B.C., investigated "truth." This led to a critical attitude toward the sacred and mythological conceptions of mental disease. The "physiologists," as they were called by Aristotle, studied a primary, fundamental matter, supposed to constitute the "nature" of the soul, which they considered to be related to active and passive metabolic processes, both anabolic and catabolic, of "generation" and "corruption." Psychopathology is related to the structure of the soul and to the variations that it undergoes through pathologic processes of "transmutation."

The interpretive model for psychoses, called "of elements and qualities" and elaborated by the physician and philosopher Empedocles of Agrigentum, was based on the hypothesis of a biological equilibrium or homeostasis as the basis of mental sanity. Only a biochemical disequilibrium of the humoral metabolism could bring about a substantial alteration of the physiochemical balance of the brain. This phenomenon would then be the cause of a "transmutatio cerebri" physically homologous with the physical characteristics of the humors.

The phlegma (i.e., the pituita), the humor selected by the pituitary gland (i.e., epiphysis), the liquid of the cerebral ventricles, is similar to "insipid" water. Because of its physical characteristics, this humor, a concrete element of the body, assumed a relevant value in the etiopathogenic dynamics of schizophrenia.

Between the 7th and 6th centuries B.C., the physicians of the Italic school—particularly Alcmaeon of Croton, Philolaus of Croton and Philistion of Locri (all followers of the Pythagorean trend)—had already succeeded in identifying in this simple element the etiologic factor of the psychosis called "hebetudo." It was physically "cold and moist"; therefore, it had an inhibiting function on the psychic activities, causing a slowing down and weakening of the cerebral chemism. If the quantity of pituita inside the brain exceeded certain levels, it would overpower the other humors, causing a homologous modification of the brain, which would therefore become colder and moister than normal.

This slow, viscous, insipid, cold, and watery humor would be imbibed by the cerebral tissue, causing a sort of precocious senility. It was, in fact, the same humor that also prevailed in old age and during winter. A young person affected by this biochemical anomaly, instead of having a "hot and dry" brain (i.e., a rapid and strong biological factor), would be in a condition similar to that of an old person. Pituita and hebetude were therefore related, as the physical characteristics of the humor corresponded in all respects to the psychotic symptomatology. The physiologically "tempered" cerebral tissue was subject to an "intemperies" (i.e., to a change brought about by the pituita). Feelings, emotions, affections, and sensorial and intellectual operations were all obliged by the pituita to deviate in the biopsychological direction willed by that humor. Therefore, hebephreny represented a "surrender" of psychic life to the characteristics of the prevalent humor; there was, in other words, a "permissio rationis."

A young person affected by hebetude was, in fact, stolid, fatuous, capricious, voluble, unfit for life, and silly—all qualities that corresponded to the characteristics of the pituita (soft, watery, insipid, weak, cold). An excessively moist brain was therefore at the basis of hebephreny. The hebephrenic psychosis, according to this vitalistic approach, was the sign of a "general weakness of the nerves and spirit." The individual was indolent, apathetic, abulic, and lacking in vitality. Thus the Latins described a "secors," from "sé-cors" meaning "without a heart" (i.e., lacking in vital tone, strength, and courage), since the heart was considered the very seat of the basic biological impulse of each individual.

The soul is the seat of metabolic processes of a physical and chemical nature, which are reflected in a particular type of emotional, affective, and psychological life. The substance of which the soul is made carries out a continuous internal activity, through processes of rarefaction, condensation, cooling, heating, and so forth. When the interaction of these mechanisms results in homeostasis (equilibrium due to a balancing action), there is psychic health. When there is a disequilibrium due to the excess of one factor, there is a psychic disease. The latter is always the expression of the action of one factor that predominates over the others, augmenting its "power" and establishing a "monarchy." The power of one single physical element implies a correlated and homologous state of the soul (25, 26).

The Vitalism of Heraclitus of Ephesus (520–460 B.C.)

The thinker who stressed the value of this biophysical model of the soul and who used it to interpret the psychopathology of "foolish folly" was the great Heraclitus of Ephesus, who laid the foundations for the model of both normal and pathologic mental life, which was to lead to the formation of a scientific psychopathology. Heraclitus set the limits of a complex range of reciprocal relations between the original matter and psychic life, which in turn depend on the mutations of the substance that constitutes the soul: fire, an element that is by nature fast, active, hot, and dry. Different factors may alter the physical state of the original matter of the soul, especially water, the element that involves a diminution, an extinguishing of the vital heat (it makes the soul "moist and cold").

According to Heraclitus, in fact, the "foolish psychosis . . . is brought about by a soul which has become too moist, as happens in those who swallow much wine." A "hot and dry" soul is wise, whereas a moist and cold one induces "foolishness." The foolish, superficial, and unbalanced behavior that occurs in this morbid state is comparable to that of "a young boy who has not yet developed, so that he staggers and does not know in which direction he is going." Therefore, according to Heraclitus, a soul with a metabolism that has slowed down because of a moistening action is the cause of an extinguishing of emotions and the loss of a unified psychic life (12, 13, 16, 22, 27–32).

Hippocrates of Cos (460–377 B.C.)

In the year 460 B.C., when Heraclitus of Ephesus died, Hippocrates was born on the island of Cos. He was a member of the cult of Aesculapius, and the first person in history to give clinical psychiatry a biological basis. Hippocrates' thinking was an attempt to establish a relation between the symptom, the morbid process, and the physiopathology of the humors by going back to the model of the physiologists. Hippocrates thus set up a nosology of psychic diseases in terms of biohumoral etiopathogenic models.

Hippocrate's vast clinical experience enabled him to set the limits of the manifestations of melancholy that would arise in certain individuals following a "motivated sorrow." Such an event would play a decisive role, as he had seen in many cases—particularly that of a girl from Thasos—only if the particular type of character, now called "schizoid," was also present. In fact, the depressive symptomatology appeared to be atypical, due to the presence of violent psychomotor agitation and "delirious ideas." However, only the presence of a particular psychopathic personality, called "morose" by Hippocrates, could trigger a psychosis, which modern psychiatry would classify within the category of affective schizophrenia. In fact, in such cases there was a typical personality that was always present: "sad, rigid, shy, scarcely affective and with introverted character."

However, in Hippocrates's work we find no other elements that allow us to make further reflections on this acute syndrome, which has the form of a schizophrenic reaction. His remained a mere clinical observation, as did the remarks on those psychomotor disturbances he defined "catatonic."

Hippocrates had pointed out the presence of a muscular rigidity and of a certain "vacillating of the mind." For this reason it had seemed to him that this disturbance was much akin to the febrile organic psychosis, which he had defined as phrenitis. He had also noticed many cases of individuals "on a borderline with folly" who would lead an apparently normal life. However, if a pathogenic factor (e.g., "a slight inflammation, excess of food or wine") interfered and was such as to set off folly, then a psychotic symptomatology would also appear—that is, "the subjects would become insane."

There were three different clinical experiences, with different symptomatologies, in which the mental disturbance was set off by various pathogenic factors. The mental disturbances presented themselves to Hippocrates in their changing, many-sided nature. Only an organistic model, such as that elaborated by the philosophers of nature, could perhaps define these disturbances in a correct and rational way (17, 33, 34).

Hippocrates brought together the biopsychological intuitions of the thought of Heraclitus and clinical observation. In his opinion, normal life is related to a balanced "temperament" of the soul, which is fed by a "pure fire." Any modification "corrupting" the physical qualities of fire, usually "hot-dry," also involves the onset of the symptoms of mental disease. Hippocrates also thought that an increase in the water content of the brain would induce a psychotic condition: "torpor, inability of sensorial synthesis and foolish desipience," or in semiological terms, psychic blunting, mental dissociation, and a weakening of the emotional life.

Hippocrates thus defined the limits of the concept of this psychosis on the basis of *desipience*, a term signifying unreasonable behavior and stupidity, that is, a foolish and antisocial attitude that is such because of a detachment from reality. At the basis of dementia praecox then, according to Hippocrates, there is a "mutation" of the physiochemical qualities of the soul that, from hot-dry, becomes excessively "moist-cold" (17, 22). The physis of the soul is altered anomalously by the cerebrospinal liquid. The "pituitary" humor, similar to water, if its quantity in the brain is excessive, brings about "stupiditas." A humoral imbalance, with the increase in "power" of the pituita, is the etiopathogenic mechanism that induces a "trasmutatio" of the soul, the cause of "stultitia."

The "humoral secretion," which takes place in balanced "circuits" to produce an equilibrium between the various humors, puts an excessive quantity of pituita into circulation. This happens in pathologic states, because of the influence of genetic, climatic, and nutritional factors and of factors connected with age. The pituita, a "cold and moist" humor, increases in winter, in people approaching old age, and in young people with a "predisposition." As an increase of black bile induces melancholy and that of yellow bile induces mania, so an excess of pituita brings about the foolish psychosis, characterized by "irritability, laziness, slothfulness, incoherence of psychic life, sometimes excessive ingenuity or a difficult and hostile temperament."

Hippocrates's biochemical hypothesis on psychoses is based on clinical data that he saw as the expression of an underlying dysmetabolic process. Thus "desipientiae" with "gayness and laughter" were induced by yellow bile, whereas those with "sadness and preoccupation" were induced by black bile. The brain according to Hippocrates was "a gland secreting humors," above all "pituita"; the mind is alienated only in that the cerebral tissue is "perturbed" by a metabolic dysfunction (11, 17, 18, 35–37). Hippocrates's great achievement was to unite psychiatric semiology with the humoral conception of psychoses so as to relate certain clinical pictures to a specific endogenous dysmetabolism.

Another of Hippocrates's merits lies in the fact that he established a correlation between the psychiatric symptomatology and the physical characteristics of the humors; the pituita, a cold and moist hormone, thus has an inhibitory action both on the intellectual faculties and on the emotional ones. "Stupiditas" is therefore an epiphenomenon of a physical modification of the brain due to the action of the pituitary humor (11, 35).

Hippocrates distinguished the "real" endogenous psychoses of the kind of "desipientia stupida" from some forms that present an analogous symptomatology; in their case, however, the symptoms arise as a consequence of internal and neurologic disease, which he called "a morbis" (i.e., symptomatic).

Hippocrates also provided a description of dementia praecox in which he stressed the aspect of psychic dissociation, the theme of delirium, the hallucinatory phenomena, and the anxious-depressive aspects:

> The ill person often weeps without reason; unimportant things make him afraid and sometimes also sad, [he is] frightened though without reason . . . he talks about things which bear no reference to his life and do not concern him . . . he takes an interest in subjects of which he is obviously ignorant . . . often in things which only interest scholars . . . sometimes he sees images as if in dreams . . . , at some moments he may become sub-furious. (17)

Hippocrates's contribution relating to the mental disease called "hebetudo" was considered clinically well aimed and scientifically correct until the work of Morel in the mid-19th century. This disease originates from an inversion of the physiologic ratio inside the brain; of the balance of the two components of the soul; of that biological energy that supports neuropsychological activities and the affective, instinctive, emotional, and sentimental spheres.

The water content of the brain, due to an augmenting of the pituita (i.e., of the cerebrospinal liquid, the typical humor of a deficient mental life) becomes higher than that of the "fire" (i.e., of the substance that is energetic, active, and vital) because it is fast. Thus a slow and retarded cerebral metabolism prevails, bringing about an intellectual defect, called "stoliditas" by Hippocrates. People affected by this anomaly are not insane, but rather they are oligophrenics, idiots, with "slow sensory-perceptive processes." They are individuals whose brain "canaliculi" are invaded by a soul that is slow because it is watery. They are incapable of grasping sensual-perceptive data. They are slow in providing verbal and psychomotor answers. The soul of "intelligent" individuals, to the contrary, has a higher fire content. Their mental processes are active, energetic, and with precise aims. They are, as Hippocrates stressed, "active and constant in relationships." The "substantial difficulty in grasping reality" that pertains to stolid individuals does not yet make them into insane persons. They are merely examples of human variety, characterized by a biological factor, to be considered as incapable persons.

If a higher quantity of water is imbibed in the cerebral tissue, due to a further excess of pituita, the cognitive capacity will be further reduced, and real signs of mental disease will appear (mainly, "the incapacity of grasping reality"). In this case, wrote Hippocrates, " a specific kind of insanity arises, which is called 'desipientia' by some, 'atony' by others and 'stupidity' by yet others." If stolidity indicated a foolish individual, the three terms used for real insanity designated a severe accentuation of the symptomatology; for instance, the appearance, as we have seen, of ideo-verbal incoherence, of emotional blunting, and of vague delirious ideas. However, in this case, the nucleus of the mental disease is characterized by a foolish and extravagant folly, behavioral attitudes marked by stupor, absent-mindedness, foolishness, fatuousness, and emotional inadequacy. The individual appears to be dumb, slow in comprehending, stupid. Hippocrates, in short, described the clinical picture later to be defined by Morel, Kraepelin, and Bleuler as that of dementia praecox, in its varieties: simplex and hebephrenic.

However, Hippocrates also isolated cases of personality alterations that he considered "on the border" with real insanity and that he denominated with the terms *simplex* and *segnis*, thus designating individuals who were ingenuous, imprudent, credulous, apathetic, indolent, and lazy. Finally, on a borderline with hebetude he also considered the so-called subfurious (i.e., individuals at the limit with mental disease who, due to "emotions, excessive wine-swallowing or fever may become insane").

Physiologic normality consists in a dynamic stability, thanks to which the various metabolic processes are equivalent, so that the physical and chemical characteristics of the soul remain constant. Taking this perspective, Hippocrates wrote: "because of a defect of the fire of the soul and of its force, because of an accumulation of pituita inside the brain, 'stoliditas' arises . . . , the patient becomes listless and indolent" (17, 30, 38). This psychosis, which Hippocrates called "hebetudo" because of its psycho-pathologic features and because of the fact that it arises in youth, is brought about by a dysmetabolism of the pituita, "a nativitate." The symptoms of hebetudo, such as the superficiality of emotional reactions (which appear extremely weak), the grossness of behavior, and the incoherence of thought, are all epiphenomena of a weak and listless vital tone. Ths may be observed, Hippocrates thought, by checking the quality of the arterial pulse, the expression of the biological force of "vis vitalis": one whose elbow artery pulsates strongly is irritable and a maniac; whereas one whose elbow artery is weak and cannot be seen pulsating "suffers from hebetude."

According to Hippocrates, an excessive quantity of pituita or water inside the brain brings about a change in the direction of cold and damp, so that the "soul" (i.e., the general factor of intelligence, physiologically "hot and dry") loses tone and vigor. Thus, a biohumoral condition would arise, which was necessary to induce the appearance of "desipience" (i.e., a mental state characterized by senselessness). However, psychosis ensues only when the brain is extremely imbibed with pituita, so that in such cases, together with desipience, there is also stupidity, manifested by slow, obtuse, clumsy, and "stupefied" behavior. According to Hippocrates, the individual suf-fering from hebetude is specifically a "stupid desipient" (17, 39).

There is an incongruity in Hippocrates's work concerning the seat of the lesion, which varied according to whether the anatomic seat of the soul was considered to be the brain or the heart. In his *de morbo sacro* (40), Hippocrates indicated the brain as the anatomic seat of all the soul's functions, from the neurologic to the psychological and emotional ones. In his work *de corde* (41), on the other hand, he wrote that the seat of the soul was in the "left heart ventricle." However, according to Hippocrates, there was no doubt about the seat of the etiopathogenic mechanism involved in dementia prae-cox. The heart was the source of the pure vital tone, whereas the brain constituted the structure designed to transform these energies into formal operations. In this connection, the heart-brain dilemma, in relation to de-mentia praecox, was acutely analyzed by a 17th-century physician, Giovanni Marinello, in his interpretation of dementia praecox as it was seen by Hip-pocrates. The Italian scholar wrote:

> The Hippocratic perspective sees both the heart and the brain as the cause of foolish dementia, in the same way as the roots, trunk and branches of a tree, respectively and symbolically the heart and the brain, are the creators of the fruit and the cause of its characteristics. (19)

The male sperm, according to the pre-Socratic theory of elements and qualities, had the same characteristics as water and therefore as the pituita. Moreover, it was a sort of "corrupt" pituita, and it could bring about hebephrenic psychosis if it was not emitted. Hippocrates was therefore adamant on this subject: "coitus morbis ex pituita commodus" (19, 39–41).

Plato (428–347 B.C.)

Hippocrates's humoral approach was also accepted by Athenian philosophical circles connected to Plato's academy, which had, in any case, always assimilated the biological teachings on mental disease of the medical school of Magna Grecia. The most severe psychic disturbance was considered to be "stultitia," also in the opinion of Plato, who was influenced in this by his contemporary Diocles of Carystus (384–322 B.C.). This morbid form had always been striking because of its obvious synthesis of two components: foolishness and extravagant folly.

The "fool" is a person who is ill in his or her soul, due to certain obvious disturbances affecting humors. These, especially pituita, become corrupt; they decay and alter, thus forming certain aerial substances called "vapors," as Diocles of Carystos affirmed, which intoxicate the mind. In "foolishness," in the sense given to the word by Heraclitus, and also in Plato's view, the soul, whose seat is the brain, becomes "watery due to an excess of corrupt pituita" (42).

The Vitalism of Aristotle (384–322 B.C.)

Plato's pupil, the philosopher and biologist Aristotle, reversed the "neurocentric" hypothesis concerning the soul; he considered its seat to be the heart and the vascular system. The soul is a "directive" force, autonomous with respect to the body, "as a line which is tangential to a sphere in one point." Body and soul coexist as "form and matter." The soul, according to Aristotle, "is the act of a natural organic body." If the body is considered homologous to the eye, the soul is the "visual function." The soul is the act of life; it regulates all vital faculties: sensitive, nutritive, appetitive, and intellectual. The soul is not an abstract entity, but rather "matter which expresses itself in its own physical temperament." Blood is the element that determines the force of the soul: "if it is warm and mobile the soul is strong and wise . . . and so are, consequently, the nutritive, sensory and intellectual faculties . . . , if the blood is excessively moist and dense, then the soul is weak and fragile" (24, 43).

According to Aristotle, life is "heat"; an organic structure dominated by cold and damp undergoes corruption and then death. All cold and moist substances ought to be emitted for health reasons (e.g., sperm through frequent sexual acts). The forming of residues of the pituita gives rise to psychic disturbances.

The soul of a mentally sane person is comparable to solar light, whereas that of the insane is similar to moonlight: soft, weak, pale, limp, moist, and liquid.

In time, a "metaphysical" view of hebephreny took root, so that this disease was seen as the sign of the influence of destructive, lunar forces, demoniac and female. The hebephrenic was as a small man, weak and timid because he was dominated by the Moon and the Great Mother Cybele and he was but a humble servant of the Great Mother's power. Instead of rising to the solar sphere, he would live in heavy, opaque, sublunar spheres (i.e., irrational spheres dominated by dense and opaque humoral secretions). This demonological outlook to hebephreny was further developed on the grounds of an exasperated Neoplatonism and Neoaristotelism by the philosophers Filon, Plotinus, Jamblicus, Porphirius, and Proclus, from the beginning of the vulgar era to the 5th century A.D. (44–46).

The Stoics (4th century B.C.)

With the decline of the civilization of the "polis," a new culture began to flourish that was far from the Hellenic tradition; it developed according to vaster, more articulate, and more complex models. Within this culture, which historically is called Hellenism, there was the assertion of a philosophical tend that stressed the value of Aristotle's "cardiocentric" conception of the soul and constituted Stoicism. The Stoic philosophers—Chrysippus, Zenon, and Posidonius—called the soul "pneuma," and they compared it to an aerial, hot, and moist substance circulating in the cardiovascular system. The characteristics of the pneuma differ in the transition from the inorganic bodies to the vegetal ones, to the animal ones, and finally to the human body. In the case of humans, the faster, hotter, and more subtle the pneuma, the higher the psychic functions it will sustain; the pneuma of the "logos" is subtle, very fast, hot, and extremely pure (47, 48).

Mental sanity and psychic disease both depend on the characteristics of the "tone of the pneuma," which, like an elastic substance, is diffused through the whole body. The self, the hegemonic, usually utilizes an active and fast pneuma. A diseased pneuma is dense, opaque, slow, and turbid; it determines the activity of the self and "subjugates" it. The "logos" of foolish persons is diseased because "sullied" by a pneuma charged with humoral substances, put into circulation by exaggerated emotional reactions. It is "pathos," brutal emotion, which brings about "stultitia"; the individual is then guided by a "logos" that is irrational because troubled by passions, by humors, and by instinctive pulsions. The pneuma endures the emotions. Because of them, it becomes hotter, drier, colder, or moister; it "subjugates" the logos in its turn. A "cold and moist" humor brings about homologous states in the logos and in the hegemonic, and it causes "stultitia" (i.e., "insanitas animi").

This approach, which was based on an ethical rationalism derived from Socrates and partly from Plato, was spread throughout the Roman world by Cicero with his *Tusculanae Disputationes* and Seneca with his *Letters* and his *De Gra*. Thus a dichotomy originated between morbid somatic forms and diseases of the soul. The Stoics, in fact, separated bodily diseases from psychiatric ones, seeing the latter as the sign of an "exaggerated passion" subjugating the self, the hegemonic. Melancholy arose out of sadness and anger; mania arose from hate and wrath. In the same way, the "insanitas animi" called *stultitia* had its origin in an intellective defect, in a lack of knowledge. "Foolishness" was therefore the expression of a behavior that was completely opposite to that of the "wise" person. Thus the foolish person was wholly determined by the "irrational" soul, the lowest, most wicked part—the psychological structure that was almost bodily, and therefore opposite to the rational sphere. Thus, just as a balanced temperance of the structures of the body implies physical health, an equilibrium between rational and irrational parts of the soul promotes mental health. The mentally sane person is such because of a "strong soul," which is fearless, knows no sadness, and therefore does not elaborate "phantasms" on which erroneous judgments leading to foolish behavior are based (15, 47, 49, 50).

Aesclepiades of Prusa (1st Century B.C.)

Acute schizophrenia, which was included within the concept of *mania*—a term used to indicate expansive dysthimiae as well as acute paranoid psychoses—and catatony provided rich material for the mechanistic approach of Aesclepiades of Prusa. This scholar gave interesting interpretations of these two mental disturbances, based on the idea of a state of irritation of the central nervous system due to a "tight" state of the atomic structure. This was caused by a diminution in the canaliculi's diameter, an increase of the atoms' speed, and higher frequency of "collusions" between the atoms themselves. Hebephreny, due to the scarceness of obvious symptoms, was little studied. Aesclepiades admitted the existence of a "spiritual" structure formed by minute and extremely fast atoms.

In stupid insanity there was supposed to be a certain turbidity of spirit giving rise to a negative symptomatology, with deficiencies. Thus the use of ethical terms (e.g., prudence, temperance) was to be avoided, because they indicated nothing but "generical concepts, with no meaning at all" (51).

The Solidists (1st Century B.C.)

The Solidist physicians who followed the atomistic theories of Leucippus and Democritus, applied to psychiatry in the 1st century B.C. by Aesclepiades of Prusa, focused their attention above all on acute schizophrenic psychoses whose semiological aspects seemed to lend more weight to the atomistic hypothesis of the human mind. In fact, in acute psychoses, dissociation, incoherence, and confusion appeared clearly. According to the followers of Aesclepiades, these indicated an underlying dissolution of the ties between the atoms that form the human mind (i.e., *leptomeres*). The delirious and hallucinatory phenomena could be interpreted using the concept of tightness, which indicated an increase in the speed of the atomic structures and an obstruction of the nervous ducts called channels.

In this perspective, the acute schizophrenic psychosis was described thus by Demetrius of Apamea, an author who lived in the 1st century B.C., as follows: "It is a sudden whirlwind of the mind accompanied by a slackening, *extentio* of the mind's ties . . . it manifests itself essentially as an alteration of all the senses" (52).

With the death of Aesclepiades, it was Themison and subsequently Thessalus who led the Solidist school of thought. Mnasea, one of Thessalus's pupils, deemed that a slackening of the mind's associative links, accompanied by atoms, their speed, and the ratio between the diameter of the canaliculi and the quantity of atoms, would lead to acute insanity. In acute schizophrenia, there was a definite disorganization of the neuro-organic atomistic structure.

According to Mnasea, who also lived at the end of the 1st century B.C., acute schizophrenia, called "acute mania," was brought about by a dissolution of the atomic ties of the brain (i.e., by a *laxatio animi*, a process of *diaschisis*) (52).

Aulus Cornelius Celsus (25 B.C.–A.D. 50)

The vitalist physician Athenaeus of Attalia and the eclectic Aulus Cornelius Celsus defined dementia praecox in terms of two qualities: "ingenita et adventitia." In both psychoses it is the brain that "becomes cold . . . as in old age." The value of this psychobiological trait of hebephrenia was stressed about one century later by Claudius Galen, who compared it to the symptomatology that shows itself in "evirated" young men. The nucleus of the psychosis is described by Celsus and Athenaeus as consisting in "ignavia, pigritia, fatuitas et marcor" (6, 47, 53).

As regards dementia praecox, Celsus isolated a variety of schizophrenic psychoses analogous to the "paranoid" psychoses—later to be called "paraphrosyniae" by Archigenes and Galen—precisely on the basis of a "chronic" development. These are mental disturbances specifically characterized by delirious-hallucinatory phenomena. Celsus wrote: "This kind of chronic insanity can be divided into two groups, for in one hallucinations are present (i.e. false perceptions) whereas in the other delirious ideas (i.e. ravings of the mind) may be observed" (54).

In addition to describing epileptic psychoses, hebetude, phrenitis, hysteria, melancholy, and euphoric mania, Celsus reported a form of "mental alienation" with a chronic course, resembling what we now call paraphrenia:

It is a form of insanity with a chronic course, which does not constitute an excessive obstacle to (a normal) life and which arises in young people with a robust temperament. There are two clinical varieties: in one case the patients suffer from visual and auditive hallucinations, in another case these are absent and an alienation of the mind prevails, with delirium. In both cases affectivity is stricken either with false euphoria or with depression. (54)

Athenaeus of Attalia (1st Century A.D.)

According to ancient scholars, hebetude, the fundamental nucleus of the psychoses later called schizophrenia, should present no "delirious" disturbances, the pathognomonic symptoms of that disease being mainly behavioral disorders and emotional blunting. As Aetius of Amida was to state later on, the hebephrenic in certain cases appears to be "abulic and apathetic, but his thought is coherent," whereas in other cases, there is "a disorder in action and speech."

Athenaeus of Attalia, a follower of the vitalistic trend who lived during the 1st century A.D., thought that the main characteristic of hebephreny was "stupidity"; the patient affected by such a morbid form was "bardum and nescium." At the basis of this disease there was supposed to be an "affection of the whole brain," so that hebephrenics were popularly known as people "who do not even know how many feet they (have)"; they were "ex cerebratos: i.e., without a brain" (5).

Aretaeus of Cappadocia (A.D. 135–200)

The work of Aretaeus of Cappadocia, a physician of the vitalistic school and a much appreciated semiologist in the sphere of psychiatric clinical science, carried out a unitary operation that was to be of decisive importance in the future of the nosology of dementia praecox. He collated under the concept of "mania" all those psychoses not classified in the category of "melancholy." He thought that this morbid form "manifests itself through many symptoms, but that they only express one kind of insanity" (55). Dysthymic mania, paranoid delirious psychoses, the paranoia called "fanaticism," delirious catatonies, and hebetude represent phenomena of an homologous psychotic process. The symptomatology varies because of the action of a mixture of humors, which vary in quality and quantity.

During this historical period, Rome was invaded by Oriental religions whose followers carried out strange and peculiar rituals in honor of various deities. This religious extremism was defined in the medical world as "furor divinus," but not all doctors considered it a sign of mental disease. According to Aretaeus (55), however, it was the expression of an underlying psychosis:

These are people troubled by pious superstitions and ill thoughts, who whip themselves thinking that they can thus gratify their god . . . they play music and drink, as happy as drunkards . . . for they are affected by a divine afflatus . . . ; I consider that in reality they are affected by a disease of the body.

According to Aretaeus, some psychotic manifestations that for centuries had been considered under the heading of stoliditas were really forms of mania:

> They occur in young people . . ., who become melancholic. . . . they have pathological ideas . . . , they think that they are philosophers, scholars, poets . . . ; this disease of young people may also be caused by lust with venereal excesses and excessive use of wine.

Aretaeus distinguished acute psychoses "caused by alcohol and herbs such as mandrake" from "chronic delirious mania." This is a delirious manifestation due to "a hot brain . . . i.e., inflammation." Aretaeus also considered among such cases fanaticism (i.e., severely altered behavior on the grounds of religious belief). On this much discussed clinical picture, he wrote:

> Fanaticism is a variety of chronic furor, these ill people beat their own limbs and tear them off, sacrificing to their god, as if he had requested this. This kind of insanity has its origin in certain beliefs. Such ill people are otherwise modest and temperate in their social life . . . but they only get excited . . . as though inspired by gods . . . they are also pale, thin and their bodies are covered with wounds.

Aretaeus was known for providing a precise identification of bipolar cyclothymia, a disease that would "suddenly pass from melancholic torment to merriness and joy."

The unifying attempt of Aretaeus was not very successful at the time, because the work of Galen returned dementia to the domain of Hippocrates. However, some centuries later, with Byzantine and Arab psychiatry, dementia praecox was considered, as by Aretaeus, as a variety of melancholy or mania (46, 55).

Claudius Galen (A.D. 129–199)

Claudius Galen, at the epoch of the Emperors Antoninii, examined the problem of dementia praecox, which he restored to the Hippocratic domain. Galen stressed the value of the lesson given by the biopsychological school in psychiatry in that he considered the soul an active form with a physical structure: "the soul has a physical temperament . . . also in its rational part." The psychiatric symptom is the expression of a "function" of the soul altered by pathogenic factors: "The black bile sets off melancholy, yellow bile mania, fever phrenitis . . . , wine and hemlock alter the mind . . . , the pituita brings about 'stoliditas'." Any physical, chemical, infective, toxic event can bring about psychiatric symptomatology because "it makes the soul a slave to the body" (10).

Psychoses have their genesis in a somatic dysfunction that is reflected in the brain, or in a primary disorganization of the "animal activities" (i.e., what we now call neuropsychological functions).

Combinations of humoral factors, genetic data, and even the somatic constitution determine both character and the predisposition to psychiatric disturbances. "Mores" can also be inferred from the *forma corporis*. "Morositas," "paraphrosyniae," and foolishness originate from humoral or neurophysiologic disturbances; an excess of pituita in the brain is sufficient to bring about stultitia (i.e., "slothful" behavior) (6, 56–60).

According to Galen, the brain is the seat of "animal functions"—that is, of the higher neuropsychological activities that are deranged in the course of psychoses, such as "the chronic disease called 'fatuitas' . . . due to an excessive cooling of the brain" (61, 62).

Fatuitas is a "morbus" connected with an "intemperies cerebri" of the structures of the soul, situated by Galen "at the basis of the brain . . . , near the third ventricle"; these structures are physiologically "hot." In fact, according to Galen, the soul is "a hot substance, which contains its own vitality and innate purpose" (63).

According to Galen, the processes of mental disease are always set off by an organic factor; in particular, in dementia praecox, the "corruption" of the soul gives rise to a "weakness" of the same. This usually occurs in individuals presenting a congenital fragility of the soul, so that, also according to the physiologists, sexual intercourse was the cause of a weakening of the vital tone (6, 64). The pituita "moistens" excessively the brain tissue and makes it similar to that "of a child." As a consequence, the main characteristic of that disease is "indolence"—that is, affective impoverishment and the weakness of will, which brings about a behavior that is socially inappropriate because it is listless and not sufficiently vital (10, 58, 59, 61, 62).

In Galen's view, the primary symptom that characterizes dementia praecox consists in the deadening of the affective and emotional life, in its "leveling." He defined it thus: "the individuals affected by 'morositas' or 'fatuitas' primarily display a deadening of the life of the emotions" (65).

According to Galen, a person is worthy if he or she has "an acute reason and a strong heart." With fatuousness, on the contrary, we are in the presence of an individual "who has no brain and owns a timid and pusillanimous heart." For this reason, Galen wrote, patients affected by fatuousness are commonly designated as individuals "sine cerebro" (i.e., with a poor mind). This disease always makes itself manifest "sine delirio," and all attempts to activate a "moist and cold" brain lead to nothing, so that this disease is to be considered incurable. The patient may also be designated by the terms *nescius, bardus, or stupidus* (58, 59, 62, 65).

Thus identified, the psychotic nucleus of dementia praecox excluded any confusion with other forms of psychosis, either catatonic or paranoid, between which Galen, in fact, made a rigid distinction. He distinguished with respect to foolishness the delirious paranoid psychoses called 'paraphrosyniae" (i.e., "delirious insanities") in which "the imaginative functions are altered" so that this psychosis manifests itself through a "delirium of the imagination." There are also hallucinations, "spectra," and psychomotor agitation with "strange and rash acts" (6, 65).

"Cathoco" is another psychosis that Galen distinguished from dementia praecox both on an etiopathogenic level, because he thought it was caused by the "black bile," and on a symptomatic level. In fact, it shows three kinds of symptoms ("tria genera"): "one [kind] with sopor alternating with wakefulness, [another] with muscular block and [another] similar to hysterical fits of anguish" (63).

Mental disturbances have their basis in a functional disorganization of the "animal" activities of a hegemonic kind—that is, of the higher psychic functions, subdivided by Galen into imaginative, rational, and mnesic activities.

The three fundamental psychoses of the schizophrenic group—that is, catatony, paraphrosyniae, and foolishness—depend, respectively, on a "block" of the imaginative function, on a "depravation" of the same, and on a "diminution" of the rational activities (59, 65).

Galen thought that psychoses, "alienationes mentis," were characterized by behavior that was "detached from the usual social customs." For this reason, he did not include in the sphere of psychopathology "fanatismus religiosus," also called "enthusiasmos" or "furor divinus," as this was supposed to be "a particular state of the mind" that brought about "a perversion supported by particular religious ideas."

Unlike Galen, the physician Rufus of Ephesus, who followed the Hippocratic and Aristotelian trend, considered the fanatics real "delirious men" who behaved abnormally because "they hated humanity and acrimoniously condemned sexual activity, which, on the contrary, by dilating the canaliculi and expelling the pituita actually has an hygienic and therapeutic effect on such patients."

Although he maintained they were distinct from dementia praecox, Galen included among insanities those psychoses he called "explesis"—that is, a physical state of panic, bewilderment, and dismay. By this he meant "an alteration of the mind related to external events"—that is, a psychogenic psychosis in modern nosologic terms. Another acute psychosis, called "extasis," was "a brief and acute insanity" (26, 42, 54, 63, 66, 67).

He explained the clear-cut separation between dementia praecox and the other psychoses that are now considered related to it, such as catatony and acute chronic paranoid psychoses, on the basis of a blunting of the intellectual and affective-emotional life in the former morbid form. This could be interpreted using a vitalistic biological model.

Catatony

Catatony was for the first time acknowledged as a psychiatric form by Hippocrates, who called it "cathoco"; with time, the cataleptic symptom became synonymous with the morbid form, which was thus denominated *catalepsy*. It was also called *oppressio, apprehensio, detentio, congelatio*, and *extasis*. Praxagoras called it *comatode*, and Antigenes Cleophantinus called it *anaudia*. The name of the disease, as may be noted, was given according to the value attributed to the considered pathognomonic symptom: muscular rigidity, mental confusion, sopor, verbal negativism.

In the 1st century A.D., Agatinus, Magnus, and Archigenes distinguished it from the organic psychoses, such as lethargy, phrenitis, and hysterical sopor. The symptoms considered fundamental in "cathoco" were muscular rigidity, negativism, and, above all, catalepsy, due to which the patient would "hold the positions which were imposed upon him."

However, Galen had often noticed how the outcome of the morbid picture did not lead to mental deterioration and how the ill person would "remember all that he had seen and heard." According to Galen, the etiopathogenic mechanism consisted in a "temporary block of the imaginative function." The modern scholar might translate this as a loss of control over the superior symbolic functions: language, bodily schemata, and motor schemata. Intelligence was only temporarily "blocked," while only the "imaginative [function] of movement" was affected (5, 58, 68).

The vitalistic and humoral paradigms, however, could not be used to interpret catatony because of its psychomotor symptoms. In fact, the importance of this psychosis was stressed by the physicians of the "solidist" trend, who had chosen, as an approach to mental disease, the atomistic philosophy of Democritus and Epicure.

Mental diseases were due to an "anomalous movement of the corpuscles." These were supposed to move inside the "nervous canaliculi," with greater or lesser speed, thus bringing about certain psychoses caused by a "strictura" and others by a "lax" state; if the two states coexisted, there was a "mixed" state. Catatony was related to an obstruction of the corpuscles, called "leptomeres," inside the canaliculi of the brain and the meninges, which brought about a secondary "strictura cerebri" (52, 54, 63, 69–73).

According to the psychopathologic approach of the atomistic school, catatony was caused by a "tight" state of the brain due to an "oppilatio," a clogging of the organic atoms in the "meata" of the brain.

As a follower of the vitalistic school, the physician Archigenes of Apamea (2nd century A.D.), on the other hand, considered catatony as a psychosis brought about by a de-structuring of the state of wakefulness, more than as a phenomenon of mechanic hyperstimulation.

The "cathoco" is a disease that affects young people and is situated in between lethargy and phrenitis:

It is a sort of amential delirium . . . the patients are immobile . . . they seem not to hear . . . they do not speak . . . , if one passes one's hand in front of their eyes their eye-lids do not move . . . ; the disease is due to the action of the black bile. (26, 74)

Between the 1st century B.C. and the 3rd century A.D., some scholars of a mechanistic and vitalistic orientation took an interest in cathoco. Among the first to do this were Aesclepiades of Prusa, Themison, Philippus, and Soranus of Ephesus, followed by Agatinus of Apamea and Magnus of Sparta.

The fundamental symptom is catalepsy, because the muscular fiber is supposed to have become "dry and cold." The cathoco is considered an autonomous psychosis, although very near to "hebetudo." The value given to the importance of the action of the black bile is based on the frequent observation of depressive aspects: "dejection, affliction, and sadness." However, other symptoms—such as rigor, stupor, and negativism, as a result of which the patients "clench their teeth and do not eat"—directed the diagnosis toward a form of mental disease that was independent of mania, melancholy, and dementia praecox.

As we have seen, in Galen's opinion, cathoco was the expression of a dysfunction, a block of the "animal" functions called imaginative (i.e., symbolic). The catatonic individual had lost the schemata of movement and thought. Catatony was a secondary disturbance, a "paralysis" of the imaginative activity, a function having its seat in the brain, under the direction of the "animal" functions and with a directive center situated, according to Galen, around "the medium cerebral ventricle." It is in this very area, as Galen also proved with his experiments on animals, that a small lesion would "cause catatony and sopor."

The basic symptom of catatony (i.e., "catalepsis") originates from a block between the imaginative and the motor function, because the "directive" animal forces have been damaged. For these etiopathogenic reasons, cathoco vaguely resembles an organic psychosis, both because of the psychomotor block and the blunting of the sensorium; indeed, Galen thought, it is situated "between lethargy and phrenitis" (58, 65, 75).

According to Paulus Aegineta (76), cathoco is characterized by muscular tension, sopor, a mental block, and catalepsy; for this reason he considered it something in between lethargy and phrenitis. He deemed it useful to warn physicians that this morbid form was quite rare in women, in whose case such clinical pictures are of a psychoemotional kind—that is, they are due to "strangulatio uteri," the mechanism fostering hysteria. The various catatonic clinical pictures are to be recognized through negativism: "the refusal of food and drink" and catalepsy, which is the peculiar phenomenon in which "the patients remain in the position in which they have been put" (76).

The Byzantine Period (5th–8th Century A.D.)

With the work of Galen, at the beginning of the 3rd century A.D., the great phase of classical psychiatry came to an end, and a period of decline that was to continue during the Byzantine period commenced. At the time of the emperor Valens, in the 4th century A.D., there was still the work of the physician Posidonius, which was indeed closely linked with the models of the past. He observed that "fatuitas," a disease that was typical of "youngsters and adolescents," was characterized by a process of disintegration and regression, as it would affect individuals "whose rational mind had previously been intact" and then lead to a state called "dementia" by Posidonius (26).

The period of Byzantine psychiatry goes from the end of the 5th century to the end of the 8th century A.D. The scholars of that period of involution merely reported whole passages of the works of physicians of the past: Claudius Galen, Aesclepiades, Rufus of Ephesus, Archigenes, Posidonius, and Soranus of Ephesus.

Aëtius of Amida (A.D. 502–575)

The first physician of the Byzantine epoch, Aëtius of Amida, was the personal physician of the emperor Justinian. Aëtius focused the course and the demential outcome of fatuitas: "those affected are young people with a modest but intact mind, who after the disease appear as though [they were] demented" (26). Aëtius insisted, as Galen had already done, on distinguishing the hebephrenic psychoses from the paranoid ones; in his experience, individuals suffering from dementia praecox "hardly ever suffer from deliria."

Catatony is, in the view of Aëtius, a mental disturbance differing both in its symptomatology and etiopathogenesis from fatuity. It is a mental alienation whose genesis is to be sought after in a disturbance of a confusional kind. It is situated, according to Aëtius, "halfway between phrenitis and lethargy and is a variety of amential delirium."

The etymology of this term, amens, indicated a clinical picture based on a partial or complete block of mental functions. This same mechanism would bring about, as a secondary effect, "immobility . . . absence of speech . . . retention of faeces and urine . . . and a secondary dementia" (26).

Alexander of Tralles (A.D. 525–605)

With Alexander of Tralles, who was also an acute semiologist of organic psychoses, we see a return to the tendency to include dementia praecox among other forms of mental disease, and thus to deny it nosologic autonomy. The psychiatry of the Byzantine epoch was oriented toward a synthesis that abstracted the clinical data and thus united all "insaniae" under the concept of melancholy. The semiological differences between the various psychoses were explained on the hypothesis that there was a multiformity of pathogenic factors due to the different actions of the four humors. The association of a dysmetabolism of the black bile and of the pituita thus engendered a particular melancholy in which, in young patients, "incoherent speech . . . and laziness" were predominating.

Alexander of Tralles observed in these schizophrenic psychotics also (and especially) emotional and affective blunting, abulia, apathy, and negativism: "they are sleepy, indolent and they [refuse] to answer questions" (77). He then described some chronic delirious forms of psychosis, in which the affected people "are afraid of being killed . . . or they think they can predict their future . . . and in such cases the patients are always in a continuous state of folly" (77).

According to Alexander of Tralles, paranoid deliriums are part of a variety of melancholy. They are characterized by both negative and productive symptoms: "torpor, laziness, and deliria as the patients think that they can foresee the future" (77). This disease has a chronic course and its outcome is often "dementia." Alexander of Tralles thought that melancholy included three subgroups: somatic, hypochondriac, and mental. In the latter morbid form, the mind was "affected" so that the patient would manifest "mystical and religious deliria." In the course of this kind of paranoid delirious melancholy, attacks of "delirious furor" might appear (77).

Paulus Aegineta (A.D. 625–690)

Paulus Aegineta was a physician who became historically important. As a teacher of medicine, gynecology and obstetrics at the University of Alexandria, he was responsible for transmitting classical psychiatric culture to Arab scholars. He lived in Asia Minor and in Alexandria after these regions had fallen under the dominion of the Arabs. He was much appreciated both as a translator of classical texts and as a practicing physician; he was head of a school of midwifery in Egypt. Paulus Aegineta tended to classify dementia praecox with other psychoses, but above all with those of a psycho-organic kind. In fact, according to this scholar, "fatuitas" was part of group of diseases with an organic psychopathology: "disturbances of memory, alterations of the reason and tendency to sopor" (76).

Having learned the traditional clinical lesson, based on semiological experience—which saw in catatony a disease situated between organic delirious psychoses and confusional states—Paulus Aegineta called this disturbance also "vigil sopor." This disease is characterized by the presence of "total immobility, apparent absence of breathing and the retention of faeces and urine" (76). Paulus Aegineta also noted an active negatism: "If one tries to feed them they even reject the food and discharge back through their nostrils." A female patient affected by catatony might even lead to think of "uterine suffocation." In this case, Paulus wrote: "The differential diagnosis is easy—for a woman who is prey to such an hysterical state feels, perceives and reacts intermittently with violence, and then falls into sopor" (76).

Paulus Aegineta noticed that one characteristic of catatony (a disease caused by damage to the pituita) of the "rear ventricle of the brain" was catalepsy, so that "the patient remains still and immobile in the position in which he has been placed" (76). For this reason, ancient observers called the disease "cathoco" (i.e., "motor block" and, also referring to the latter semiological aspect, "catalepsis") (76, 78, 79).

The death of Paulus Aegineta at the end of the 7th century A.D. marked the beginning of Arab psychiatry. This new direction did not contribute new data to dementia praecox, since the Arab scholar as a rule merely translated the work of Aristotle, Plato, Hippocrates, and Galen, and the pharmacology of Dioscorides Pedacius (80).

The Arabian Phase (7th–12th Century A.D.)

Dementia praecox, as an autonomus psychosis, had lost interest and value, so much so that one of the first great Arab physicians, Rhazes, (81) (judging from the documents that have been handed down to us) seemed not to mention it at all. He described summarily some psychoses, such as melancholy and phrenitis, but he did not mention specific clinical pictures resembling dementia praecox. He only described some physical and physiognomic aspects of individuals having a "natura hebes" or a "natura morosa" (81).

Avicenna (A.D. 980–1037)

The physician Avicenna mentioned dementia praecox in reporting the interpretation of this psychosis given by Galen. He thought that the typical symptoms of dementia praecox, affecting "the imagination" or "the intellect," were due to a dysfunction of the frontal and median cerebral lobes, where the imaginative and the intellectual functions, respectively, were situated. According to Avicenna, dementia praecox is a psychosis based on three pathognomonic symptoms: "stoliditas," "amentia," and "fatuitas." These symptoms may be slight when they are due to a functional alteration involving only a "diminution" of the activity of the nerve centers or severe "when these centres are blocked" (6, 8).

Avenzoar (1091?–1162)

The last Arab physician, who lived in Sevill and died there in 1162, was Avenzoar. He had a direct influence on medieval psychiatry, above all on that of the University of Montpellier, which, a few decades before, had been acknowledged as a cultural center by a special papal law. Avenzoar was faithful to Aristotle's biopsychology and to his "cardiocentric" approach. Dementia praecox, according to this theory, originates from a "weakening of the heat of the blood." This diminution of the "power" of the physical foundations of the soul is supposed to reflect on the brain, which, in turn, becomes "excessively cold." This mechanism is supposed to bring about a "weakening of the centre of the animal faculties . . . as may also happen in an oily and heavy climate" (82).

Conclusion

Having reached the end of our historical exposition and having compared the views of the various classical psychiatrists on schizophrenic disturbances, we are forced to recognize a substantial identity between the ancient and the modern approach. There seem to be no remarkable differences between the nosology of schizophrenic disturbances proposed by the American Psychiatric Association's *Diagnostic and Statistical Manual of Mental Disorders* (83) on the one hand and classical nosology on the other. This statement is very important from a scientific viewpoint, for it confirms the existence, above all, of interpretive models of natural psychiatric entities that have been modified only marginally by historical and social development.

I trust that I have also demonstrated the richness and complexity of ancient thought with respect to the mental disturbance now called schizophrenia. The ancient scholars were able to identify this disease, describing its semiological aspects and providing an adequate nosology for it, as well as creating various interpretive schemas of a monistic and organistic type.

It is my conviction that the modern psychiatrist can profit greatly from a "dialogue" with the scientific contributions we have inherited from ancient scholars on the theme of schizophrenia (84).

References

1. Kraepelin E: Psychiatrie, Vol. 2. Leipzig, Von Johann Ambrosius Barth, 1904
2. Bleuler E: Dementia Praecox or the Group of Schizophrenias. New York, International Universities Press, 1961
3. Bellack L: Dementia Praecox. New York, Grune & Stratton, 1948
4. Fish FJ: Schizophrenia. Bristol, John Wright & Sons, 1962
5. Mercurialis J: de cognoscendi et curandis corporis humani affectibus. Venetia, B Giunta, 1606
6. Perdulcis B: de morbis animi. Paris, L Boullenger, 1639
7. Menninger K: The Vital Balance. New York, Viking, 1963
8. Robin L: La pensée grecque at les origines de l'esprit scientifique. Paris, Albin Michel, 1951
9. Zeller E: Die Philosophie der Griechen in ihrer geschichtlichen Entwicklung. Hildeskeim, Georg Olms, 1963
10. Galenus C: Quod animi mores corporis temperamenta sequantur, in Opera Omnia. Venetiis, V Valgrisium, 1562
11. Hippocrates: de natura homini, in Opera Omnia. Venetia, Radiciana, 1737
12. Pohlenz M: Der Hellenische Mensch. Gottingen, Vandenhoeck & Ruprecht, 1947
13. Laurenti R: Eraclito. Bari, Laterza, 1974
14. Aristotle: Metaphysics. Cambridge, MA, Harvard University Press, 1961

15. Diogenes L: Lives of Eminent Philosophers. Cambridge, MA, Harvard University Press, 1964
16. Plutarch: Moralia. Cambridge, MA, Harvard University Press, 1967
17. Hippocrates: de diaeta, in Opera Omnia. Venetia, Radiciana, 1737
18. Hippocrates: de morbis, in Opera Omnia. Venetia, Radiciana, 1737
19. Marinellus J: Commentaria, in Opera Omnia Hippocratis. Venetia, Radiciana, 1737
20. Lloyd GER: Magic and Experience. Studies in the Origin and Development of Greek Science. New York, Cambridge University Press, 1979
21. Jager W: Paideia. Berlin, W de Gruyter and Co, 1936
22. Gomperz T: Griechische Denker. Berlin, W de Gruyter, 1922–1931
23. Garrison FH: History of Medicine. London, WB Saunders, 1968
24. Aristotle: On the Soul. Cambridge, MA, Harvard University Press, 1962
25. Castellus B: Lexicum Medicum. Patavia, J Manfré, 1721
26. Aetius A: de re medica. Parisiis, Henricus Stephanus, 1567
27. Burckardt: Griechische Kulturgeschichte. München, GmbH & Co, 1977
28. Aristotle: On the Heavens. Cambridge, MA, Harvard University Press, 1971
29. Hippocrates: de carnibus, in Opera Omnia. Venetia, Radiciana, 1737
30. Mieli A: La scienza greca:i prearistotelici. Firenze, Libreria della Voce, 1916
31. Heraclitus: Fragmenta. Bari, Laterza, 1974
32. Kahn CH: The Art and Thought of Heraclitus. New York, Cambridge University Press, 1979
33. Galenus C: Hippocrates praedictionum commentarium, in Opera Omnia. Venetiis, V Valgrisium, 1562
34. Galenus C: Hippocrates de morbi vulgaribus commentarius, in Opera Omnia. Venetiis, V Valgrisium, 1562
35. Hippocrates: de homini structura, in Opera Omnia. Venetia, Radiciana, 1737
36. Hippocrates: de glandulis, in Opera Omnia. Venetia, Radiciana, 1737
37. Galenus C: Hippocratis commentarius in aphorismos, in Opera Omnia. Venetiis, V Valgrisium, 1562
38. Jaeger W: Die Theolögie der frühen griechischen Denker. Stuttgart, W Kohlhammer, 1953
39. Hippocrates: de morbis popularibus, in Opera Omnia. Venetia, Radiciana, 1737
40. Hippocrates: de morbo sacro, in Opera Omnia. Venetia, Radiciana, 1737
41. Hippocrates: de corde, in Opera Omnia. Venetia, Radiciana, 1737
42. Plato: Timaeus. Cambridge, MA, Harvard University Press, 1975
43. Aristotle: Parts of Animals. Cambridge, MA, Harvard University Press, 1979
44. Aristotle: Problems. Cambridge, MA, Harvard University Press, 1970
45. Macrobius T: Convivia Saturnaliorum. Torino, Utet, 1967
46. Mercurialis J: Variarum lectionum in medicinae scriptoribus. Venetia, B Giunta, 1606
47. Pohlenz M: Die Stoa. Göttingen, Vandenhoeck & Ruprecht, 1959
48. Sambursky S: The Physical World of the Greeks. London, Routledge & Kegan, 1956
49. Plato: Prothagoras. Cambridge, MA, Harvard University Press, 1976
50. Pigeaud J: La maladie de l'âme. Paris, Les Belles Lettres, 1981
51. Gumpert CG: Fragments of Asclepiades of Bithynia. New Haven, CT, Licht, 1955
52. Aurelianus C: de tardis passionibus. Ludguni, G Rovillium, 1566

53. Galenus C: de semine, in Opera Omnia. Venetiis, V Valgrisium, 1562
54. Celsus AC: de medicina. Patavii, J Cominus, 1750
55. Aretaeus Cappadocensis: de causis et notis diuturnorum morborum. Parisiis, H Stephanus, 1567
56. Siegel RE: Galen, on Psychology, Psychopathology and Function and Diseases of the Nervous System. Basel, S Karger, 1973
57. Galenus C: Hippocratis de humoribus commentarius, in Opera Omnia. Venetiis, V Valgrisium, 1562
58. Galenus C: de locis affectis, in Opera Omnia. Venetiis, V Valgrisium, 1562
59. Galenus C: de symptomatis causis, in Opera Omnia. Venetiis, V Valgrisium, 1562
60. Galenus C: de termperamentis, in Opera Omnia. Venetiis, V Valgrisium, 1562
61. Galenus C: de praesagitione ex pulsibus, in Opera Omnia. Venetiis, V Valgrisium, 1562
62. Galenus C: de Hippocratis et Platonis decretis, in Opera Omnia. Venetiis, V Valgrisium, 1562
63. Galenus C: Medicae definitiones, in Opera Omnia. Venetiis, V Valgrisium, 1562
64. Alexander A: Problemata, in Phisici et medici graeci minores. Amsterdam, AM Hakkert, 1963
65. Galenus C: de symptomatum differentiis, in Opera Omnia. Venetiis, V Valgrisium, 1562
66. Plato: Phaedrus. Cambridge, MA, Harvard University Press, 1975
67. Taylor AE: Plato. London, Methuen, 1966
68. Galenus C: de uso partium corporis humani, in Opera Omnia. Venetiis, V Valgrisium, 1562
69. Aurelianus C: de acutis morbis. Ludguni, G Rovillium, 1566
70. Cocchi A: Discorso secondo sopra Asclepiade, in Consulti medici. Milano, Classici italiani, 1824
71. De Renzi S: Storia della medicina italiana. Napoli, Labezio, 1845
72. Cicero MT: Tusculanae disputationes, in Opera Omnia. Torino, I Pomba, 1828
73. Galenus C: de historia philosophica, in Opera Omnia. Venetiis, V Valgrisium, 1562
74. Le Clerc D: Storia della medicina. Napoli, V Manfredi, 1762
75. Galenus C: de causis pulsuum, in Opera Omnia. Venetiis, V Valgrisium, 1562
76. Paulus Aegineta: de re medica. Parisiis, H Stephanus, 1567
77. Alexander T: de arte medica. Parisiis, H Stephanus, 1567
78. Le Clerc L: Histoire de la médicine arabe. Paris, E Leroux, 1876
79. Zilboorg G, Henry WG: History of Medical Psychology. New York, WW Norton, 1941
80. Freind J: Historia medicinae a Galeni tempore usque ad initium saeculi decimi sexti. Neapoli, A Cervonius, 1758
81. Rhazes AB: de re medica. Basilae, H Petrus, 1544
82. Avicenna: Liber Canonis. Venetiis, 1505
83. American Psychiatric Association: Diagnostic and Statistical Manual of Mental Disorders, 3rd Edition, Revised. Washington, DC, American Psychiatric Association, 1987
84. Roccatagliata G: A History of Ancient Psychiatry. Westport, CT, Greenwood, 1986

.

CHAPTER TWO

Schizophrenia
in the Medieval Period

John G. Howells, M.D.

Although authorities vigorously debate the definition of the term *medieval*, they at least agree that no precise beginning or end can be given to the period of time it covers. Usually, it is deemed to cover from the decline of the Roman civilization to the Reformation. Here the period taken is that between A.D. 1000 and A.D. 1600, and thus it includes part of the Renaissance. The area for study is that of Western Europe. The medieval period saw the beginning of Christian care for the mentally infirm. Institutional care for the mentally ill and physically sick also existed in Western Europe and the Arab world, and organized medical care was being established. Toward the end of the period, we see the slow breakaway from Greco-Roman medicine and more dissemination of knowledge through the invention of printing.

Academic medicine early in the medieval period was passed down from master to pupil; after the 12th century, it was taught in university medical schools. It was based on the writings of Hippocrates (A.D. 460–377) and, more especially, Galen (A.D. 129–199), and also the 6th and 7th century physicians such as Alexander of Tralles (A.D. 525–605) and Paul of Aegina (A.D. 625–690). Greco-Roman medicine had been retained and developed in the Islamic world from Persia to Spain; this was also influenced by the local medical traditions. Academic medicine returned to Europe in the 12th century. Two particular Arab physicians influenced our period: Rhazes and Avicenna. Rhazes (A.D. 864–925), a Persian physician, published a classi-

29

fication of physical and mental conditions in *The Spiritual Physick of Rhazes*. Avicenna (A.D. 980–1037), a Persian poet, published his *Canon of Medicine* based on Galen and influenced the Islamic as well as the Western European world; mental diseases were included in a chapter on head diseases. As time went on, the traditional Galenic medicine was challenged by new findings such as those by Vesalius (1514–1564) in 1543 on anatomy and by the views of figures such as Paracelsus (1493?–1541) and Felix Platter (1536–1614). There were physicians among the monks but the rise of medical practices in the towns and of medical studies in the new universities put monastic medicine into a backwater after A.D. 1200. Physicians could still be influenced by the prevailing interest in astrology. They took the available knowledge and applied it as best they could to the practical problems of the ill and mentally ill. In addition, there was folk medicine.

Care for mental patients was given by municipalities, by hospitals, and, for clerics, by monasteries. The system of monastic and church-door poor relief had begun to break down a long time before the Reformation. The methods of charity practiced by the monasteries had been indiscriminate, property of the hospices had often been diverted from its intended use, and the hospitality of monasteries or hospices had frequently served the rich rather than the poor. The Council of Vienne (1313), after condemning corrupt adminstrators of leprosariums, hospices, and hospitals, had forbidden the transformation of charitable foundations into clerical benefices. The edict was renewed by the Council of Trent (1545–1563). Thereafter, in many countries, attempts were made to transfer the administration of foundations to secular control. Thus in France from the time of Louis XII, a series of ordinances sought to reorganize the administration of philanthropic institutions and to take them out of the control of religious bodies. The same tendencies were found in England. These were the circumstances from which evolved the policy of public support through compulsory taxation to relieve extreme poverty through the enactment of poor laws.

Municipalities made provision for the care of the mentally ill in their budgets. Hospitals began to give care. In England, for instance, there were 18 hospitals in 1120 but by the 12th century there were 166, 80 of which were leper houses. Later, these hospitals began to include accommodation for the mentally ill; in 1403, for instance, Bethlehem in London had nine inmates of which six men were "deprived of reason." In the second half of the medieval period, there began to develop hospitals for the insane alone. Some were founded as such and some made use of the leper hospitals as they became available.

Kroll (1), Neugebauer (2, 3), and Neaman (4) all argued strongly and convincingly that public as well as professional opinion in the medieval period attributed lunacy to naturalistic rather than demonological ideas. Kroll and Bachrach (5) put this view beyond reasonable question by their careful study of 57 descriptions of mental illness in the middle ages. In only 16% of these descriptions did the source attribute the mental illness to sin or wrongdoing. The researchers concluded: "The medieval sources indicate that the authors were well aware of the proximate causes of mental illness, such as humoral imbalance, intemperate diet and alcohol intake, overwork, and grief." According to Howells and Osborn (6), natural causes were emphasized as the source of mental illness by writers of the time: Roger Bacon (1214–1294), Bartholomaeus Anglicus (died 1260?), Gilbertus Anglicus (1250), Johannes Actuarius (?–1283), Cornelius Agrippa (1486–1535), Juan Luis Vives (1492–1540), and Reginald Scott (1538–1599). Bartholomaeus Angelicus expressed himself thus on this issue:

> Madness cometh sometime of passions of the soul, as of business and of great thoughts, of sorrow and of too great study, and of dread; sometime of the biting of a wood-hound (mad dog), or some other venomous beast; sometime of melancholy meats, and sometime of drink of strong wine. And as the causes be diverse, the tokens and signs be diverse.

Our quest is to discover whether the condition that we now term *schizophrenia* was recognized at this time by whatever practitioners served the mentally ill. We would also like to know how they described it. Given its identification, it would be intriguing to know how they visualized its cause. For the practitioners of that age to state their case to us today presents them with formidable obstacles: written records were scant, notions of pathology were primitive, and their nomenclature was different from ours. These obstacles are discussed in the introduction to this book. While the more direct evidence that we seek will come from clinical sources, valuable indirect sources exist, such as legal codes and literary allusions.

Clinical Sources

General

In the medieval period, largely following Galen, there were three main elements to views held on mental disorders (7, 8). First, views on etiology were based on aberrations of the four humors. Second, there was an early attempt to localize mental dysfunction, disorders of the head, around the cerebral ventricles. Mania or madness was ascribed to "infection of the foremost cell of the head"—the anterior horns of the lateral ventricles and the frontal lobes. Melancholy was ascribed to "infection of the middle cell"—the body of the lateral ventricles and the parieto-temporal regions. Forgetfulness was ascribed to the "hinder cell"—the posterior horns of the lateral ventricles and the occipital lobes. Third, there were attempts at classification. Disorders of the head had three common conditions: melancholie (common), phrenitis (common also), and mania (less common and least mentioned in medieval literature); each of these conditions is worthy of more discussion here.

Melancholie was distinguished by manifesting no fever and was due to an excess of black bile. Galen even asserted that there were three types. In the first there was a disease of the blood and a darkening of the skin. In the second, the brain was affected. The third was regarded as hypochondriacal (i.e., having its origin in the hypochondrium); the brain was secondarily involved when "the vapours" rose to "the head." Melancholie was thought to be more common in men but more serious in women. It was precipitated by physical causes (e.g., dietary irregularities) and by psychological causes. It manifested itself in two groups of symptoms. The more common group had symptoms turning around sadness, fear, and anxiety; these patients were usually able to continue life. The less common group had delusions as their main feature (e.g., that they were made of glass, that people were against them, that they were dead). This group of patients were said to be in continual madness, and the term *insania* was used to describe them. The descriptions raise the possibility that schizophrenia might be included in this less common group.

Phrenitis was a disorder of the head characterized by fever. It was assumed to indicate an inflammation of the brain or meninges. Phrenitis was differentiated from delirium caused by infections elsewhere in the body than the head. The humoral imbalance was an excess of yellow bile.

Mania was characterized by a tendency to restlessness, wildness, and excitement, but in the absence of fever. There was an imbalance of yellow bile. It was precipitated by physical reasons (e.g., drunkeness, drugs) as well as by emotional causes. It is a possibility that states of acute schizophrenia might be classified here.

Less common conditions included catalepsy, lethargy, lycanthropy, incubus, hysteria, love sickness, and being "possessed." Catalepsy was characterized by stupor. In lethargy there was stupor, but with fever. Lycanthropy was a form of melancholie when patients went out at night imitating wolves. In incubus there were frequent nightmares. Hysteria was a disorder of the uterus in women and marked by a loss of consciousness and convulsions; the uterus caused "suffocation." Love sickness is reactive to romantic misadventure. Possession, first described by Paul of Aegina, was characteristic of patients who thought themselves possessed by divine influence and with a gift of prophesy; it was a form of melancholy and the patients were not demoniacs. Epilepsy was also described as a separate condition from the above. It can be seen that some of the symptoms of schizophrenia could be identified in these less common conditions.

Schizophrenia was not recognized as a clear-cut disorder. States of schizophrenia characterized by a lack of florid symptoms, and especially marked by delusions, might well have been classified under melancholie. Excited schizophrenics might have been classified under mania. Others might be regarded as cataleptic or suffering from possession or even lycanthropy.

Major Texts

Study of nosologic schemas in some of the main texts in European psychiatry will be considered for evidence that schizophrenia was recognized.

Bartholomaeus Anglicus. An English Franciscan friar, Bartholomaeus Anglicus (died 1260?) (6, 9) became professor of theology in Paris. Between 1230 and 1240 he compiled an encyclopedia, *De Proprietatibus Rerum (The Properties of Things)* (10), which was translated into English by John of Trevisa in 1398 and printed by Wynkyn de Worde in 1495. This was a very popular treatise in the medieval period and the first book to be printed on paper made in England. In Book 7, he considered conditions of the "head." There are no case histories to clarify the nature of the disorders mentioned. He followed humoral theory and the influence of location in one of the three brain ventricles: the foremost, middle, or hinder cells. *Frenesis* is said to be a meningeal lesion related to the action of red choler; it shows itself in restlessness, insomnia, crying and laughing, aggression, and fever. He thus seemed to talk of an infective delirium. He distinguished it from *parafrenesi*, a delirium due to infection other than in the brain. Amentia is equated with madness: "Amencia and madnes is al one." Madness includes raving madness, or mania; as elsewhere mania connotes restlessness from any origin. *Melancholie* appears to include what would be termed *neurosis* today together with the condition of delusional states—thus suggesting the possibility of schizophrenia. "Gaurynge (staring) and forgetfulness" could be stupor and dementia in present-day nomenclature; both might have affinity to schizophrenia—stupor in a catatonic state and dementia in the form in which it presents in the young.

Gilbertus Anglicus. Gilbertus Anglicus (fl. 1250) (6, 9) was an English author of several works of medicine. The oldest manuscript of his famous work, *Compendium Medicinae*, is dated 1271. His theories were mainly derived from Galen and Constantine the African (1020–1087). He did not recognize diabolic possession as a cause of insanity. Mania was an infection of the front cell and produced a disorder of the imagination; he gave an example of a son hitting his father through lack of recognition. Melancholie was an infection of the middle cell. He also recognized a condition of lethargy termed a "cold insanity" (i.e., an insanity without fever). He gave examples of symptomatology, some of which might relate to schizophrenia: auditory hallucinations, visions, irrational fears, suspicion, and withdrawal.

Arnold of Villanova. Arnold of Villanova (1240?–1313?) (6) was probably born in Catalonia, Spain. He taught theology, law, philosophy, and medicine at Barcelona, Paris, and Montpellier. His most important medical contributions are the *Breviary of Practice* and the *Parabolae*, 345 aphorisms. He described "mania" and advocated perforation of the skull so that both devils and vapors could escape. He described hallucinations and epilepsy. He recognized emotional phenomena.

Bernard de Gordon.   Said to be of Scottish origin, Bernard de Gordon (died 1320?) (6, 9) practiced in France and taught at the medical school of Montpellier from 1285 to 1307. He was a medical reformer and in 1305 produced a book *Lilium Medicinae* (11) in manuscript form; in 1480, it was printed in Naples and in 1496 in Venice. He recognized the following mental disorders: "lethargia vera" (eyes closed), "lethargia nonvera" (eyes open), stupor, mania, melancholia (corruption of the mind or "foolish insanity"), phrenesis, and incubus. The lethargic conditions appear by his description to be organic states. Stupor was a partial sensory or motor loss (i.e., a neurologic condition). Mania no doubt represented states of agitation and restlessness. He regarded melancholia as a generic term covering a number of conditions, including the condition stolidatas. Stolidatas was caused by an imbalance, both in quality and quantity, of humors; here he referred to the fact that in "juvenile stoliditas the patients pronounce empty words having neither head nor tail, the speech is broken and incomplete, nor do they themselves realise what they are saying." Although an incomplete description, all that is described here would be recognized in patients today considered as having simple schizophrenia. Phrenesis denoted delerious states of infective origin. Incubus was a sleep upset by demons. He also described "congelatio," a state in which the patient suffered a general loss of sensation and remained in the position in which he or she was placed (perhaps catalepsy?). Of some interest to the schizophrenic theme is his reference to disorders of speech—talking to oneself, childish silliness (word salad?), remarks without head or tail (disorganized thinking?), failure to finish sentences (thought blockage?), and an inability to explain sentences (loss of abstract thought?). He also referred to wandering here and there and odd movements of the limbs, tongue, and eyes (mannerisms?). Bernard de Gordon was not averse to treating "lethargia vera" by plaguing with squealing pigs or the noise of trumpets and drums, but for melancholia and mania, he advocated rest and beautiful surroundings, unless the patient was disobedient, in which case he or she should be punched and thrashed.

John of Gaddesden.   John of Gaddesden (c. 1280–1349) (6, 9, 12) was an English physician and clergyman who practiced medicine in Oxford and London and was court physician to Edward II (1284–1327). Around 1314, he wrote a compendium of medicine entitled *Rosa Medicinae,* or *Rose Anglica* (12). In it, he relied on humoral theory and was influenced by Bernard de Gordon. He described mania as noisy aggressive behavior. Under melancholie he included emotional states, depression, and also withdrawal and talking to oneself. Like de Gordon, he recognized the condition of lethargy.

Andrew Boorde.   Andrew Boorde (1490?–1549) (6) was an English physician, a Carthusian monk, and Bishop of Chichester. After 20 years, he left his order to study medicine in Europe, North Africa, and the Near East. During practice in Montpellier, he wrote two medical books: *The Dietary of Health* (1542) and *The Breviary of Health* (1547). The latter contains material of psychiatric interest. He recognized psychosis and neurosis as two separate clinical entities, saying: "This impediment may come by nature and kynde, and then it is incurable, or else it may come by a great feare or a great study." Of insanity, he said: "there be four kyndes of madness, Mania, Melancholie, Frenesis and Demoniachus. This latter doth passe all manner of sicknesses and disease." He regarded mania as restlessness without fever; fever is characteristic of frenesis. Melancholie appears to cover a group of people with fantasies and delusions. Boorde's Book II, Chapter 11 contains a case history of a German madwoman with her examination and treatment by exorcising.

Johann Weyer.   Johann Weyer (1515–1588) (6) was a Dutch physician who studied under the German physician Cornelius Agrippa. He was court physician to Duke William of Cleves. In *De Praestigiis Daemonum* (13) he maintained that abnormal behavior was due to sickness and not possession, thus putting himself in conflict with the church. He described symptoms that would be attributed today to schizophrenia. He was also probably the first to describe the phenomenon of pathology occurring on the same day each year (i.e., the anniversary reaction).

Philippus Aureolus Paracelsus.   Philippus Aureolus Paracelsus (1493?–1541) (6, 9, 14) was a pseudonym assumed by Theophrastus Bombastus von Hohenheim, a Swiss physician, to proclaim his superiority over Celsus. His ideas were revolutionary. He threw the Canon of Avicenna on a bonfire and condemned Aristotle. Life, he believed, was dictated by a pervading principle he called "archeus," with each star corresponding to a single passion. Lunacy was the victory of one's "animal nature" over the divine spirit of humans. He was professor of medicine at Basel until forced to leave. One of his books was on mental disorders; entitled *Diseases that Deprive Man of his Reason*; it was published posthumously in 1567. Despite the originality of his views, Paracelsus's tangled concepts give no reliable insight into nosology, and no case history allows us to judge whether he knew anyone with schizophrenia.

Felix Platter.   Felix Platter (1536–1614) (6) was a Swiss physician and anatomist who studied medicine in the universities of Montpellier and Paris before settling in Basle as Professor of Medicine. In his best known work, *Praxis Medica*, published in 1602 and translated into English in 1662, he discussed in detail mental disorders and their etiology, course, treatment, and classification. This classification, although true to humoral theory, was a new departure. His *Observationum Libri Tres*, translated into English in

1604, contained psychiatric case histories. Platter distinguished two types of mental disorders: natural and unnatural. Unnatural disorders he dismissed from the medical sphere as he attributed them to the devil; they were a matter for the clergy. In the etiology of natural disorders, he emphasized heredity, lesions of the brain, rising vapors, poison, excess of blood, humoral imbalance, and dryness of the brain. He classified natural disorders according to observable symptoms as follows: "mentis ibecilitas (mental deficiency), mentis consternatio (cerebral vascular accidents and epilepsy), mentis alienatio (psychosis), and mentis defatigatio (sleep disturbances). Students of Platter (15, 16) have found probable descriptions of schizophrenia in his writings.

Timothy Bright. Timothy Bright (c. 1550–1615) (6) was an English physician born in Cambridge. He studied medicine at Trinity College in Cambridge and in Paris, where he witnessed the St. Bartholomew's Day massacre in 1572. He was a cultured, if erratic, man, who was versed in music, languages, and literature. His first book, published in 1580, was *The Sufficiencie of English Medicines,* in which he praised the qualities of medical remedies made from native herbs. This work was followed by two more volumes, which were based on his lectures on medicine delivered at Cambridge. In 1585 he as appointed physician to St. Bartholomew's Hospital in London. There he wrote *A Treatise of Melancholie,* the first book on mental disorders to be written in English. It was quoted by Robert Burton and was said to have inspired William Shakespeare. Bright then turned his efforts toward devising a system of shorthand, which he dedicated to Queen Elizabeth, who granted him exclusive teaching and publishing rights. The neglect of his clinical duties led to his dismissal in 1591. He became more involved in religious activities.

A *Treatise of Melancholie* set forth the cause of melancholia, described its psychological and somatic symptoms, differentiated between melancholy and "afflicated conscience," and offered spiritual advice as well as physical prescriptions. It is interspersed with "philosophical discourses" for the entertainment of the reader. Thus Bright concentrated on what we would term neuroses and reactive depression today and makes no useful comment applicable to psychoses and schizophrenia. This attitude he shared with Robert Burton (1577–1640), whose *Anatomy of Melancholy* (17) was first published in 1621.

In addition to academic texts there were "leech books," collections of herb remedies and folk medicine. The best-known, written just before the medieval period, but influencing it, was *The Leech Book of Bald.* It was written by Bald (A.D. 900–950), an early physician, and written down by the scribe Cid. Leech books often contained simple descriptions of mental disorders.

Case Histories

The most direct link with schizophrenia is through case histories. Here we can consider four groups of patients from the medieval period. The greatest certainty comes from considering individual case histories in detail. This is rarely possible. However, information on royalty is usually abundant, and here we can consider the cases of an English monarch, Henry VI, and a French monarch, Henry's maternal grandfather, Charles VI.

The St. Bartholomew's Group of Patients (12th Century) (9, 18). A

shrine was attached to St. Bartholomew's Hospital in the city of London. (The case records are published in *The Book of the Foundation of Saint Bartholomew's Church in London* [19]. The original manuscript was written between 1174 and 1189.) Shrines attracted individuals seeking miraculous cures of intransigent conditions. Occasionally, records would be kept. Here there are two sets of cases, one at the time of Henry I and the other in the reign of Henry II making up the recorded group. Of the total of 40 cases in the group, more than one-third were connected with problems other than sickness. Wilmer and Scannon (20) listed 22 cases as neuropsychiatric. Of these, some included gross hysterical states presenting in a neurologic guise. Of the 22, 9 were regarded as psychotic. Jeste et al. (18) quoted four cases from Book II that might be considered schizophrenic from Wilmer and Scannon's series. These are mentioned here.

A young man (case 2) had a hallucinatory experience following which he "lost his wits, and his reason was deprived of all power, and he did not know what to do or not do. Controlled by madness, he wandered, running now this way, now that way. Not knowing what he was doing, he went wherever the impetuousness of the evil madness drove him."

A man (case 3) who became "mad and seized by a terrible unreason . . . wandered in the woods and . . . in the hills, slid down from his horse and rent his clothes, threw stones at the people he met, scattered the money, mixed among the crowd, threatening or frightening those whom he met."

Another concerned a girl (case 5): "the virgin's nurse, coming in, marveled at whom the girl was speaking, for she heard some speaking but saw no one but the girl." Another time, the patient "filled the house with great cries." But "when the servants ran to see where the noise was coming from," they saw only the patient.

One young woman (case 8) "completely lost her mind, tore her clothes with her hands, her tongue was unbridled to blasphemy, and ribaldry; and when her madness became worse, she was restrained in straight bonds."

Clarke (9) quoted a case from Moore's (19) book, which although it may lack detail, could suggest that it is the first recorded case of childhood schizophrenia: "A woman brought their small son on the feast day to be cured of his madness. He had lost all reason and was in distress."

Becket Shrine Group of Patients (12th Century) (6, 9). Canterbury Cathedral in England was the scene of the martyrdom of Saint Thomas à Becket (1118?–1170) in 1170. The shrine of Saint Thomas became a focal point of miraculous cures. Four of the cases will be mentioned here.

A 13th-century window in the Trinity Chapel depicts a bound maniac being beaten with birch rods and dragged to the shrine of Saint Thomas where he is cured.

A similar episode is recounted in the chronical edited by E. A. Abbot, *Life and Miracles of Saint Thomas of Canterbury*. A madman, Henry of Fordwick, is dragged struggling and shouting to the tomb of the saint. He spent a day and night in the church and returned home cured.

In the Trinity Chapel, three stained glass windows also depict the story of Matilda of Cologne (8) who is recorded as insane in the above chronicle. She is described as shouting, using foul language, and striking out. She was tightly bound with ropes. After raving for some hours, she came to, declaring that she had seen Saint Thomas in a dream.

Clarke (9) quoted a case from the shrine taken from 350 cases recorded by J. C. Robertson (21). This is a letter of Roger of Berkeley, who stated the case of a "wild man" who had withdrawn from all social contact under the troubles of a demon and had lived an entirely animal life, until taken to a chapel and there brought back to his right mind.

Henry VI Tomb Group of Patients (15th Century) (6, 9). Henry VI (1422–1471) of England was murdered, at first buried in Chertsey, and then moved to Windsor in 1484. His tomb at Windsor became a shrine. To establish Henry's case as a saint with the papal authorities, an unusually careful record of miracles was kept. Grosjean (22) reported 174 cases involving people from all over England and Wales in the period 1484–1500. The original record was in English, later translated into Latin; this is the text that is available. Of the 174 cases, 90 concerned illnesses, 61 accidents, and 23 are nonmedical. Of the 90 cases of illnesses, 24 could be considered psychiatric; in the sample of 66 other cases of illness, there is evidence of neurotic and hysterical states.

Clarke (9) selected the following four instances of severe mental breakdown from the sample of 24 psychiatric cases. These instances have a psychotic flavor.

One case (case 168) (1485) merely records that a madman was restored to his "integrity of mind."

Agnes Green (case 119) (Sutton Courtenay, Berkshire, 1485–1486) was distracted, lost her normal discretion, seemed to do nothing "in a human way" and was wilder than the beasts. She raged at all around her and could not be pacified or controlled. She was then shut away by herself in a strong hut ("munitissimam domunculam") so that she should not be disturbed. She began to think of religion. Then a handsome man appeared, spoke very soothingly, hung two coins round her neck, and told her to go to Windsor. She at once ceased raving and became as mild and sensible as usual.

The wife of Geoffrey Brawnston (case 2) (Ashby St. Leger, Northamptonshire, 1486) became disturbed on a hot July day. The onset was sudden and the build-up to fury rapid. She roamed about, lost to modesty, and became a pest not only to officials and townsfolk but even to the idiots and children. After a day's "delirium," she came to the church when the congregation was gathering. She,

> delirious or full of a demon," shouted at some, made terrifying rushes at others, and set the rest laughing with her silly and dirty ramblings. The respectable ones wanted to bind her with ropes, but the vicar forbade unkindness and urged them to "bind her with compassion by praying to the Virgin and to Henry." She waited quietly in a corner and slipped home afterward. She raved again at midday but became steadily milder and was composed and sane on the third day.

Agnes Leveryche (case 72) was horribly troubled by a demon and entirely lost her reason until her son prayed for her. She also recovered in 3 days.

The Case Histories of John Hall (Early 17th Century).   John Hall (1575–1635) was a medical practitioner in Stratford-on-Avon and married Susanna, Shakespeare's daughter. He was highly regarded in the area, as can be seen from the inscription on his tombstone. Hall collected together two notebooks of observation on his patients. His first notebook was translated from Latin to English after his death and appeared in 1657 as a book entitled *Select Observations on English Bodies,* now available in a facsimile edition (23).

As reported by Howells and Osborn (24), Hall recorded 180 patients; they analyzed the group of patients to see the clinical composition of the group. This group differs in an important way from those of the patients attending shrines in that it conforms more closely to the day-to-day illnesses in a local community. Of the total sample of 180 patients, 52 (29%) were found to display presenting, and usually primary, symptomatology suggesting emotional disorder. This incidence is very close to the 30% estimated by the Royal College of General Practitioners in the United Kingdom for contemporary practice (25). In Hall's group, the proportion of females (75%) was greater in those displaying symptoms of emotional disorder; this matches contemporary studies. Our present interest is to ask whether any psychotic, especially schizophrenic, patients appear in the sample. None were present. The closest example was a postpartum delirious state of short duration. This finding is not surprising, as can be seen in a consideration of a contemporary analysis of a British general practice (26); the researcher found 3 schizophrenic patients in the general practice of about 3,000 patients. By chance it would not be expected that a schizophrenic patient would appear in a sample of 180 patients.

The Case of Henry VI, a King of England (8).   Henry VI (1422–1471) succeeded his father when he was less than 12 months old. A pious and weak-willed man, he was ruled by his uncles and by his strong-willed and power-hungry wife, Margaret of Anjou (1430?–1482). He was a protector of learning and founded Eton and King's College in Cambridge. In 1453, he became insane, lost his memory, and was paralyzed, which led to the election of Richard of York (1411–1460) as protector. The Privy Council gave John Arundell and other physicians the authority to treat Henry. They used the then standard treatment of purges, baths, and shaving of the head. Henry recovered for a brief period and resumed power but again suffered episodes of insanity with visual and auditory hallucinations that lasted until his death. He was imprisoned in the Tower of London by his rival, Edward (1442–1483), son of Richard of York, who had him murdered. For some time after his death he was considered a saint and a martyr.

The account of Henry's first breakdown is as follows:

> But after he had reached Clarendon about the feast-day of St. Thomas the Martyr, he fell, through a sudden and unexpected fright, into such an illness that for a full year and a half he was without natural sense or intelligence adequate to administer the government. No doctor or medicine had power to cure that illness.

Clarke (9) quoted an account of a visitation to Henry by a group of peers in March 1454 during this first breakdown:

> to the which matters nor to any of them they could get no answer nor sign, for no prayer or desire, lamentable cheer or exhortation, nor anything that they or any of them could do or say, to their great sorrow and discomfort . . . . And so after dinner they came to the King's Highness in the same place where they were before; and there they moved and stirred him by all the ways and means they could think to have an answer of the matters aforesaid, but they could have none; and from that place they willed the King's Highness to go into another chamber, and so he was led between two men into the chamber where he lies; and there the Lords moved and stirred the King's Highness the third time by all the means and ways that they could think, to have answer of the said matters, and also desired to have knowledge of him, if it should like his Highness that they should wait upon him any longer and to have answer at his leisure. But they could have no answer, word or sign; and therefore with sorrowful hearts come their way.

Henry's paralysis seems to have been in the nature of a catatonic stupor. His passive nature, withdrawal, lack of judgment, and monosyllabic speech would suggest a schizophrenia of lifelong duration, punctuated by catatonic episodes; other mental illnesses could fit the clinical picture.

The Case of Charles VI, a King of France (8).   Charles VI (1368–1422) was Henry VI's maternal grandfather. Clarke (9) reported his first break-down as follows:

> He collapsed dramatically in August 1392 at the age of 24, while pursuing the would-be assassin of Olivier de Clisson, constable of France. On the journey he had been making silly remarks and acting in an undignified way—but this may be observation with hindsight, for he was not in any case solemn or a serious talker. In the forest of Le Mans, startled by a beggar warning him of treason ahead and by the crash of a lance, he broke down, lashing out with his sword—and killing four before it snapped, it was said. Charles was in a coma for a while and recovered slowly over several months.

His next breakdown (9) was seen as follows:

> In the next breakdown [June 1393 to January 1394] undignified behaviour led on to a state when "his spirit was covered with shadows so dense" that he forgot basic facts about himself and took to violence. [His breakages appear in the royal accounts over some 13 years.] But he was orientated in the early phases, and his disorientation consisted of saying he had no wife and no children, that he was not king but a man called George; and he defaced the royal arms on vessels. His signature became boldly schematic, but it is noticeable that it retained its basic form firmly.

The breakdown of 1395 (9) was similar: he lost his memory, called himself George, ran wildly about, acted obscenely, and hated his doctor (Renaud Freron). Poor attention was noted in the short remission of 1397. Later he became quite indifferent to deaths among family and friends and fell into a listless state. By 1405 he was verminous as well as infected through having dug a piece of iron into himself; he had to be forcibly washed and retrained to look after himself. Charles relapsed almost at yearly intervals but the remissions became shorter, and ultimately his disorder was permanent.

Legal Sources

No period of history, or country, has a monopoly on humanitarian attitudes and actions. Plato (427–347 B.C.) in The Laws XI, 934 stated "if anyone be insane, let him not be seen openly in the town, but let his kinfolk watch over him as best they may, under penalty of a fine."

The Romans (6) legislated to protect the insane. In the "Twelve Tables," the earliest code of Roman law evolved in the 5th century B.C., there were provisions for the mentally ill. It differentiated between the insane and fools. Domitius Ulpianus (A.D. 160–228), a Roman jurist, asserted that an insane individual could not be responsible for criminal acts. In "Corpus Juris Civ-ilis," the main body of Roman law codified in the time of Justinian (A.D. 483–565), legislated for the mentally ill; it defined their criminal responsi-bility, their ability to testify, their ability to make a will and to marry and divorce, and their ability to dispose of goods.

According to Walker (27), the Penitentials of Egbert, the 8th century Archbishop of York, were protective of the insane:

> If a man fall out of his senses or wits, and it come to pass that he kill someone, let his kinsmen pay for the victim, and preserve the slayer against aught else of that kind. If anyone kill him before it is made known whether his friends are willing to intercede for him, those who kill him must pay for him to his kin.

A Welsh Celtic king, Hywel Dda (A.D. 909–950) (28), codified the regulations of his people in "The Laws of Hywel Dda." The laws reveal well-defined attitudes to the mentally ill. Idiots and madmen were differentiated. In the 10th century Laws of Aethelred (960–1016) (27), we find:

> And if it happens that a man commits a misdeed involuntarily, or unintentionally, the case is different from that of one who offends of his own free will, voluntarily and intentionally; and likewise he who is an involuntary agent of his misdeeds should always be entitled to clemency and better terms owing to the fact that he acted as an involuntary agent

that is, those with no intention, such as the insane, were not held culpable. A similar note is found in the laws of Cnut (1035) (27): "we must make due allowance and carefully distinguish between age and youth, wealth and poverty, freemen and slaves, the sound and the sick."

Henry I (1068–1135) reformed the English legal system. His laws stated that the mentally ill should be cared for in a benevolent fashion by their parents: "Insane persons and evildoers of a like sort should be guarded and treated leniently by their parents."

Henry De Bracton (?–1268) (27), an English judge, wrote in 1260 a treatise on the laws of England in the Middle Ages entitled *De Legibus et Consuetudinibus Angliae*. He held that a madman should not be held responsible for his actions.

The 15th Council of the Roman church, The Council of Vienne (1313), held that if a child, a madman, or a sleeper killed or injured someone he was not to be held culpable.

In the reign of Edward II (1284–1327), in 1324, a statute of English law, "Statute De Prerogativa Regis" (27) decreed that a distinction be made between lunatics (or persons non compos mentis) and idiots (or natural fools). The estates of idiots were vested in the king, after provision for the welfare of the patient, presumably because there was no hope of recovery of the patient. The estate of a "lunatic" was administered by the crown on the patient's behalf. The matter of legal incompetency was tried before a Chancery court, and the process was termed an *inquisition*.

Legal sources rarely give clinical descriptions. The codes refer to a class of people such as the "mad" who require legal provision for their welfare or the welfare of the public. The "mad" would be a heterogeneous group of people, among whom might be schizophrenic individuals. There have been very few studies of the legal codes of the medieval period. Neugebauer's (2, 3) work is an excellent exception. It produces interesting information. He studied the records of the Chancery courts referred to above. Neugebauer's work demonstrates that the lunatics came from all social groups. As long as a lunatic had property, however small, the law protected the property and the lunatic's interest in it. That lunacy covered a heterogeneous group of patients is suggested by the common reasons given for the start of the lunatic's condition. The most common was illness. Another cause was injury. Yet another was old age. A further factor was fright or emotional shock. The etiologic factors do not suggest that they were dealing with schizophrenics; indeed most of these conditions were either neurologic dysfunctions of the brain, the dementias, or the neuroses. Perhaps we are close to schizophrenia when we read such phrases as "distraction of his wits" or "distempered and weakened in his senses" or "infirmation of the mind." However, such terms could be applied to toxic psychosis.

Literary Sources

In medieval literature there is occasional reference to madness, or a mad person, or a delusion or hallucination. Clarke (9) quoted Edmund Spenser (1552–1599) (29) and his unfinished poem *Faerie Queene*; he described a man wounded by Furor. Spenser's work is more illuminating about depression (8). Chaucer (1340–1400), an English poet, gave a description of melancholy in his *The Boke of the Duchesse*. His *Canterbury Tales* produces only passing reference to emotional and mental disorders. Thomas Hoccleve (1368–1437) (8), an English poet, gave some vivid portraits of the mentally disturbed; his work may be autobiographical. The portraits, however, are of melancholics. In his *Don Quixote* (1605), a parody of Spanish society in the 16th century, Miguel de Cervantes (1547–1616) described abnormal behavior. As a child he was acquainted with the mental hospital at Valladolio and may have acquired his knowledge there. In none of the above work does a clear picture of a schizophrenic emerge.

Wright (30) outlined some examples of medieval French literature, ranging from the 12th to the 14th centuries, rich in descriptions of psychoses. These included Chrétien de Troye's *Yvain, Amadas et Ydoine*, the prose *Lancelot* and prose *Tristan, La Dame à la Lycorne* and *Ysave le Triste*, in *La Folie Tristan*, and in Adam de la Halle's play, *Le Jeu de la Feuillée*. Alas, all except one are descriptions of reactive conditions, usually a reaction to unrequited love. An exception is Adam de la Halle's play, *Le Jeu de la Feuillée*. According to Wright (30):

> Its "dervé," or madman, is presented altogether realistically, and although the cause of the psychosis is not intimated, its manifestations are described quite fully. The "dervé" is apparently a paranoiac, with delusions of grandeur and

of persecution (he thinks that he is king or pope, and that his father wishes to kill him). He has "ideas of reference," believes that people are talking about him, and that they plan to murder him. At one point he thinks that he is a toad; again, that he is a bridegroom. He is destructive, restless, noisy, indecent and sexually uninhibited. He insults his father and threatens to strangle him.

The view that schizophrenia is a recent phenomenon (31–33) has led others (34) to claim a clear description of schizophrenia in the works of William Shakespeare (1564–1616); this is Mad Tom in the play *King Lear*. *Tom O'Bedlam* (4) was a term used to describe beggars who pretended to be patients of Bethlem Royal Hospital in London to induce sympathy and gain money or shelter. The hospital did not authorize begging; the governors of the hospital issued disclaimers of this practice in 1675 and again in 1676. King Lear was a striking portrait of an agitated dement, with good cause for his agitation in the betrayal by his daughter Regan. In the play, the character Edgar simulates a Tom O'Bedlam. Errors must creep into such a portrayal: a true awareness of mental patients is not to be expected in a feigning beggar. The picture depends on the beggar's supposed notion of insanity. The picture is changed by the beggar to make the impression that is desirable to gain an end in that social situation. We have to ask how accurate is Shakespeare's notion of a Tom O'Bedlam. The dramatist needs to make the maximum effect on his audience—especially the need to dress the stage to match the agitated dement.

Nevertheless, there are occasional snippets of information about the insane in Shakespeare, especially in characters that pretend insanity: Hamlet in *Hamlet,* Malvolio in *Twelfth Night,* and, of course, the character Edgar in *King Lear* (as reported above).

The author Edgar (35) stated:

> There are numerous maniacs, melancholias, imbeciles, morons and feigners of madness introduced by most of the Elizabethan dramatists. Hieronimo of Kyd's *Spanish Tragedy,* Memmon of Fletcher's *Mad Lover,* Penthea of Ford's *Broken Heart,* Venelia of Peele's *Old Wives Tale,* Sir Giles Overreach of Massinger's *A New Way to Pay Old Debts,* Trouble-All of Ben Jonson's *Bartholomew Fair,* Lucibiella of Chettle's Tragedy of *Hoffman,*—these are only a few of the psychotic characters in general Elizabethan drama.

Conclusion

That schizophrenia was recognized in the medieval period is highly likely, although it lacks final proof. The educated strove then as they do now to care for the mentally ill, and they did so with an equal sense of humanity. Although schizophrenia was not identified as a discrete entity, it could have existed in several parts of the prevailing nosologic schemes in this period. More exactitude comes with a description of a patient at length. That by Bernard de Gordon is suggestive, as are some of the descriptions of patients attending shrines, but more conviction comes with the lengthy case histories of Henry VI of England and Charles VI of France. Even here there has to be caution; George III proved to be a sufferer from porphyria rather than schizophrenia. There are formidable obstacles to communication between ourselves and practitioners in previous centuries, as reported in the introduction of this book. If there is no final proof that schizophrenia existed in the medieval period, then there is no final proof that it did not.

References

1. Kroll J: A reappraisal of psychiatry in the middle ages. Arch Gen Psychiatry 29:276–283, 1973
2. Neugebauer R: Treatment of the mentally ill in medieval and early modern England: A reappraisal. J Hist Behav Sci 14:158–169, 1978
3. Neugebauer R: Medieval and early modern theories of mental illness. Arch Gen Psychiatry 36:477–483, 1979
4. Neaman J: Suggestion of the Devil: The Origin of Madness. New York, Doubleday, 1975
5. Kroll J, Bachrach B: Sin and mental illness in the Middle Ages. Psychol Med 14:507–514, 1984
6. Howells J, Osborn M: A Reference Companion to the History of Abnormal Psychology. Westport, CT, Greenwood Press, 1984
7. Jackson SW: Unusual mental states in medieval Europe, I: medical syndromes of mental disorder: 400–1100 AD. Journal of the History of Medicine 27:262–297, 1972
8. Diethelm O: Medical Dissertations of Psychiatric Interest (before 1750). Basel, Karger, 1971
9. Clarke B: Mental Disorder in Early Britain. Cardiff, University of Wales Press, 1975
10. Bartholomeus Anglicus: Reprint of the Properties of Things (1495). Oxford, Oxford University Press, 1975
11. Gordonius Bernardus: Lilium Medicinae Inscriptum. Edit, Venice, 1496
12. Cholmeley HP: John of Gaddesden and the Rosa Medicinae, 1912
13. Wier J: De Praestigiis Daemonum (Reprint). 1967
14. Pagel W: Paracelsus. Basel, Karger, 1982
15. Talbott JH: A Biographical History of Medicine. Orlando, FL, Grune & Stratton, 1970
16. Diethelm O, Heffernan TF: Felix Platter and psychiatry. Journal of Behavioral Science 1:10–23, 1965
17. Burton R: The Anatomy of Melancholy (1621). Reprint 1964
18. Jeste DV, Del Carmen R, Lohr JB, et al: Did schizophrenia exist before the eighteenth century? Compr Psychiatry 26:493–503, 1985
19. Moore N: Book of the Foundation of St Bartholomew's Church in London. Oxford, Oxford University Press, 1923
20. Wilmer HA, Scannon RE: Neuropsychiatric patients reported cured at St Bartholomew Hospital in the 12th century. J Nerv Ment Dis 119:1–22, 1954
21. Robertson JC: Materials for the History of Thomas Becket (6 Vols). 1875
22. Grosjean P: Henrici VI Angliae regis miracula postuma. Brussels, 1935

23. Joseph H: John Hall: Man, Physician. Hamden, CT, Archon Books, 1964
24. Howells JG, Osborn ML: The incidence of emotional disorder in a seventeenth century medical practice. Med Hist 14:192–198, 1970
25. Council of the College of General Practitioners: Working party report. Br Med J 2:585, 1958
26. Kessel WIN: Psychiatric morbidity in a London general practice. British Journal of Prev Soc Medicine 14:16, 1960
27. Walker N: Crime and Insanity in England. Edinburgh, Edinburgh University Press, 1968
28. Howells JG, Osborn ML: Great Britain, in World History of Psychiatry. Edited by Howells JG. New York, Brunner/Mazel, 1975, p 168
29. Spenser E: Faerie Queene. Furor & Pyrocles II: 6, 41, ff
30. Wright EA: Medieval attitudes towards mental illness. Bull Hist Med 1:352–357, 1939
31. Torrey EF: Schizophrenia and Civilisation. Northvale, NJ, Jason Aronson, 1980
32. Hare E: Schizophrenia as an infectious disease. Br J Psychiatry 135:468–470, 1979
33. Cooper J, Sartorius N: Cultural and temporal variations in schizophrenia. Br J Psychiatry 135:468–470, 1977
34. Bark NM: Did Shakespeare know schizophrenia? Br J Psychiatry 146:436–438, 1985
35. Edgar II: Shakespeare, Medicine and Psychiatry. New York, Vision, 1971

CHAPTER THREE

Concepts of Schizophrenia: 1600–1860

Mark J. Sedler, M.D.

In the field of medicine, conceptual histories frequently, and not surprisingly, focus on the development of specific disease concepts. This is particularly so since the notion of specific diseases achieved widespread currency in the 19th century following the advent of pathologic anatomy and the subsequent discoveries of tuberculosis, general paresis, and eventually the germ theory itself, all of which supported the idea of diseases as entities. Despite the often valid criticisms of this medical "ontology," we think today of diseases in terms that continue to invoke its language and precepts: the disease has a nature of its own, a mode of attack, a multitude of forms in which it may appear, a range of outcomes, visible marks of its presence (e.g., lesions), and most importantly a determinate etiology, a definable cause.

For this reason, a conceptual history of schizophrenia presents special difficulties in that schizophrenia has failed to live up to the requirements of medical ontology despite the fact that it was precisely these conditions that Kraepelin had in mind when he so persuasively formulated his dementia praecox concept. On the one hand, we speak, think, and conduct our research as though this name *schizophrenia* designated some thing, that is to say something provisionally unitary; on the other hand, we recognize the great probability that it serves to delimit only vaguely a markedly heterogeneous collection of morbid processes. Therefore, to investigate the history of schizophrenia is much more like asking about the history of "essential fever" than it is like asking about the history of, say, neurosyphilis. As a result, we find that both the concept and any presumed unity among the various phenomena it seeks to make coherent literally disintegrate as we pursue the origins of schizophrenia to that period of psychiatric germination antecedent to the research of Bleuler, Kraepelin, Kahlbaum, and Hecker (i.e., into the 17th, 18th, and early 19th centuries).

Inevitably, this conceptual disintegration opens the field of study to a very wide range of documented clinical events and, at the nosologic level, devolves into nothing less than the reemergence of those generic notions of insanity so familiar to the ancients—such as delirium, mania, melancholia, and dementia—notions whose persistence throughout the history of psychiatric thought bears witness both to their inherent clinical plausibility and to the intractable obscurity of the diseases these designations have sought to embrace. The "prehistory" of schizophrenia is nothing less than the history of insanity prior to the mid-19th century.

In the place of so comprehensive a survey, it must suffice to examine in some detail a few of the early psychiatric conceptualizations of mental disturbances that we would today be inclined to group with the schizophrenias. In doing so, we shall keep in mind the Kraepelinian formulation of dementia praecox as a hypothetical *telos*: a deteriorating condition whose onset in adolescence or early adulthood brings with it an insidious disintegration of the whole psychic personality with characteristic disturbances developing in the intellectual, emotional, and volitional spheres of mental life. With this in view, let us now consider how such disorders were apprehended in the "premodern" period of psychiatry's history.

17th and 18th Centuries

Psychiatry as it stood in the early 17th century was theoretically and practically no farther along than it had been in Greco-Roman times. Much of its practical efforts were dedicated simply to establishing mental disorders as falling within the jurisdiction of medical authority and in seeking to dispel the obstinate incursions of superstition and the hegemony of the Church. Psychiatric theory consisted, with certain exceptions, almost entirely of recapitulations of the doctrines of Celsus, Aretaeus, and Soranus, often transmitted through secondhand medieval sources. It is true that in the 16th century Paracelsus had proffered an unusual taxonomy and that somewhat later Felix Platter had suggested an alternative to traditional classification based on his personal observations. These innovations had little effect on the mainstream of psychiatric thought, however, which was largely content to recover the knowledge of the ancients.

A representative exponent of this tradition was Lazarus Riverius (1589–1655), physician to Louis XIV, whose general medical writings included extended treatments of received psychiatric categories (1). Thus he followed many 16th century predecessors in dividing the domain of mental illness into three principal forms: phrenitis, mania, and melancholy. *Phrenitis*, or phrenzy, he defined as an "Inflammation of the Brain, and its Membranes with a continual dotage, and a sharp constant Feaver." By "dotage" he referred to the presence of delirium, a crucial term designating a disturbance of reason: it was this conjunction of delirium with fever that constituted the essence of phrenitis.

Counterposed to phrenitis stood those deliria that occurred without fever: mania and melancholy. Since both mania and melancholy involved disorders of reason, one would not expect them to be differentiated by the presence of delusions, eccentricities of thought, or confusion. Rather, the distinction turned on emotional and behavioral criteria. Mania was marked by fury, rage, and boldness; melancholy was marked by fear and sadness. Interestingly, it was mania that was identified with madness, per se. Here we see what appears to constitute the original division between the "schizophrenic" disorders and the "affective" disorders with the as yet disjunct (and undiscovered) "manic-depressive illness" straddling the fence.

However, one should not make the error of simply identifying mania with schizophrenia and melancholy with the later concept of depression. Not until one has thoroughly grasped the fact that this classical nomenclature cannot simply be superimposed onto modern taxonomies is it possible to make sense of the formidable epistemic barriers to the emergence of the notion of schizophrenia that existed. Consider, for example, that the hallmark of the melancholic (in addition to fear or sadness) was the prominence of the delusions to which they subscribed. Riverius (1) told us next to nothing about the phenomenology of simple depression, but he described at length the delirium of melancholy. He observed that in

> many Melancholick people there is much laughter and appearanse of joy. For some laugh, some sing, some think themselves to be very rich Kings and Monarchs. . . . Others, that they are made of Glass, or Potters-Clay; or that they are barely Corns ready to be devoured by the Hens. Some think they are melting Wax, and dare not approach the Fire; Others, That they are Dogs, Cats, Wolves, Cuckows, Nightingales, or Cocks, whose voyces they imitate. Others fancy themselves dead, and will neither eat nor drink. Others dare not piss least they should drown the World by a second Deluge. Some think they have lost their heads, or some other Member, or that they carry the world upon their fingers end, or that they have Sparrows in their heads, or Serpents, Frogs, Lice, and other Creatures in their bellies. (p. 49)

Let us take stock a moment. From this description of the ravings of those with melancholia, it is apparent that while they might have suffered from "delusional depression," they may just as well have been suffering from paranoid schizophrenia or even bipolar mania, to use current nomenclature. Of particular note is Riverius's (1) remark that some melancholics are gay and expansive, an observation that rings true to the form of "bipolar" illness but not to his avowed definition, which cites fear and sadness. Moreover, fear and sadness, when they occur, are hardly pathognomonic of depression in the modern sense. In fact, the notion of schizophrenia as it evolved in the 19th century German literature was indebted to the "unitary psychosis" model, which recognized in depression but the first stage of that ultimately malignant process.

On the other hand, what of mania, or madness? Riverius (1) had a number of very specific observations to make. He noted that "Men are more often mad [maniacal] than Women . . . . Madness comes oftener to yong men than to boyes and old men" and he described a variety of clinical symptoms. Often the illness was heralded by complaints of

> constant pain in the head, watchings, short and little sleep, troublesom dreams, cares, and thoughtfulness, frights from smal causes, a rash and often fury from none, or the smallest occasion, eyes not enduring light, noise in the ears, an unaccustomed desire of Venery, Nocturnal pollutions often, laughter unaccustomed and without Reason, much talk not formerly used, and somtimes much silence. These shew that a Mania is begun. (p. 46)

Once "fury and boldness" develop, the clinical picture is complete. The astuteness of these observations allows us to recognize in mania the familiar onset of many schizophrenic disorders, although again it is impossible to rule out the mania of bipolar illness. What we can now appreciate is that from this strictly cross-sectional, symptomatologic point of view, the terms *mania* and *schizophrenia* frequently are not clinically distinctive, an observation that gave rise to the current provisional diagnostic term *schizophreniform disorder*.

In addition, Riverius (1) realized that:

> diverse are the kinds of Dotage or Delirium in divers sick men, and at divers times they come according as the cause is more or less vehement; for some have a rash madness, and seize upon every man they meet, tear their own cloathes, sometimes lay violent hands to destroy themselves. Others are milder and tamer, and hurt no body, but speak distractedly and ridiculously, somtimes they sing, somtimes they laugh, and have divers whimseys and symptomes much like those in Melancholly men and fools. (p. 46)

("Fools," of course, are born mad.) This clinical heterogeneity to which Riverius so eloquently attested has the paradoxical effect of bringing us closer to a concept of schizophrenia even as it accedes to the elusive and protean character of the illness.

Without restructuring the basic definitions, the only remaining clinical information that might aid in subclassification is the prognosis. In this respect, Riverius offered a few highly suggestive comments. Of the prognosis of mania, he wrote:

> A Mania is a strong Disease, and continueth not only months, but years, even to death, especially if it be haereditary. All Diseases of black choller are hard

to be cured, and this especially, because the Patient will not be ruled, and take their Medicines as prescribed. A Mania which comes with laughter, and those light symptoms is easier cured than that which comes with sadness and fury. (p. 46)

The validity of these prognostic insights is nothing short of astonishing. Clearly, those patients with unremitting, hereditary disease who are unruly and morbidly preoccupied are those most likely to have been afflicted with what we would call schizophrenia. The better outcome afforded the patient with bipolar mania is, of course, signaled by the patient's high spirits, gaiety, and laughter.

The melancholic patient, we have seen, is characterized as much by the presence of delusions as by a disturbance of mood. As a result, both paranoia and schizophrenia may have been so classed. In keeping with this, Riverius (1) noted that "the Disease is dangerous, if Chronical, of long continuance, and very fixed" (p. 50). On the other hand, he observed that "a newsprung melancholly coming of immediate Causes, is easily cured" (p. 50). That is, acute, "reactive depressions," even when they involve delusions, have a good prognosis.

It is clear that lodged within the mania-melancholia matrix elaborated by 17th century psychiatric thought are a variety of profound mental disturbances. Moreover, our distinctions among types of schizophrenia, paranoia, bipolar mania, delusional depression, and even severe forms of obsessive-compulsive neurosis and other anxiety disorders were inextricably enmeshed within this matrix. Insofar as this matrix was grounded, explicitly or contextually, in a humoral doctrine, the protean manifestations of mental illness presented no particular difficulties. The prevailing Galenic medical philosophy was fundamentally attuned to the dynamic aspects of disease and allowed for endless symptomatic transformations within the same individual. The imbalance and malproportion of physiologically active humors obeyed the logic of qualities not of autonomous disease processes. Thus the evolution of a severe, chronic affliction might necessitate a number of diagnostic designations before terminating in dementia.

By the latter part of the 17th century, Galenism had for most intents and purposes succumbed to the new spirit of empiricism, but psychiatric thinking lagged behind. This is clearly demonstrated by the fact that in matters neurologic, the great Thomas Willis (2) worked at the cutting edge, whereas his psychiatric knowledge was little advanced from that of Riverius (1). His eristics on the nature of the soul were too idiosyncratic to have much advantage over traditional theory for he complicated the Galenic doctrines with his even more abstruse notion of "animal spirits" and an admixture of prevailing iatrochemical speculations. His general view of insanity recognized the effects of "perverted imagination" on the "mind and will," but he continued to invoke the language of humoral pathology when trying to account for the fluctuation in symptoms. Nosologically, he followed traditional thinking: in general, the varieties of "foolishness" were divided into acute and chronic deliria. Among the chronic affections, those without fever included "raving" or "madness," "sadness" or "melancholy," and "stupidity" or "common foolishness." He dissected his subject with greater precision than did Riverius, but we learn very little about schizophrenia that cannot be found elsewhere.

19th Century

The first fully coherent description of schizophrenia as a clinical entity is not found until John Haslam's memorable treatise *Observations on Madness and Melancholy* (3), published in 1809. Rather than simply detail a particular case, Haslam provided a general account that aimed to define a "form of insanity that occurs in young persons."

> As far as these cases have been the subject of my observation, they have been more frequently noticed in females. Those whom I have seen have been distinguished by prompt capacity and lively disposition. . . . This disorder commences about, or shortly after, the period of menstruation and, in many instances, has been unconnected with hereditary taint as far as could be ascertained by minute enquiry. The attack is almost imperceptible; some months usually elapse before it becomes the subject of particular notice; and fond relatives are frequently deceived by the hope that it is only an abatement of excessive vivacity conducing to a prudent reserve and steadiness of character. A degree of apparent thoughtfulness and inactivity precede, together with a diminution of the ordinary curiosity. . . . Their sensibility appears to be considerably blunted; they do not bear the same affection towards their parents and relations; they become unfeeling to kindness, and careless of reproof. To their companions they show a cold civility, but take no interest whatever in their concerns. If they read a book, they are unable to give any account of its contents; sometimes, with steadfast eyes, they will dwell for an hour on one page, and then turn over a number in a few minutes. It is very difficult to persuade them to write . . . much time is consumed and little produced . . . the orthography becomes puzzling and by endeavoring to adjust the spelling the subject vanishes. As their apathy increases they are negligent of their dress, and inattentive to personal cleanliness. Frequently they seem to experience transient impulses of passion, but these have no source in sentiment; the tears, which trickle down at one time, are as unmeaning as the loud laugh which succeeds them; and it often happens that a momentary gust of anger . . . ceases before the threat can be concluded. As the disorder increases, the urine and faeces are passed without restraint, and from the indolence which accompanies it, they generally become corpulent. Thus in the interval between puberty and manhood, I have painfully witnessed this hopeless and degrading change, which in a short time has transformed the most promising and vigorous intellect into a slavering and bloated ideot. (p. 64)

Here we see plainly the characteristic clinical picure—its onset, course, and termination—rendered in a manner that might easily allow subsequent clinicians to link their experience to a well-delineated apprehension. But Haslam's (3) "form of insanity that occurs in young persons" remained just that, nameless and unmoored. It compelled no recognition in part because Haslam had fallen into some disrepute, at least in England, but more importantly because the established approach to psychiatric classification at that time was essentially cross-sectional. Indeed, this failure to adequately appreciate the course of mental disease persisted despite quite explicit discussions in the literature of intermittent and remittent forms of illness.

This point may be illustrated by briefly considering that masterpiece of 19th century psychiatry, J. E. D. Esquirol's (4) justly celebrated *Mental Maladies: A Treatiese on Insanity*, first published in 1838. His incomparable chapters on mania and dementia together reveal from a descriptive point of view everything there is to know about the clinical picture of schizophrenia. In the chapter on mania, he observed that the onset is insidious, often signaled by a "general and unaccountable uneasiness," by various somatic symptoms, and by insomnia and moodiness. He noted that although the age at onset varies, in general the "number of cases are very considerable from twenty to twenty-five years of age, and still greater, from twenty-five to thirty. The proportion increases from fifteen to thirty, while it decreases from thirty to sixty years, and above" (p. 379). He described in exquisite detail the typical delirium of mania:

> Maniacs are remarkable for their false sensations, illusions, and hallucinations, and for their vicious association of ideas, which are reproduced, with extreme rapidity, without order or connection. They are also remarkable for their errors of judgment; the perturbation of their affections; and in fine, for their freaks of volition. This class of patients possess great nervous excitability, their delirium is general, and all the faculties of the understanding are exalted and overthrown. (p. 378)

Finally, in the phase of resolution of the acute attack, Esquirol distinguished recovery with and without persistence of the delirium. In the former instance, the prognosis is very poor; the outcome for mania not cured is dementia. Where resolution is complete, the prognosis is much better, although relapse was known to be a serious problem. Dementia, on the other hand, is "usually chronic." It is characterized by a "weakening of the sensibility, understanding and will. Incoherence of ideas, and a want of intellectual and moral spontaneity, are the signs of this affection" (p. 417).

Although Esquirol (4) had much more to say about mania and dementia, most of it remarkably astute, for our purpose it suffices to note that what prevented him from delineating schizophrenic illness as a distinct clinical entity was the inherent taxonomic gap that then separated mania and dementia. He recognized the variety of outcomes to which mania tended— continued, remittent, intermittent—but these differing fates did not essentially alter the nature of the affliction.

A mutation in the nosologic discourse was required to create a framework capable of comprehending the essential elements of schizophrenia. What was needed was a set of nosologic postulates that ordered along new lines observations that were already age old. Between 1822 and 1863, these postulates were in fact articulated, making Hecker's pivotal statement of 1871 on hebephrenia possible (5). I have chosen this historical frame based on the publication of two seminal works: in 1822, A. L. J. Bayle's *Recherches sur l'arachnite chronique* (6) and K. L. Kahlbaum's revolutionary *Die Gruppierungen* (7) published in 1863. Within this frame, a series of conceptual elements were precipitated: a longitudinal, prognostic viewpoint; a principle of presumed etiologic unity; a clinical, pathologic method; a phenomenology based on a psychology of intellect, affect, and volition; and a diagnostic scheme that recognized the importance of "age at onset."

In 1822, relying on meticulous postmortem examinations, Bayle (6) demonstrated the encephalic lesions of general paralysis, thus establishing a prototypic correlation between a clinical form of mental disturbance and a demonstrable pathology. For nearly a century, this discovery, and the research it engendered, was something of an obsession among psychiatric theorists. As late as 1874, K. L. Kahlbaum (8) wrote that the "extraordinary importance" of the GPI (general paralysis of the insane) concept had so monopolized the attention of psychiatric researchers that "most additions to the psychiatric literature for many years have been almost exclusively works dealing with this subject" (p. 2). For the history of schizophrenia, it played a major role.

First of all, the clinical course of general paralysis taught an important lesson. Initially, paralysis was considered by many, including Esquirol (4), to be a mere complication of insanity. Eventually, however, it became apparent that the course of the disease was such that any number of clinical forms might appear (e.g., depression, mania, or dementia) in the earlier stages of the illness but that "general paralysis" defined an invariable end point. This progression underscored the importance to nosology of longitudinal follow-up, and it was precisely to this prototype that both Falret (9) and Hecker (5) were to refer in their attempts to establish "circular insanity" and "hebephrenia," respectively, as distinct clinical entities.

In addition, the distinction between the evolving symptom picture and the underlying disease process challenged the validity of simple symptomatic diagnosis. Later, this idea was taken to an extreme by the doctrine of the "unitary psychosis," which held that all mental disorders were but the expression of one pathologic process. Although it was not long before the absolute hegemony of this model was seriously questioned (e.g., by Kahlbaum [7] and Hecker [5]), it performed an invaluable service to psychiatric diagnostics and taxonomy by temporarily reducing traditionally distinct conditions (e.g., mania, melancholy) to phases of a presumed underlying morbid process. This "phenomenological reduction," to borrow a phrase from Husserl, suspended all previous assumptions concerning the natural divisions and boundaries between diagnostic categories. A number of nosologic innovations were to emerge out of this melting pot. Meanwhile, careful attention had been focused on the various courses of insanity.

The discovery of paralytic insanity encouraged another line of research that also served to prepare the way for schizophrenia. The clinical pathologic investigations of the French school had made the search for a specific lesion immensely compelling and the invocation of a somatic cause increasingly credible. At the same time, substantial evidence was accumulating that many severe mental diseases were hereditary. The most illustrious proponent of this latter view, B. A. Morel, played a dual role in fostering the appearance of the fledgling entity, dementia praecox. In his influential treatise of 1860, Morel (10) summarized the theoretical schema that would come to dominate psychiatric thinking until the advent of psychoanalysis. Describing his own methodology, Morel announced:

> We shall be occupied by the etiology of insanity and by its symptomatology. The onset of the disease, its course, its diverse manifestations, and its outcome will be set forth in a manner that allows the physician to form an idea of the principle types of insanity, to arrive at the diagnosis and the prognosis, and to ascertain the relationship between insanity and the lesions found post-mortem. (p. 76)

Kraepelin later followed this concisely formulated program with little deviation, although he naturally made recourse to chemical and physiologic hypotheses, and to methods borrowed from experimental psychology as well.

Kraepelin recalled Morel's work in a second respect as well. As early as 1852, Morel (11) reported the existence of a "large number of young persons of both sexes who have fallen prematurely into dementia" and he noted that the "name of *démence juvénile* is employed by us nearly as often as that of *démence sénile*" (p. 234). Some years later, the famous case report of "démence précoce" to which Kraepelin explicitly referred appeared not by way of erecting a new clinical entity but rather as evidence for Morel's pet theory of "hereditary degeneration." Because of its historical importance, I offer a translation of Morel's case report extracted from *Maladies Mentales* (10):

> I recall with sadness a case of progressive insanity that occurred in a family I knew well when I was growing up. The unfortunate father consulted me one day about the mental condition of his son, aged 13 or 14, in whom a violent hatred toward his father had supplanted the most tender feelings. The child, whose head was well proportioned and whose intellectual faculties surpassed those of many of his fellow students, struck me offhand as a case of arrested physical development. He related the beginning of his difficulties to an insignificant cause, one which was far from being the actual source of his singular emotional anomolies. He said he was despondent about being the smallest boy in his class, although he was always first in composition, and this without much effort or work. . . . He gradually lost his good nature and became

sombre, taciturn, and reclusive. At first one might think this was due to a penchant for masturbation but such was not the case. The boy's depression, his hatred for his father which gave rise to murderous thoughts, had another cause: his mother was insane and his grandmother extremely eccentric.

I ordered an interruption to his studies and confinement at a hydrotherapeutic institution. Gymnastic exercise, baths, and manual work provided him with the most up to date hygienic therapies. . . . He gained considerable weight but soon a more ominous symptom came to dominate the situation. The young patient progressively forgot everything he had previously learned and his once brilliant intellect suffered a disturbing arrest. A type of torpor seen in hebetude replaced his earlier activity, and when I saw him again, I knew that the inevitable transformation into a state of premature dementia (*démence précoce*) was in progress. (p. 566)

Conclusion

Everything now was in readiness. The clinical picture had been described in general by Haslam and in particular by Morel. An interest in the longitudinal dimension of mental illness had emerged. Hereditary and somatic etiologies were well established. A theoretical framework adequate to assemble the requisite elements was available. Yet schizophrenia as a concept required another 50 years to attain full maturity and to command general recognition. German psychiatry was still catching up to the modern methods of the French, and not until 1861, with the second edition of Griesinger's (12) *magnum opus*, was the absolute supremacy of Esquirol's achievement seriously challenged. French psychiatry went on to define a variety of paranoid disorders, states of organic delirium, and refinements of paralytic insanity, but precisely by pursuing these directions it failed to subordinate intellectual symptoms to the peculiar affective and volitional symptoms that were to prove pathognomonic in the formulations of Kahlbaum and of Hecker. Moreover, the importance of "age at onset" was not grasped prior to Kahlbaum's original idea of the "paraphrenias," or age-bound psychoses. Thus not before 1863, and quite possibly later, can the "age of schizophrenia" truly be said to have begun.

References

1. Riverius L: The Practice of Physick. London, Peter Cole, 1655
2. Willis T: *Two Discourses Concerning The Soul of Brutes*. Translated by Pordage S. London, Peter Cole, 1683
3. Haslam J: *Observations on Madness and Melancholy*. London, G. Hayden, 1809
4. Esquirol JED: Mental Maladies: A Treatiese on Insanity (Fr 1838). Translated by Hunt EK. Philadelphia, PA, Lea & Blanchard, 1845
5. Sedler MJ: The legacy of Ewald Hecker: a new translation of *Die Hebephrenie* (1871). Translated by Schoelly ML, Sedler M. Am J Psychiatry 142:1265–1271, 1985
6. Bayle ALJ: Recherches sur Parachnite chronique. Thèse, Paris, 1822

7. Kahlbaum KL: Die Gruppierung der psychischen Krankheiten und die Einteilung der Seelenstorungen. Danzig, AW Kafemann, 1863
8. Kahlbaum KL: Catatonia (1874). Translated by Levijy, Pridant. Baltimore, MD, Johns Hopkins University Press, 1973
9. Sedler MJ: Falret's discovery: the origin of the concept of bipolar affective illness: translation of Falret's *La folie circulair* (1854). Translated by Sedler M, Dessain E. Am J Psychiatry 140:9, 1983
10. Morel BA: Maladies Mentales. Paris, Masson, 1860
11. Morel BA: *Études Cliniques*. Paris, JB Baillière, 1852
12. Griesinger W: Mental Pathology and Therapeutics, 2nd Edition (Ger 1861). Translated by Robertson, Rutherford. London, New Sydenham Society, 1867

CHAPTER FOUR

The German Classical Concept of Schizophrenia

U. H. Peters, M.D.

The philosophy of German Idealism, German Romanticism, and French Sensualism must be considered to a different extent as the complicated roots of the German classical concept of schizophrenia. Its beginnings date back to the end of the 19th century; it was finally completed around 1932. As with physicians in other countries, German physicians had been aware of madness since the Middle Ages and defined it as the absence of reason. The roots of the German word for madness, *Wahnsinn*, are Germanic and originally do not refer to a disease. In Old High German (starting from the 6th century) you already have the word *wanawizzi*, which gradually becomes *wahnwitz* (an adjective) and has to be translated into English as "of poor reason" ("wahn" meaning empty, poor, not full; "witz" meaning reason, intellect). Since the 15th century, there is also the word *wahnsinnig* with the same meaning. The old word *wahnwitzig* was gradually replaced by *wahnsinnig*. The weaker expressions *Irrsinn* and *Verrücktheit* were added after that. *Irrgang* (maze) still meant walking aimlessly, an aimless walk, or a path that leads nowhere. Although I cannot do so here, it would be very interesting to compare the German etymology with the English and the French etymology. The Germanic connotation "of poor reason" later entered the classical concept of schizophrenia and has remained there up to the present.

The English Empiricism influenced the treatment of the mentally ill in Germany insofar as the nonrestraint and the moral-treatment movements were adopted, but apparently this did not really influence the theoretical concept of mental diseases. The French sensualists (e.g., Étienne Bonnot de Condillac, 1715–1780), however, actually tried to see all mental processes from memory to thinking and the will as transformations of sensory perceptions as the only source of cognition. They were succeeded by people like Helvetius, Condorcet, and Pinel, who consequently tried to describe what they could actually perceive with their senses. Pinel introduced a completely new way of looking at the insane, as Gilman (1) showed. It then became necessary, but also sufficient, to describe individual case histories. This radical empiricism—describing only what one can perceive with the senses, ears, and eyes—actually led to the introduction of portraits of the mentally ill in addition to the case histories in psychiatric literature, so that observer and observable fact could face each other directly. This new French view was directly adopted by German psychiatrists. After the French Revolution and at least until the end of the Napoleonic Era (1815), Germany was deeply influenced by French culture. The learned person was able to speak French fluently (and did this even at home), was an eager reader of French literature, and traveled to France whenever possible. The works of Esquirol and Pinel could be found everywhere in Germany where mentally ill people were treated. Despite this, it was considered necessary to translate the main works into German immediately. Pinel's (2) main work, for example, was translated immediately into German in 1801, the year it was published.

The way French clinicians described diseases was maintained in Germany during the whole 19th century, even when the description gradually shifted from individual psychiatric cases to the "Klinisches Bild." It is quite significant that there has never been an adequate English word for this expression that can carry its full meaning. Because the literal translation—"clinical picture"—is unclear and can be misunderstood, similar expressions (e.g., clinical feature, vignette, clinical description) were introduced. In the 19th century, the clinical "Bild" meant creating a more and more complete picture by gradually combining increasingly complex details derived from individual cases, similar to a portrait that gradually looks more and more like the original. This is why Kraepelin (3) needed 356 printed pages in the 8th edition of his textbook for the mere description of dementia praecox after already having explained the general psychopathologic basis on 228 previous pages. Only after the complete English translation becomes available can the reader possibly get an appropriate impression of the "Bild" of dementia praecox in classical German psychiatry.

Independent of the adoption of the ideas of French psychiatry (but not independent of the ideas of the French Revolution) at the same time (i.e., at the beginning of the 19th century), a second completely new, and completely German, tradition began to develop within the Romantic movement. In German psychiatry, however, this Romantic tradition was never predominant, not even in the first half of the 19th century. In the second half of the 19th century, it was treated partly with scorn by the positivists and partly forgotten. Toward the end of the century, however, these very ideas entered into the newly formed "classical concept" (or "Bild") of schizo-phrenia, and this is why they should be explained here in detail. Since medicine and poetry were linked in an unusually close way at that time in Germany, two Romantic poets are of particular importance: Hoffmann and Novalis.

Hoffmann

Ernst Theodor Amadeus Hoffmann (1776–1822) was one of the most pro-ductive writers, painters, and composers of the Romantic period. His name was actually Wilhelm, a typically Prussian name, but he replaced this name with Amadeus because of his great admiration for Mozart. His main oc-cupation was that of a judge and civil servant, and he actually left several volumes of juridical writings. Hoffmann was familiar with all the essential psychiatric literature of his time, which included, for example, Joseph Ma-son Cox's (1763–1818) book (4). This book was not only part of his forensic psychiatric reading, because Hoffmann also took complete case histories from the book and used them almost unmodified in his fictional fantasy writings. Madness plays a central role in Hoffmann's literary works. Three of his four narrative cycles (5) deal with madness in some way or other. Serapion, the central figure in the cycle "The Serapion-brothers," can be identified quite clearly as a schizophrenic. The "Night Pieces" also deal with the psychology of the unconscious. "Princess Brambilla," for example, one of his "Later Works," centers around Hoffmann's "theory of duplicity." Madness is explained as the loss of the recognition of duplicity, which is the loss of recognizing that there is a subjective inner world inside of us that is fundamentally different from the "objective" external world. Nor-mally, we know when we refer to objects of the subjective world or to objects of the objective world. Madness, however, leads to the loss of this ability. This split already anticipates quite clearly the later concept of schizo-phrenia as a split personality. In "Princess Brambilla," a young man suffers from:

> a disease that may well be called one of the strangest and at the same time most dangerous diseases we know and it can really only be healed through an "Arkanum" [which means the possession of secret devices and arts] for which one first has to possess magic wisdom. The young man is suffering from chronic dualism. (p. 311)

This "chronic dualism" was actually nothing else, he continued, "but the strange folly that estranges one's own self from one's self itself, which makes the personality unable to cling to itself." As an illustration, Hoffmann used strong metaphors—for example, the story of the two princes whose bodies have grown together but who have different heads that think different thoughts, "so that neither [of the twin princes] really knew if he had actually thought himself or if it had been the twin; and if that is not confusion then I do not know what is."

Another of Hoffmann's metaphors for "chronic dualism" is the image of the magic glasses. Whoever wears those glasses no longer sees the objective world as it is but sees a changed subjective world according to his or her own inner needs. In his opera *Les contes d'Hoffmann* (1880) Jacques (Jacob) Offenbach made Hoffmann himself wear these glasses and fall in love with Olimpia, an artifact figure who is not a real person. Thus Hoffmann's dualism-glasses become a kind of common property of Western culture.

Novalis

Novalis (1772–1801), or rather Georg Friedrich Philipp Freiherr von Hardenberg, lived only 28 years. He has always been associated with ideas of the personification of Romantic work and life. His main occupation, however, was that of an administration official and a mining official. Only after the publication of his complete works in five volumes (1968–1981) (6) could a general view of his work become possible (at least in the German language; the complete works have not yet been translated). Novalis was one of the most important theoreticians of modern medicine. He had strong personal ties to Romantic psychiatry since Johann Gottfried Langermann (1768–1832) had been his personal teacher for 10 years. Langermann was appointed the director of St. Georgen, an asylum near Bayreuth, and later councillor of state and administration official for the Prussian public mental health services; this was due to Novalis's intervention. Novalis developed a theory of the independent nature of diseases. He thought a disease to be an animated organism, a parasitic plant of its own species on the human organism. A disease follows "its own laws, had its own strivings and course." Thus Novalis was the first to introduce the concept of schizophrenia as a plant, so familiar to us today. According to Novalis, the disease has its origin (seed), forms roots, grows, develops, blossoms, and finally withers. It is a parasitic plant that lives on humans and develops its own "egotism of disease." According to this Romantic concept of disease, the symptoms are linked systematically due to the plant-like character of the disease. In this view, it is not at all enough simply to describe what one sees or even to compile symptom lists, like the French clinicians used to do, it is also necessary to explain the general context.

Kraepelin

One normally dates the modern history of schizophrenia back to Kraepelin's lecture in Heidelberg in 1898 (7) and the sixth edition of his textbook in 1899 (3). In this lecture, Kraepelin linked several "Bilder" or concepts of madness together that had been described separately up to that time. Kraepelin combined them to a uniform concept. Kraepelin was not aware of the Romantic roots of his concept, but referred to a theoretical work by Kahlbaum (8), which has never been translated into English. Bacteriology had just started to develop rapidly and thus provided a matrix for new concepts. To this day, infectious diseases provide the most obvious paradigm for the model of diseases of classical German psychiatry. But Kraepelin completed a model with two important elements taken from tradition. Both are of irrational nature, although Kraepelin considered himself the perfect rationalist.

The concept implies that mental diseases are diseases of the brain and has been accepted since the middle of the 18th century. Kraepelin formulated it in 1899 as follows: "*I cannot have any doubt* [emphasis added] judging from the known clinical and anatomical facts that we are actually dealing with very serious lesions of the cerebral cortex that as a rule can only be regenerated in parts, if at all." With this pathogenetic concept in mind, Kraepelin later founded the Deutsche Forschungsanstalt für Psychiatrie and invested an immense amount of energy and money in the research of the anatomic lesions of "morbus schizophreniae," although as we know without any success. It has remained a fiction.

The other element is called "eigentümliche Schwächezustände," or "peculiar states of mental weakness." This element later became famous in the name "dementia praecox" and has led to misunderstandings right from the beginning (and not only in the antipsychiatry movement). For Kraepelin, dementia praecox refers to the familiar observation (in German psychiatry) of the strange fact that the mentally ill (in contrast to patients with organic dementia) are in possession of their reason, but peculiarly enough do not fully use it and thus also seem demented. Whenever Kraepelin explained that this Krankheitsbild of dementia praecox leads to such "states of weakness" or Schwächezustände (note the image of the withering flower!), he never forgot to add the adjective *eigentümlich*, a word that can be quite aptly translated with the English word *peculiar* (Latin: proprius). It has to be added, however, that it is meant in the word's original sense, which means a feature belonging exclusively to some thing. This peculiar quality, characteristic only for schizophrenia, of not using one's mental apparatus in an appropriate way, which Kraepelin considers the unifying link of all that can be called schizophrenic, is up to now "intuitively" understood as the most significant feature of a schizophrenic by every psychiatrist trained in Germany, but does not appear in any list of symptoms and is therefore also missing in the DSM-III (9).

Apart from that, Kraepelin did for dementia praecox what Mayer-Gross (10) in 1932 critically called a "mosaic-like listing of all that turns up based on a completely general psychological frame." As a faithful student of Wundt, Kraepelin simply listed perception (Auffassung), orientation (Orientierung), awareness (Bewusstsein), sensory perceptions (Sinneserfahrung), attention (Aufmerksamkeit), memory (Gedächtnis), train of thought

(Gedankengang), reasoning (Urteilsfähigkeit), behavior (Benehmen), and action (Handeln), and described what is actually altered or noteworthy about it and what is not. "Mosaic-like" actually means that these descriptions, which can be endlessly long and very boring to read, are not held together by some overall idea or concept.

Bleuler

Despite the impact Bleuler had on classical German schizophrenia, he does not have to be dealt with in detail here. Compared to the other authors, he is relatively well known to the English reader because his work on schizophrenia (11, 12) is also available in English. The application of the association theory, the outline of the understanding of symptoms in theory and the study of signs, and his coinage of the name *schizophrenia* are some of his contributions.

Concerning the causes of schizophrenia, Bleuler (12) quite clearly adopted the concept of disease of Novalis, Kahlbaum, and Kraepelin:

> But it is highly unlikely that this actually caused the disease [namely life events, experiences or conflicts]. These psychological events spark off the symptoms but not the disease itself like a physical strain in a phthisic can cause a bleeding in the lungs. (p. 281)

For Bleuler, too, schizophrenia is more a result of an infection.

The association theory of Locke also had a great influence on German Enlightenment philosophy. Kraepelin, too, often fell back on the association theory (e.g., when explaining mania). Strangely enough, however, Kraepelin did not refer to associations in the case of dementia praecox. On the other hand, Bleuler maintained the association theory to be the central theory for explaining and categorizing psychological manifestations of schizophrenia. Bleuler (12) used the association theory particularly to explain, as has been mentioned before, what in Germanic-German tradition was the most essential issue: the disturbance of reason. However, we find association disorders in the primary symptoms: "It is as if links and inhibitions formed by experiences had lost some significance. The associations find new channels more easily." These association disorders are considered primary:

> as far as the slackening off or levelling of affinities is concerned. Now as a direct result of the slackening off of associations the usage of more conceptual fragments is added to the process of thinking with its incorrect results, displacement, symbolization, condensation, and its incoherence of thinking. (p. 285)

One of the reasons for Bleuler's success in the English-speaking world is certainly the fact that he adopted the association concept, which was deeply rooted there.

Bleuler (12) categorized the incoherent "mosaic" into two systems that were not compatible with each other: a theoretical system and a diagnostic system. The theoretical system consisted of two theories. Primary symptoms (Primärsymptome) are symptoms that are directly caused by hypothetical processes of the body. Secondary symptoms "are partly psychological functions under changing conditions and partly the results of more or less successful or unsuccessful attempts to adapt to the primary disorders" (p. 288).

Primary and secondary disorders are theoretical distinctions and cannot be used for clinical diagnoses. Bleuler therefore designed a second system that contained basic symptoms (Grundsymptome) and accessory symptoms. Basic symptoms are "as far as we know typical for schizophrenia while the accessory symptoms can also appear in other diseases." The division of schizophrenic manifestations under different symptom-groups can be disregarded at this point because they can be found in every textbook. Unfortunately, Bleuler's own use of terminology has led to much confusion. "Primärsymptome" and "Grundsymptome" can both be translated into English as "primary symptoms." Both have association disorders as their main characteristic. Yet they meant something completely different for Bleuler. However, it must be stressed once more that Bleuler was the first to introduce theoretically ordered symptom lists.

With the term *schizophrenia*, however, Bleuler goes back to Hoffmann's theory of duplicity, to the twin-prince, an idea that was entirely alien to Kraepelin. Bleuler said the patients were "split into different persons according to their complexes." He stressed his theory with a footnote quotation of Wernicke: "The patient as it were consists simultaneously of several different personalities" (12, p. 295). "Complexes" are not meant to be understood in the narrow psychoanalytical sense, but in a general psychological sense as "psychological events that have a uniformed effect." His general popularity in the cultural world is apparently due to the attractive and simple metaphor of splitting. The covers of books about schizophrenia and television films about split personality hardly ever go without referring to it.

The Heidelberg School

It is astounding to what extent one single hospital, the Heidelberg psychiatric clinic, has defined the theory and semiology of schizophrenia of the present. If one goes beyond the boundaries and takes into consideration those researchers who had closer links to the Heidelberg school after or before they carried out research on schizophrenia, this statement gets an even more general validity. Kraepelin formulated dementia praecox first during the 10 years of his work in Heidelberg. In Vienna, Josef Berze, whose books on schizophrenia (13–15) have always been recognized by

German psychiatry, wrote a book (16) together with Gruhle, who came from Heidelberg.

The Wilmanns school with Mayer-Gross, Gruhle, Beringer, Steiner, Homburger, and others represented the actual Heidelberg school, which marks the climax and the end of classical German psychiatry. Under the leadership of Wilmanns (17), this school jointly wrote a book about schizophrenia. This book on schizophrenia, which up to now has not been translated into another language, is the most important work of the entire movement. Unfortunately, it was published in 1932, immediately before the Nazi takeover in Germany. The Nazis destroyed the Heidelberg work team within a few weeks. This was not because the Nazis had something against classical psychiatry, but individual persons were forced to emigrate inwardly or abroad; others were able to continue their work in other towns or places.

According to the Heidelberg school, the natural history of schizophrenia is strictly biologistic. The organogenesis of schizophrenia is regarded as a fact and hence not only removed from all discussion but also already determined concerning its future direction of investigation. This becomes quite clear in some of the thoughts Mayer-Gross (10) expressed in the chapter "psychological causation":

> If there is agreement concerning schizophrenia in its basic structure being an organic disease, then it is likely that the possibility of a psychological causation is regarded most sceptically. . . .
>
> The symptom formation of some symptoms may be instructive and interesting for the life history of the individual patient, but for the etiology of his schizophrenic psychosis which is just not simply a 'pathological reaction" or "neurosis", it has no value. (p. 112)

Gruhle (18) closed Wilmanns's (17) book with the following words: "Since the psychology of this disease seems to be almost completely understood . . . the disclosure of new *physical* symptoms will probably be the best method to cast some light on this matter" (p. 713)

Thought Disorders

According to Germanic tradition, the discussion of the disturbed mind is very important. Like Bleuler before him, Gruhle (18) stressed the fact that "the schizophrenic person is temporarily impeded from using formal intelligence—at times for many years—while the intelligence itself remains intact." At the same time, Gruhle coined another description, which has entered most German textbooks of psychiatry in a slightly modified version:

> Complicated tasks bring about difficulties. One should not suspect this to be the manifestation of an extensive fatigue (as is often the case with focal brain

diseases). The schizophrenic patient already fails when he has to comprehend a complicated process of thinking. Mastering several requirements at the same time, maintaining a particular thought for a longer period of time (letting a tendency determine itself for some time) without going astray; comprehending a content of thinking directly and symbolically at the same time; drawing conclusions from the actual content of a picture or a metaphor that have to be reinterpreted retrospectively and the like—all this exceeds the thinking capacity of a schizophrenic at times. The range of thinking is missing, the "intentional curve" is lacking (Beringer). The schizophrenic likes clinging to details and loses the main thought, he draws an enormous amount of correct individual conclusions but fails completely when it comes to synthesizing them. If one provides him with the right approach he succeeds in drawing the right conclusions but he cannot find the right approaches by himself. (p. 152)

The Heidelberg school stood in a critical opposition to Kraepelin that may seem peculiar to us now. Kraepelin was reproached for his lack of structure. The Heidelberg school maintained that Kraepelin would never have been successful if Bleuler had not first given the concept of schizophrenia the plausible form that appealed to many readers in his book (12). Gruhle (18) in particular exposed Kraepelin's weaknesses in sharp words. But he gets entangled in very difficult formulations that are hard to follow when he introduces his own thoughts that are based on the assumption that the essence of schizophrenic thought disorders and hence schizophrenia itself lies in the disturbance of some kind of *thinking initiative*, a term he does not explain:

Schizophrenic thought disorder is therefore essentially a disturbance of the "highest" part of the personality, the initiative of thinking. The poor results in the explanation of proverbs thus stem from a lack of spontaneity of contrasting opposite pairs (no weight: a lot of weight; dead donkey: living horse; hat in the hand: hat on the head; new brooms: old brooms); but this does not mean a lack of memories or associations, nothing got lost, nothing got "loosened up" [a criticism of Bleuler's central theory of symptomatology]. Because it is a big difference remembering something when dealing with something else (this has remained intact) or spontaneously contrasting these two things concerning their consequences. The bad results also stem from a lack of ideas concerning the relation between the symbols. One has to actually get the idea that something may mean something else, only then is it possible to actually be able to remember a specific symbolic content (allegory). And if we spoke about the "intentional curve" (Beringer) earlier on this also contains the spontaneous act of spanning ones intention that far, not only to maintain the relationship step by step (almost driven by the well preserved associations), but to urge the relation spontaneously beyond common associations (that are not at all or only badly remembered). As far as I am concerned this is also the main reason for the subjective reflection of failure, the schizophrenic helplessness. Even normal helplessness concerning a situation (practical or intellectual) is actually brought about by the lack of ideas; not of associative ideas but of productive ideas, the initiative to active behavior, i.e. to master a situation and to intervene. The moment I intervene—that is the moment my spontaneity is let loose—I stop being helpless. The essence of schizophrenic thought disorder hence seems to me to be a disturbance of initiative. The second important factor is eccentricity.

Gruhle's formulations show quite clearly that the presentation of symptomatology is combined with the attempt to explain and trace everything back to a uniform principle.

Delusion

Themes of delusion were simply listed in the earlier literature. Now there is actually an attempt to verbally grasp the essence of delusion and especially to work out the kind of delusion typical for schizophrenics. Every now and then this leads to very vivid descriptions, for example a conversation between doctor and patient reported by Gruhle (18) in which the doctor tries to find out what was so special about the (normal) perception that the schizophrenic connected with a delusional meaning:

> "There was a nanny with a pram, and the child was wearing a bonnet (well, and what was so special about that?), and then a dog went to the corner and stood there, and a man whistled (yes, but that sort of thing happens every day, what was so striking about that?), and then two young girls arm in arm, and a worker was carrying a ladder: it was simply terrible." But one never finds out what actually was so terrible or what was the essence. (p. 171)

Of course this is not the verbatim report of the conversation, but a kind of condensation meant to express what Gruhle considered most important.

Kurt Schneider (19) later reported a similar example, but he actually wrote down everything the person said and used it to illustrate delusional perception:

> A schizophrenic woman reports, "The next-door neighbours were so strange and brisk, maybe just because I was so calm and quiet that they did not want to have anything to do with me. Last Sunday my master and mistress got a gentleman visitor. This visit made me bashful. I thought this gentleman might be my real father. And later on I thought he might only have been the young master in disguise. I do not know if they wanted to test me. And then again I thought perhaps the gentleman wanted me to be his wife." This shows quite clearly how perfectly harmless observations are interpreted as something related to ones own person without any tangible reason. (p. 107)

Surely every modern psychiatrist recognizes quite clearly from this short description that this patient must have been schizophrenic, so that Schneider was right when he maintained that such thought disorders and disturbances of perception are "always a symptom of schizophrenia," the only rare exception being symptomatic schizophrenia.

With this the Heidelberg school, and particularly Gruhle, succeeded in finding something that had been thought impossible up to then (and Schneider later even refined the theory)—namely, a sign that was not completely but almost completely specifically characteristic for schizophrenia. This advantage was limited, however, by the fact that, according to the basic hypothesis of organic causes, the question concerning the content of delusion is no longer asked but is actually frowned on and will be for a long time. Gruhle (18) expressed this in one of his apodictic personal confessions:

> Real delusion functionally has nothing to do with any past experiences of the patient, it is not caused by a specific trait of the character, has nothing to do with constitual suspicion, distrust, jealousy, uncertainty, and anxiety, etc. I disagree with many mostly Freud orientated scientists in that I am convinced that schizophrenic delusion is not an escape into psychosis, does not stem from an inner conflict, cannot be put down to complexes or similar factors, even if past experiences do appear as its contents. The interest is not mainly directed towards the question after a specific content of the delusional idea (i.e. why is he being persecuted by a married couple), not even towards the question of why he is being persecuted at all, the question is: why has someone got delusional ideas to start with? I consider real delusion a primary symptom of schizophrenia, a symptom that cannot be deduced or understood and that is organic. (p. 178)

Ego Disturbances

Another contribution of the Heidelberg school is the theory of ego disturbances. Again and again schizophrenics report that certain events that are thought to be intrapsychic by the people around them are not part of them but alien.

The fact that the theory of ego disturbances was formulated at the same time as psychoanalytic ego psychology often leads to misunderstandings now. Gruhle's ego disturbances, however, have nothing to do with the ego described by Sigmund Freud, Schilder, and Anna Freud. Gruhle's descriptions of ego disturbances go back to Husserl's phenomenological philosophy, according to which the ego takes itself as the "pure ego" that is directed toward what it perceives. Gruhle (18) himself gave summary of the ego disturbances:

> The ego content of the state of consciousness, of the process of consciousness is quite different from the brightness and the affiliation to the "Duree", but still belongs to consciousness in the same way they do. Whenever I pursue a mental process, be it perceiving, or imaging or thinking, having moods etc., all these processes have an ego content. This content has different grades. The sensory impressions seem to me to be fairly independent of myself and yet they are my perceptions. When a tune comes to my mind while looking at a picture then I did not intend this tune, but I was the scene of it, but I nevertheless conceive this tune as something familiar that I experienced before. Even if I

cannot get the tune out of my head—something that is similar to an obsessional idea—if I cannot get rid of it so to speak, then I may well be reluctant about it but I would never actually believe that this tune was due to some foreign ego-alien power that has put a spell on me. In schizophrenia this is exactly what happens. Any mental process can suddenly become foreign to the ego. The content is not important. Whether a schizophrenic housewife decides to put water near the fire or the scholar Staudenmaier experiences influences of thinking through "personification" or his usual way of chest breathing is changed into an extreme belly breathing: in all these cases the schizophrenic person "knows" that all this is not due to his own decisions, wishes, intentions, etc. but is being "done" to him. (p. 188)

Although theory and observation are connected in a way that is very difficult to understand, the ego disturbances (Icherlebensstörungen and Ichstörungen) have entered the traditional description of schizophrenia.

The classical German psychopathology that saw its main task in explaining the "psychology of schizophrenia" as one understood it at that time ends just here. In 1932 Gruhle considered this problem solved, and Kurt Schneider spoke of the "harvest being gathered in." Speaking about the "end" simply means that no new thoughts were added to this theory of schizophrenia, it was merely passed on unchanged.

Schneider

Yet present psychopathology, for example the DSM-III, does not directly take up the classical German tradition but starts with Kurt Schneider. Although after World War II Kurt Schneider was the director of the Heidelberg Hospital for several years (1946–1955) and at that time became the mediator of classical psychiatry for the first postwar generation of psychiatrists, he himself did not really belong to it. He had been deputy medical director to Gustav Aschaffenburg in Cologne, who had been Kraepelin's first student. In 1931 he became the director of the clinical institute of the Deutsche Forschungsanstalt für Psychiatrie in Munich, which had been founded by Kraepelin in 1918 to unite all ancillary sciences of psychiatry under one roof and was the first of its kind in the world. According to Kraepelin's theory of schizophrenia, one floor of the three-story building was occupied by the neuropathologic department. The floor underneath was the department of heredobiology and belonged to the geneticists who provided the scientific justification for the killing of 100,000 mentally disturbed people some years later. The rooms of the clinical department run by Schneider were on the same floor. Karl Stern (20) who became a member of the institute in 1932, described Schneider in his memoirs as follows:

> The clinical professor was a slim man of medium height with dark, piercing eyes and a sharp profile: which somehow made you think of a half-open pocket-knife that might snap close any minute. There seemed to be something spartanic and soldier like about him; hiding a tender sensitive core. It was common

knowledge that he possessed a collection of the poems of the German Romantics bound in pretty flexible Moroccan leather. (p. 127)

This was the setting where Kurt Schneider first listed the first-rank and second-rank symptoms of schizophrenia. They were first published in 1938 in the *Nervenarzt*, the journal of neurology and psychiatry that had been the most popular one of its kind since 1929, but was not paid too much attention to at the time. In 1939 Kurt Schneider (21) published the symptoms for the second time, this time in a leaflet of 27 pages entitled "Psychischer Befund und psychiatrische Diagnose" (Mental State and Psychiatric Diagnosis) that was meant to be read by general practitioners and medical health officials. Wagner (22) praised it for being particularly useful for expert genetic opinions as an easy method for determining which persons were designated for compulsory sterilization. Hence the little leaflet was reprinted several times up to 1946, with Schneider making small editorial changes every time. Therefore, the description of first-rank and second-rank symptoms had nothing to do with statistical calculations nor did it provide symptom lists. The only aim was to offer a simplification of classical psychopathology to enable physicians inexperienced in psychiatry to diagnose schizophrenia more easily as classical German psychiatry had defined it. It has always been maintained that not only the clarity of Schneider's description but also its brevity and simplicity have been the main reasons for the lasting popularity of this leaflet, which was finally translated into English as well. Most probably it is also the first inclusion list similar to the one that became the basic concept of the DSM-III in 1980.

Conclusions

Concerning therapy, classical psychopathology remained sterile. This was not only due to the general spirit of the time, which also coined the slogan "therapy is unscientific" in internal medicine in hospitals (23), but the classical theory of schizophrenia also did not provide a therapeutic technique. It was more important to provide a clearer diagnosis for the schizophrenia groups to be more able to find the somatic cause. If the cause could be found, this would, as it was felt, lead to the proper therapy (as had been the case with general paresis of the insane). As long as the causes could not be found, therapists would be unable to provide apt treatment.

There is a second reason why classical psychiatry became popular again in Germany after World War II up to the beginning of the era of psychopharmacology (at about 1955). German psychiatry was deeply compromised by Nazi rule and had lost many of its psychiatrists. Several hundreds of them had been forced into emigration from 1933 to 1938, and many psychiatrists who remained in Germany had become participants of the mass murder of mental patients. The psychiatrists who had become prominent under Nazi rule lost their positions in 1945; some of them committed suicide.

Classical German psychiatry, however, seemed to be free of any ideology. This explains why Schneider was offered the influential Heidelberg chair of psychiatry at the unusual age of 59. Only then did he start to form a school that was still classical and that many modern psychiatrists—such as Meyer, Kranz, Janzarik, Wieck, Scheid, Mattussek, Bronisch, Rauch, Wendt, and Huber—have considered as their psychiatric origins. It goes beyond the scope of this chapter, however, to report about this.

References

1. Gilman S: What looks crazy: towards an iconography of insanity in art and medicine in the nineteenth century, in The Turn of the Century: German Literature and Art 1890–1915. Edited by Chapple G, Schulte HH. Bonn, Bouvier, 1981
2. Pinel PH: Traité médico-philosophique sur l'aliénation mentale. Paris, Brosson, 1801 (German translation by Wagner M: Philosophisch-medicinische Abhandlung über Geistesverwirrungen oder Manie. Wien, Schaumburg, 1801)
3. Kraepelin E: Psychiatrie. Ein Lehrbuch für Studierende und Ärzte. Fifth edition 1896, sixth edition 1899, eighth edition 1909–1915 Leipzig, J. A. Barth
4. Cox M: Practical observations on insanity; in which some suggestions are offered towards an improved mode of treating diseases of the mind . . . to which are subjoined, remarks on medical jurisprudence as connected with diseased intellect. London, Baldwin & Murray, 1806.
5. Hoffmann ETA: Die Serapions-Brüder. Späte Werke. Juristische Arbeiten. Schriften zur Musik. München, Winkler, 1973
6. Novalis: Schriften in vier Bänden und einem Begleitband. Darmstadt, Wissenschaftl. Buchgesellschaft, 1968–1981
7. Kraepelin E: Zur Diagnose und Prognose der Dementia praecox: Heidelberger Versammlung 26/27, November 1898. Zschr Neurol Psychiatr 56:254, 262, 1899
8. Kahlbaum K: Die Gruppierung der psychischen Krankheiten und die Einteilung der Seelenstörungen, Danzig, Kafemann, 1863
9. American Psychiatric Association: Diagnostic and Statistical Manual of Mental Disorders, 3rd Edition. Washington, DC, American Psychiatric Association, 1980
10. Mayer-Gross W: Die Klinik, Erkennung und Differentialdiagnose, Therapie, in Die Schizophrenie. Edited by Wilmanns K. Berlin, Springer, 1932
11. Bleuler E: Die Prognose der Dementia praecox (Schizophrenie-Gruppe). Allg Zschr Psychiatr 65:436–464, 1908
12. Bleuler E: Dementia praecox oder Gruppe der Schizophrenien. Leipzig, Deuticke, 1911 (Dementia Praecox or the Group of Schizophrenias [1911]. Translated by New York, International Universities Press, 1950)
13. Berze J: Über das Primärsymptom der Paranoia. Leipzig, Marhold, 1903
14. Berze J: Die hereditären Beziehungen der Dementia praecox. Leipzig, Deuticke, 1910
15. Berze J: Die primäre Insuffizienz der psychischen Aktivität, ihr Wesen, ihre Erscheinungen und ihre Bedeutung als Grundstörung der Dementia praecox und der Hypophrenien überhaupt. Leipzig, Deuticke, 1914

16. Berze J, Gruhle HW: Psychologie der Schizophrenie. Berlin, Springer, 1929
17. Wilmanns K (ed): Die Schizophrenie. Berlin, Springer, 1932
18. Gruhle HW: Allgemeine Symptomatologie, Erkennung und Differentialdiagnose, Theorien, in Die Schizophrenie. Edited by Wilmanns K. Berlin, Springer, 1932
19. Schneider K: Klinische Psychopathologie. 5. Aufl. Stuttgart, Thieme, 1959
20. Stern K: Die Feuerwolke (The pillar of fire). Salzburg, Müller, 1954
21. Schneider K: Psychischer Befund und psychiatrische Diagnose. Leipzig, Thieme, 1939
22. Wagner W: Review: Schneider, Kurt: Psychischer Befund und psychiatrische Diagnose. G. Thieme: Leipzig 1939. Zbl Neurol Psychiatr 94:389, 1939
23. Weizsäcker V von: Ludolf Krchl, in Natur und Geist. 1 Munchen, Kindler

CHAPTER FIVE

Jaspers's View on Schizophrenia

John Hoenig, M.D., F.R.C.P., F.R.C.Psych, F.R.C.P. (C.)

Let it be said right in the beginning: Jaspers never proposed a "concept of schizophrenia" as such. To define such a concept is an exercise in nosology, (i.e., in special psychopathology). Jaspers's work, however, lies in the field of general psychopathology; within that, his main concern was methodology. General psychopathology has been studied as long as mental disorders have been a concern of medicine, such as when Esquirol (1) in 1838 defined the difference between a delusion and a hallucination, or when Haslam (2) in 1809 offered a definition of obsessional ideas. But these were unsystematic studies and serendipitous contributions. Not until Jaspers's fundamental work could general psychopathology be called a discipline. He defined the scope and the objectives, and most of all he created a clear and concise methodology, all of which are prerequisites for the establishment of a discipline and without which no discipline can be considered to exist.

If then Jaspers has not put forward a concept of schizophrenia of his own, why within the context of this volume is it nevertheless appropriate to examine what he wrote, and why is it of relevance to our understanding of that illness? Jaspers's work constitutes such a watershed in the history of psychiatry that nothing within psychiatry remained what it had been before him, and that includes the approach to schizophrenia. The discussions of general principles that were so much alive around the turn of the century seem to have frequently chosen schizophrenia to test their general contentions, or to illustrate their clinical applications. Jaspers, in that respect, was no exception.

To understand his contribution better, it may be helpful to recall the historical epoch, the prevailing views and trends, that he found when he entered the field of psychiatry. It may also be helpful to consider Jaspers himself, which could throw some light on the choice of his interests and the general direction of his work (3).

Historical Background

The centenary year of Jaspers's birth was 1983, and many congresses were held in all parts of the world to celebrate him. It is, however, mainly as one of the great philosophers of our century that the congresses remember him; he devoted almost his entire life to philosophy. Although these interests were already much in evidence during his medical studies, he entered psychiatry after their completion and remained a member of the university Department of Psychiatry in Heidelberg for 8 years from 1908 to 1915. The head of the department at that time was Franz Nissl, and he had a group of unusually talented men on his staff who created a lively climate of studies, with intense debates and an earnest search that never failed to inspire the new recruit:

> It was a remarkable life of great spontaneity, in the awareness, which formed the bond between us, of partaking of the advances of a magnificent universe of knowledge, with all the exuberance of knowing more than we actually did, but also with a radical criticism which took everything under the closest scrutiny. (4, p. 9)

In 1916 he transferred to the Department of Psychology; in 1921 he accepted the chair in philosophy at Heidelberg without at first entirely breaking with psychopathology. His first work after leaving psychiatry was *The Psychology of Worldviews (Die Psychologie der Weltanschauungen)* (5) which contains much of interest for psychiatrists. However, his main interest shifted further and further away. In 1936 the German government forbade him to publish; in 1937 he was deposed of the chair and of his post with the university. There began the severe hardships of his life in Germany as an internal exile during the war years, and during that time he once more turned to psychopathology and began work on a completely new edition of his *General Psychopathology* (6), a book now more than twice the size of the earliest edition.

When the United States Army occupied Heidelberg in 1945, he was reinstated in his chair and was asked by them to become the vice-chancellor, which he refused for health reasons. He presided, however, over a committee that was working on a renewal of the university, a committee that set itself the goal to begin afresh by exposing and eradicating all traces of past errors and crimes perpetrated in the name of that ancient institution during the barbaric years of its recent history. The halfheartedness of other members and the bitterness over the past soon led him to accept a call to the Chair in Philosophy in Basel, Switzerland, where he continued his work until his death in 1972. On the occasion of the 25th anniversary of the publication of Jaspers's *General Psychopathology*, Schneider (7) wrote:

> Once more we turn a final gaze on Karl Jaspers' place in the history of German psychiatry, on his psychiatric mission. A very young honorary staff physician without much clinical experience, but with a very profound clinical acumen, he, 25 years ago, laid the indispensable foundation for a methodologically clear, for the first time scientific psychopathology. Having as it were placed every-thing in its proper place for us, he left our discipline to turn to other tasks to which he felt called.

The time at which he entered psychiatry provided the topics with which he took issue. At that time, psychiatry was dominated by the ideas of Kraepelin. Kraepelin had created a psychiatric nosology that was based on Kahlbaum's idea of long-term observation of patients to arrive at disease entities. Kahlbaum himself never achieved a notable impact, but his idea came into its own in the hands of Kraepelin. Kraepelin thought entirely in biological terms, and having established the main psychosyndromes by the application of Kahlbaum's idea, expected the neurosciences to discover the pathology and etiology for each of them. The psychic abnormalities were mere symptoms of cerebral pathology. Jaspers (6) wrote:

> The basic orientation of Kraepelin remains somatic which, like most physicians, he holds to be the only appropriate medical one; not just the preferred one but absolutely the only one. The sometimes excellent psychological points he makes in his textbook succeeded as it were in spite of himself: he considers them stopgaps until the time when experiment, microscope and the test tube will have rendered everything accessible to objective investigations. (p. 711)

What psychology there was, was performance psychology as developed by Wund, Flechsig, and others, an approach closer to physiology than to psychology: the psyche was ignored. The behaviorist schools in the United States even elevated this to a principle, and turned what had been a one-sided approach, a neglect as it were, into a methodological axiom. Intro-spection, empathy, and understanding of the inner life were banished as unscientific.

In this predominantly biological atmosphere, there was the as yet small voice of Freud, who, although he too saw his work as a biological kind of psychology, nevertheless had opened the door to a subjective approach to the study of his patients. Bleuler and even more so Jung began to apply Freud's methods to the study of schizophrenia (8, 9). In his monograph *Dementia praecox oder die Gruppe der Schizophrenien*, Bleuler (10) showed that there was much in the clinical picture that could be empathically under-stood—Jung even went as far as to claim this for the entirety of the illness—

but instead of enriching the discipline of psychiatry, these efforts led to a polarization into two apparently irreconcilable camps, who were in danger of losing all common ground.

Studies in Schizophrenia

Still young and "inexperienced" (he was only in the second year in psychiatry), Jaspers soon entered the debate. Although the main controversy was concerned with general methodological principles, the chosen battleground for their application, as mentioned earlier, was largely schizophrenia. Schizophrenia became the litmus paper by which the viability of general propositions were tested, or with which the several ideas or theories were illustrated. Jaspers did the same; when we try to find what he thought about this illness, we have little trouble finding what we are looking for.

One of his earliest major articles was on "Eifersuchtswahn. Ein Beitrag zur Frage: 'Entwicklung einer Persönlichkeit' oder 'Process'?" (Delusions of jealousy. A contribution to the question: 'Development of a personality' or 'process'?) (11). As the subtitle suggests, the article deals with a problem fundamental to all psychiatry and uses the cases, all of which present with ideas of severe jealousy, to illustrate his points.

Before describing and discussing in great detail a number of such cases, he explained the meaning of the expression "development" in relation to personality:

> When in the course of psychic development, of psychic growth, we find during certain epochs an accelerated, during others a retarded pace, we are unable to understand this empathically. Just as generally in the succession of different stages of development we cannot deduce empathically the latter from the former. . . . Here we always only behold the appearances, the "symptoms"of an hypothesized underlying causally connected sequence, be that now a physical or an unconscious psychic one or both. (p. 114)

Against this background of a sequence of causal connections in which certain drives, abilities, tendencies, and modes of affect or their changes with age are taken for granted, we can empathically understand a rich variety of psychogenic developments so that in a normal person, given a full knowledge of his or her life history and characteristics, we could empathically understand a large number of detailed developments relating them to the given causally connected aspects of his or her personality.

> We have so to speak an "objective chain or matrix" in which "empathically understandable units" in large numbers are as it were embedded. Thus far we are able to conceptualize these matters. In our immediate comprehension of an individual, however, we go beyond this; as—in spite of our lack of precise concepts in relation to it—in psychiatry we make much use of this approach, we have to deal with it explicitly to clarify as much as possible what we are doing. We try to get into our grasp the total person, his nature, his development

right to the point of disintegration as a "personality". We grasp here by our detailed knowledge of the person a unit, an entity, which we are unable to define but are able to experience. . . . If we possessed more knowledge in psychology, we might get closer to a conceptualization of that entity. We . . . could grasp it as a teleological unit of personality. But of such knowledge we don't possess even a trace. We nevertheless have to work with the concept of personality whenever we speak of "development of a personality" as opposed to "process." (p. 115)

He explained that these "empathically understandable" entities are all embedded in the underlying chain of causally connected developments, and that it is therefore never possible to "understand" a personality in its entirety by tracing even in every possible detail the meaningful connections that make up these "empathically understandable" entities. For instance, we may search for and discover the history of a neurotic syndrome in terms of psychological antecedents, perhaps going back to a much earlier set of experiences, perhaps in adolescence or even childhood, but when doing so we simply take for granted the underlying chain of causally connected events of the personality development, such as the passage through the successive epochs of one's age, taking them for granted because we have those in common with the person.

The fact that the chain of objective connection which is thought to underlie the development of a pathological personality, is also present in us—although not to the same extent—becomes the criterion by which we grasp such a personality as a unified entity, and enables us to speak of a development as opposed to a process. (p. 115)

The rational or the empathically understandable developments can be clearly conceptualized, but they are only a part of the personality. When we speak of the personality as a whole, concepts are elusive, and we come to rely rather on our immediate comprehension of it. This indeed is the weak point in our usage of the term *personality*, which nevertheless has such wide application in psychiatry.

Having thus clearly established what is meant by "development of the personality"—what we can know about it and can precisely conceptualize, as well as what we do not know but use as a concept nevertheless—Jaspers explained what he meant by a "process":

. . . the personality in its uniqueness from the time of its growth to the time of its decline appears to us as an intact unity. Where we cannot achieve such comprehension of the development of a personality, we register something new, something heterogeneous to its original disposition, something which does not fit into the general development, which is no longer "development" but "process." . . . A process is an irreversible change in the psychic life, which is heterogeneous to the personality as it existed until then, and which breaks into it either just once as an isolated occurrence, or repeatedly and more general, or in all manner of combinations between those two. (pp. 116–117)

The clarification of these points has direct relevance to the concept proposed, for instance, by Jung in Bleuler and Jung (8), which tried to explain schizophrenia entirely as a development, or to later similar attempts by Kretschmer (12) with his concept of "sensitive delusions of reference," or Gaupp (13) with paranoia. The latter two authors applied their attempts to demonstrate the developmental nature only to certain subtypes, whereas Jung gave it unreserved application to schizophrenia as a whole. Jaspers's clarifications enable us to examine these claims methodologically. They are particularly helpful in our examination of Bleuler's (10) concept of schizophrenia. Stimulated by Freud's work, Bleuler was really the first who introduced a psychological approach to schizophrenia, while at the same time trying to give a more balanced view by not entirely ignoring the limits of such an approach. Bleuler "understood" psychologically the delusions, hallucinations, and other experiences of the patient, but still regarded "primary" symptoms—the four "A's" as they are sometimes called—as process bound and not understandable.

However, the attempts to "understand" schizophrenic experiences and regarding them as psychogenic developments, although they were in danger of overextending themselves, were new at the time. The prevailing and established view was the one so powerfully argued by Kraepelin—namely to ignore all these attempts and regard all the elements of the schizophrenic psychosyndromes merely as "symptoms" of the underlying somatic disease, a process conceived as a causally connected chain, devoid of any meaning. After giving a brief account of the views of Freud, Jung, Bleuler, and Abraham, Kraepelin (14) dismissed them:

I have to confess frankly, that with the best will I find myself unable to go along with the ideas of that "meta psychiatry" which, like a complex, soaks up every kind of sober clinical method of examination. As I usually tread the firm ground of direct experience, my philistine scientific conscience keeps stumbling with every step over objections, reservations and doubts, which, however, are no obstacles for the winged imagination of Freud's followers. (p. 938)

Jaspers (6), in turn, while acknowledging the tremendous achievements of Kraepelin, uncompromisingly drew attention to this lack, as he perceived it, in Kraepelin's exclusively somatically oriented approach. He continued his methodological analysis as follows:

Up to now we have completely ignored that all these processes are thought to be related to something taking place in the brain, something which represents the real nature of the disease. . . . Originally the concept of a "process" was derived from purely psychological, formal characteristics, such as the character of an irreversible change, more particularly a progressive deterioration (Verblödung). Thus defined, the concept can be applied—in certain cases—with a fair degree of confidence. If, however, one adds to the definition the relatedness of these psychic changes to an underlying cerebral change, the concept is burdened by a very hypothetical, in practice—in most cases—undemonstrable criterion. Whenever such a cerebral change can be demonstrated—everyone points here to G.P.I. [general paralysis of the insane] as an examplary model— we also speak of "process," but we must not lose sight of the fact that here the word process has an entirely different meaning. In that context it bases its criteria entirely on pathological findings, and all abnormal psychic events are seen as related to them. Our experience shows in all cases where such a pa- thology could be discovered that any conceivable variety of psychopathic or psychotic symptoms could occur; the only thing all such cases might have in common is the formation of a defect. What remains is that certain symptoms may on statistical examination be found to have a higher or lower frequency in one or another pathological state and can in that sense be seen as more or less characteristic for that underlying pathology. (6, p. 118)

He stressed that not one of those symptoms (e.g., abnormal affects, delusions, hallucinations) can be localized to any particular site in the brain, nor to any particular topology of the cerebral pathology. He made a dis- tinction between those physical-psychotic "processes" we have for instance in GPI or in arteriosclerosis on the one hand, and the "psychotic process" on the other, which is characterized only by psychic characteristics. In comparing those two heterogeneous processes to differentiate them, he analyzed the widely used concept of a psychophysical parallelism. He para- phrased that position as follows:

Wherever I have a specific cerebral process, I am bound to find parallel specific psychic manifestations as their consequence, and vice versa, wherever I have a specific course of psychic changes, I am bound one day to discover just as specific cerebral changes. The psychic processes or the psycho-physical pro- cesses must be one and the same. If on the other hand we pursue this line of parallelistic thinking, we have to note right away that up to now we don't know of a single direct parallel change which corresponds to a psychic change. . . . [All research] up to now has only brought us closer to find such parallel events but they have nowhere actually been found. (6, p. 118)

All we can say, assuming that such changes are most likely taking place in the cortex, is that this must be the substrate in which such changes are probably somehow embedded. We do not know them. They remain a postulate only. We know also that histopathologists find at times very extensive cerebral changes without any manifest psychic changes having been present in that individual, just as we observe very profound psychic changes without any histopathology whatever.

Jaspers established the relative autonomy of the psychosyndrome and its partial independence from cerebral pathology and showed Kraepelin's con- cept of the disease entity to be what it is, namely a hypothetical postulate.

The low specificity of the psychosyndrome is demonstrated in the admission statistics at Kraepelin's clinic: GPI was greatly overdiagnosed before the introduction of the serologic diagnosis of the disease.

Jaspers established three different concepts (Table 5-1.) The first is physical-psychotic, where the actual chain of events lies in the cerebral substrate while the psychic manifestations are a largely haphazard sequence of symptoms, haphazard because they are not directly dependent on the "parallel process" but in a more general way on the underlying cerebral changes. Second is the psychic process, where a single change brings about an irreversible psychic "break." Third is the development of a personality, which is radically different from the first two.

To illustrate the application of these concepts, Jaspers provided a series of extremely well documented case histories, each of them assigned to one or more of these categories. There will, of course, be transitional forms, or indeed forms not readily assignable to any one category.

> We have up to now presented our cases either as a "process" or as a "development of a personality." But we cannot expect that we will be able to subsume each and every case without any doubt under one or the other of these concepts, concepts which like all concepts are only abstractions, not concrete realities. (6, p. 135)

Meaning Versus Causality

Although Jaspers had already been using the concepts of "understanding" and of "comprehending causal connections," in a later publication he explained them more systematically and in greater detail (15). The article called "Die Phänomenologische Forschungsrichtung in der Psychopathologie" (The Phenomenological Approach in Psychopathology) is a fundamental contribution to psychopathology that has appeared in English. Because it is well known, its substance will not be elaborated here in any great detail. The direct application to schizophrenia of some of the ideas in that work are described in another article called "Kausale und 'verständliche' Zusammenhänge zwischen Schicksal und Psychose bei der Dementia praecox (Schizophrenie)" (16). Part of this article has appeared in English translation.

> Meaningful connections are something entirely different from causal connections. To illustrate this: we *understand* behavior in terms of motives, but we *explain* movements as caused by nerve impulses. We *understand* how affects arise out of certain moods, how moods give rise to certain hopes, fantasies or fears; but we *explain* (causally) how memory dispositions arise or vanish, or how fatigue or recovery from it come about.
>
> Understanding and causal explanation go hand in hand in the exploration of a human being, they are locked together in a very complex way, but with exact methodological reflections, each can be clearly and systematically discerned from the other. (p. 329)

Table 5-1.   Jaspers's view on schizophrenia

Development of a personality	Psychic processes	Physical-psychotic process
Slow development from childhood onward, analogous to the life process.	A new development with a definite onset at a certain point in time.	
	A once-only grafting on, comparable to that of a tumor.	Continued breaking in of new heterogeneous material.
Acute events do not mean permanent changes. The status quo ante is restored.	Acute processes bring an irreversible change; if an acute event ends in recovery, unless it falls under the physical-psychotic process, it will be regarded as a "reaction" or as a "periodic" event, concepts we shall not deal with here. Patients with such acute events could be subsumed under development of a personality.	Whether the change is transient or permanent will depend on the underlying physical process, not on the characteristics of the direct parallel process.
One can derive an entire life from the personality-anlage.	In deriving a life history in terms of the personality, one encounters limits where at a certain point in time something new has entered, a heterogeneous change.	The definition will in the end be determined by finding the particular physical process.
	A certain psychologically comprehensible order of the development and the course, similar to normal psychic life events, which will have a new inner unity with extensive rationally and empathically understandable connections.	A haphazard lack of order in the symptoms and the course. All the manifestations follow each other in an unconnected chaos, as they are secondary not just to the direct parallel process, but rather to the physical cerebral process.

Source.   From Jaspers (11, p. 121).

Psychological understanding is, by its nature, a subjective method. The word *subjective* in science is often given a devalued connotation. One speaks of "only subjective." In psychopathology, such judgments have no place; in fact, psychopathology without subjective psychology becomes mere physiology. In psychopathology, the subjective and objective methods complement each other and are equally indispensable. The unforgivable sin is only if the results are not kept separate, because each method produces its own kinds of knowledge; being of different orders, they must not be taken one for the other. They are governed by different rules of evidence.

In a critical evaluation of Jaspers's contribution to psychology, Lefebre (17) wrote:

> In 1912 we had a number of technical and logical research methods (memory tests, etc.) into the *objective facts* of the psyche, as we see them in such fields as somatopsychology, performance psychology etc.; for descriptions of *subjective experiences* on the other hand, which are indispensable for any kind of psychology, we did not have a precise method. . . . It was not until Jaspers' publication of his "Phenomenological research in psychopathology" that an exact description of the phenomenological method was created and phenomenology was introduced into psychiatry. (p. 468)

This introduction was a profound turn in modern psychology. It meant that a research method that gave precision to the subjective study of psychopathology had been established. Phenomenology, together with the psychology of meaning and the psychology of empathy—the precise methodology of each of these approaches—are of the most far-reaching importance for research in schizophrenia. In fact, one can go so far as to say that any research in this field that is uninformed of these methods is to that extent invalid.

In subjective psychology, the psychologist becomes a subject of methodological scrutiny as much as the matter under study itself, namely, the inner experiences of the patient. Lefebre (17) called this "the introduction of the psychologist into psychology" (p. 472):

> Jaspers, by going beyond the object of the psychologist's study and turning back to the thinking subject himself, anchors thereby psychology within the psychologist. From this follows that for Jaspers the ultimate in psychology is the way in which the psychologist thinks of a given psychic event [in the patient]. . . .
>
> Jaspers in the final analysis undertakes this relocation of psychology (into the psychologist) on philosophical grounds, but they are nevertheless, of great significance for the psychologist. (p. 477)

Within the subjective psychopathologic research itself we differentiate between rational understanding, (i.e., we analyze and follow a *logically* reasoned proposition) and empathic understanding.

In the latter we obtain by empathy a direct, immediate understanding of the feelings, wishes, fears, and the inner life in general of another person. Jaspers further explained the difference between "static" understanding, when, as in phenomenology, we try to circumscribe and define as precisely as possible particular inner experiences such as hallucinations, illusions, and depersonalizations, and "genetic" understanding where we empathically understand the patient's motives or generally how something psychic has arisen out of preceding psychic events.

Distinct from all this is performance or test psychology, which is *objective* psychology. When we attempt empathically to understand a patient's description of thought disorder (e.g, thought withdrawal), we use a subjective method (static understanding) and are methodologically engaged in something entirely different from asking the patient about the differences or similarities of various objects and establish the presence or absence of concrete thinking (performance psychology).

Empathic understanding is an immediate process and differs from "interpretation." The latter we use when understanding fails; there a connection is established by invoking a hypothetical underlying chain of events. Such a hypothetical event can be thought of as a physical cerebral event (an underlying pathology) or a hypothesized psychological event (such as when Charcot interpreted the distribution of hysterical anesthesia to be due to popular beliefs about nerve distributions), or an interpretation of a dream element as a manifestation of an archetype.

These and more clarifications point by point established, Jaspers (16) presented a number of extensive case histories to illustrate their clinical application. He described in these biographical sketches the general life history, the forefield of the psychosis (i.e., the events immediately preceding the onset of the illness), the experiences during the illness, and the passing of it. He showed how the subjective methods of phenomenology and of genetic understanding are applied, and, when their limits are reached, where causal thinking or hypothetical interpretations begin.

> There are researchers who still believe that *everything* psychic can be understood. We now realize that only certain aspects of psychic life are accessible to our understanding. (p. 333)

Where these limits to our empathic understanding are can never be entirely resolved. Understanding always brings matters, until then unnoticed, into the focus of awareness. There is, however, a difference between what has been unnoticed—certain hidden motives, feelings, or sentiments—and what is extraconscious (i.e., in principle, inaccessible). The unnoticed itself has been experienced; the extraconscious has not. The objective of the long case histories—and some contrasting ones where this was not the case—was to show the close relationships between the contents of the patient's premorbid concerns and that of the abnormal experiences during the illness.

The Reactive Psychoses

The introduction of this kind of study of the psychotic patient, the attention to the meaningful connections discerned in the content of the psychotic experiences, has in some quarters led to an attempt to establish a new category of illness. In this type of illness, a preexisting abnormal constitution *reacts* in an abnormal way to external events, only to revert to its earlier state when these events cease, as opposed to the so-called productive illness, in which, without any external causes, a process takes its course, leading to a progressive alteration in the psychic constitution. The effort to establish such categories was widespread and by no means confined to schizophrenia. In relation to affective illnesses, for example, Aubrey Lewis took issue, dismissing it as of no nosologic value (18). The *International Classification of Diseases* (ICD-9) (19) still contains a diagnostic category of reactive psychosis. The category is still used in Scandinavian countries and in the Soviet Union and perhaps one or two other countries (20). Jaspers (16) never saw it as a diagnostic category:

> In our time the view is more and more accepted that a definition of disease-"entities" can only be achieved by neuro-anatomical or other somatic research methods, and that a sharp *clinical* delineation and definition of disease-entities is once and for all an hopeless undertaking. The concepts gained by such methods, however, are by no means useless; they merely shift their significance from the field of special psychiatry into that of general psychopathology. (p. 339)

In other words, what is intended here cannot lead to a nosologic entity, but represents a particular methodological approach to the study of schizophrenic patients. In this sense, Jaspers (16) defined what he meant by "reactive psychosis":

> Under this concept are subsumed all abnormal psychic states which occur following a certain experience, are directly connected with it and are reversible, and in which the contents of the new state are meaningfully connected with the initial experience. It is irrelevant whether such a reactive psychosis occurs in a psychopath, a schizophrenic or an organically ill patient. The reactive psychosis in each such case will of course be of a very different kind. (p. 340)

Jaspers (16) thus made it quite clear that he did not assign a nosologic position to the reactive psychosis. In fact, at the end of each of his illustrative case histories, he discussed separately 1) the phenomenology, 2) the diagnosis, and 3) the meaningful connections. He also made it abundantly clear he did not mistake the meaningful connection to be the "cause":

> We hold strictly separate the causal factor from the meaningful connections, and do not believe that a mental illness can be explained by a "psychic cause" alone, even when we can to a large extent psychologically understand its mode of appearance. (p. 344)

When Jaspers described his cases, which illustrated his concept of the reactive psychosis, he clearly did not wish to establish a nosologic entity but to illustrate the application of "understanding" to the content of a psychotic illness, to show the extreme extent to which this method can almost exhaust an entire psychosis under certain conditions. It must, however, be stressed that the understanding is confined to the *contents* of the abnormal experiences. The form of the experiences—which includes delusions, delusional percepts, hallucinations, illusions, and others—are the subject of static understanding, of phenomenology; by them, the phenomena, we can characterize the concept of schizophrenia, as was later shown, for example, by Schneider (21). Content, on the other hand, is not the proper basis for diagnostic categorization. Content has its roots in the unique life of the individual and never lends itself to nosology, which represents a generalization. It is on the relative frequency of various abnormal *forms* of experience that our syndromatic classification is based.

As the understanding in Jaspers's cases is limited to the content, it is not a *full* understanding in the general sense of this concept. According to Schneider (22), for full empathic understanding, the form is as important as the content. If a patient is deeply offended and hurt by the infidelity of his wife who has run off with a lover and, in the psychosis, hears his wife's voice saying she no longer wants to have anything to do with her lover and is wanting to come back to him, but her lover's voice saying she must not go, we recognize the thematic continuity between the prepsychotic trauma (i.e., the wife's infidelity, and its intrusion into the psychotic experiences), but we cannot say that we "understand" the patient. The form in which the theme, the hurt, and wishfulness appears make full empathy impossible and defy such understanding.

> One of the patients, after emerging from the acute illness, said: "One and the same event could have had 20 meanings. Everything was so full of contradictions, 'so terribly illogical'." [And Jaspers comments:] It is therefore quite impossible to "rationalize" the psychosis, to try to project some logical reason into the psychosis. (16, p. 409)

All that can be gleaned in this mass of often only fleeting and rapidly changing experiences during the psychosis is the basic theme, which is connected with the aspirations and disappointments of the patient's life history. Jaspers also described many other experiences in the psychosis of his patient that do not seem so connected, that appear to be rather haphazard associations and reminiscences. The "meaningful" experiences have to be sorted out from all the others, which also contribute to the clinical picture.

Jaspers recognized, of course, that *all* psychotic contents must have come from somewhere in the patient's past life, but considered as relevant to the reactive psychosis only those that have decisively influenced the psychotic breakdown by their significance and their emotional impact.

The confusion about the nosologic significance of these syndromes is at least partly caused by the name Jaspers assigned to them: *reactive psychoses*. Not surprisingly, such terminology appears to some to point to a nosologic characterization of these case descriptions. In his final paragraph, however, Jaspers (16) said:

> We do not attempt here to deal with the problem of establishing "types of reactive psychoses," or perhaps to determine "the properties of schizophrenic reactivity." (p. 412)

Pathography

The detailed study of the premorbid as well as the psychotic experiences is, at all times, beset with great difficulties.

> We can only study [such experiences] with any hope for success in highly differentiated, gifted persons. Once we have them in our grasp, we shall the easier recognize them in the less differentiated form in the average case. But such gifted patients with a schizophrenic process have rarely—mainly for lack of opportunity—become the object of scientific study. (16, p. 404)

It was this that induced Jaspers to study a few such individuals—creative writers and artists—who were known to have been afflicted by a severe psychiatric illness and whose life and illness were amply documented in diaries, letters, autobiographies, biographies, or comments by contemporaries, as well as by their creative works. Examples of such studies are one of the prophet Ezekiel and one of Nietzsche.

Of particular interest here, however, is Jaspers's book on *Strindberg und Van Gogh* (23). The lives of August Strindberg (1849–1912) and of Vincent Van Gogh (1853–1890) are briefly described to provide the canvas on which their illness is then outlined. In addition to those two, there are also shorter histories of the scientist and theologian Immanuel Swedenborg (1688–1772) and of the poet Johann Christoph Friedrich Hölderlin (1779–1843), presented for various comparisons with the first two. What these four men have in common is their psychotic illness. They were all suffering from schizophrenia, or rather schizophrenia came at least first in the differential diagnosis.

Jaspers showed in these studies the application of his general concepts of differentiating between "process" and "development of a personality," between phenomenology and "understanding of meaning," and between these subjective methods and causal explaining. By looking at these lives, he tried to trace the meaningful connection between the personal development and earlier experiences with the experiences during the acute phases of the illness, as well as with the details of the residual syndromes and how the entire psychic constitution is changed in the total course of the illness. He also tried to show the effect of this change on the work of these men.

By this undertaking, Jaspers—always concerned with methodology—developed his general principles of pathography, while showing them in their application to the study of those afflicted by mental illness.

The work and indeed the decisions taken in the conduct of the lives of the mentally ill are never dismissed, even when they occur during, or are clearly influenced by, psychosis. The meaning is explored, is understood as far as this remains possible, and is appreciated in its own right. This approach, which is central to Jaspers's psychopathology, is explained in greater detail in his *General Psychopathology* (6) in parts 5 and 6:

> No man can ever be grasped in his entirety. . . . It is merely a prejudice to consider a man as an object, to believe that one can grasp him in his entirety by scientific knowledge. Hence: we should never lose our awareness of the inexhaustibility and mystery of every single mentally ill person, even when faced by the apparently most common everyday patient. (p. 661)

The productions of psychotic patients have their roots in the inner world, albeit a world formed—or deformed—by the psychosis.

> Even behind the delusions of being an inventor, for instance in the constant repetitiveness of the construction of a perpetuum mobile, there exists a reassertion of a world view by rational work. (p. 249)

Analyzing Van Gogh's letters to his brother Theo, Jaspers (23) determined the time when the illness was active. He also followed Vincent's thoughts about his work, his problems:

> These letters as a whole (only about a quarter were written during the psychosis) document a world view, an Existence, a mind of high ethos; they are the expression of an absolute honesty, of a deep irrational faith, of an unending love, of a magnanimous humanity, of an unshakable amor fati. These letters are amongst the most moving publications of our recent past; this ethos exists without any dependency on the psychosis, rather it really only comes into its own in the psychosis. (p. 109)

In the evaluation of Van Gogh's work, Jaspers (23) counted him among those artists whose creations are the expressions of a human existence, as partial solutions, steps toward a goal. He quoted Van Gogh in a conversation with his teacher: "What I want is to give poor people peace with their fate on earth" (p. 112). He wanted with his work to console. At the same time, Jaspers analyzed the changes in the pictures over time and noticed the changes that began around 1888 and culminated later in what can be seen as a "mannerism." He noticed the new kind of impact these pictures had on the onlooker, a peculiarly stirring effect. Van Gogh wrote that he really wanted to paint Christ, saints, and angels but desisted because he found it too upsetting for himself and chose instead to paint simple objects. But the religious impulse is not lost with them and is noticeable. In fact, the paintings of the years between 1888–1890, while so ill he had to live in a mental hospital, had the greatest impact. He was also most productive during those years. Only the latest paintings done during the last few weeks of his life make in parts a chaotic impression. The colors are more brutal. Their earlier inner tension is replaced by a rather chaotic character.

> The works between 1888 and 1890 contain a tension, an excitement, as if questions about life, about the world try to find expression. . . . Here is something utterly original and without affectation. They don't represent anything learned or acquired which has become objectivated, but something which in the general inner loosening by the psychosis was intensely experienced. It happened as with Hölderlin: as if the string which was mightily touched, just when sounding the right tone, bursts itself by it. (23, p. 114)

It is, of course, impossible to give even a sketchy account of this fascinating book. The above is only a sample illustrating the approach. The aspect of interest here is the illustration of the method outlined in the article on the reactive psychoses applied to highly differentiated, original, and outstanding men. It illustrates a methodologically diverse, yet integrated approach to the study of their illnesses as they are embedded and intertwined with their lives and work.

We let Jaspers (23), in conclusion, speak once more:

> Another misunderstanding has to be dealt with. When one attempts to find a formulation for the schizophrenic atmosphere in works of art, this doesn't mean that such works are "sick." The spirit is beyond such opposites as healthy or sick. However, works which have grown on the grounds of a morbid process might possess a specific character which represents an essential factor in the universe of the spirit and yet can in reality only come about when such a process has created the necessary conditions. The philistine use of the concept of "sick" to devalue, or to consider any part it may play in philosophical questions as banal, blinds one to a reality which up to now we can only grasp descriptively and which we as yet have no means to interpret. (p. 124)

Nosology

Although Jaspers did not produce a concept of schizophrenia as such, he dealt with the nosologic aspect in his *General Psychopathology* (6), but in the context of that discipline, rather than in the context of special psychiatry. He stated that Kraepelin's creation of the two large functional psychoses, although fruitful, have so far not been established as what Kraepelin conceived them to be (i.e., disease entities). They are psychosyndromes of great importance, but they do not satisfy the requirements expected of a disease entity. Their etiology and pathology remain elusive. Their delineation changes and is based at times on the course of the illness, sometimes on the psychopathologic criteria. Each approach has its own limitations. Thus the demarcation line between the two functional psychoses swings like a pendulum. The resilience of Kraepelin's work suggests a certain validity, but this must not tempt us to jump to premature conclusions about them.

Jaspers has shown the relative autonomy of the psychosyndrome. But, while sympathetic to Bleuler's efforts to introduce the subjective study to the syndrome, showed this in the hands of Bleuler to lack methodological clarity. The attention to methodology is essential to Jaspers. Every knowledge we have has to be evaluated in terms of the method by which this knowledge has been gained. In his analysis of the various theories proposed in his time or before him, he examined each view in the light of the conceptualization and methodology from the unitary psychosis of Griesinger (24) to the elaborate classification by Leonhard (25).

He reviewed the entire field, and what he showed is as valid now as it was then. There is no attempt to close the great debate, but rather to leave all doors open, subject only to methodological clarity.

References

1. Esquirol JE: Des Maladies Mentales. Paris, Bailliere, 1838
2. Haslam J: Observations on Madness and Melancholy, Including Practical Remarks on those Diseases. London, Callow, 1809
3. Hoenig J: Karl Jaspers and Psychopathology. Philosophy and Phenomenological Research. 26:216–229, 1965
4. Jaspers K: Philosophische Autobiographie, in Karl Jaspers. Edited by Schlipp PA. Stuttgart, Kohlhammer, 1957, pp 1–79
5. Jaspers K: Die Psychologie der Weltanschauungen. Berlin, Springer, 1919
6. Jaspers K: Allgemeine Psychopathologie, 7th Edition. Berlin, Springer, 1959 (In English: General Psychopathology, Translated by Hoenig J, Hamilton MW. Manchester University Press, 1963)
7. Schneider K: 25 Jahre 'Allgemeine Psychopathologie' von Karl Jaspers. Nervenarzt 11:281–283, 1938
8. Bleuler E, Jung CG: Komplexe and Krankheitsursachen bei Dementia praecox. Zentralblatt für Psychiatrie und Nervenheilkunde 3:220–227, 1908
9. Jung CG: Über die Psychologie der Dementia Praecox. Halle/S, Marhold, 1907
10. Bleuler E: Dementia praecox oder die Gruppe der Schizophrenien. Leipzig, Deutike, 1911 (In English: Dementia Praecox or the Group of Schizophrenias. Translated by Zenkin J. New York, International Universities Press, 1952)
11. Jaspers K: Eifersuchtswahn. Zeitschrift für die gesamte Neurologie und Psychiatrie. 1:567–637, 1910 (In Gesammelte Schriften zur Psychopathologie. Berlin, Springer, 1963)
12. Kretschmer E: Der Sensitive Beziehungswahn. Berlin, Springer, 1918.
13. Gaupp R: Die wissenschaftliche Bedeutung des "Falles Wagner." Münchner Medizinische Wochenschrift 61:633–637, 1914 (In English: The scientific significance of the case of Ernst Wagner, in Themes and Variations in European Psychiatry. Edited by Hirsch SR, Shepherd M. Bristol, Wright, 1974)
14. Kraepelin E: Psychiatrie, Vol 3, 9th Edition. Leipzig, Barth, 1923
15. Jaspers K: Die Phänomenologische Forschungsrichtung in der Psychopathologie. Zeitschrift für die gesamte Neurologie und Psychiatrie 9:391–408, 1912 (In Gesammelte Schriften zur Psychopathologie. Berlin, Springer, 1963) (In English: The phenomenological approach in psychopathology. Br J Psychiatry 1968: 114:1313–1323, 1968)

16. Jaspers K: Kausale und "verständliche" Zusammenhänge zwischen Schicksal und Psychose bei der Dementia praecox (Schizophrenie). Zeitschrift für die gesamte Neurologie und Psychiatrie. 14:158–263, 1913 (In Gesammelte Schriften zur Psychopathologie. Berlin, Springer, 1963) (In English [a part only]: In Themes and Variations in European Psychiatry. Edited by Hirsch SR, Shepherd M. Bristol, Wright, 1974)

17. Lefebre LB: Die Psychologie von Karl Jaspers, in Karl Jaspers. Edited Schlipp PA. Stuttgart, Kohlhammer, 1957 (In English: The Philosophy of Karl Jaspers. Edited by Schlipp PA. Stuttgart, Kohlhammer, 1957)

18. Hoenig J: Early signs of depression, in Clinical Depressions. Edited by Ayd FJ Jr. Baltimore, MD, Ayd Medical Communications, 1980

19. World Health Organization: Manual of the International Statistical Classification of Diseases, Injuries and Causes of Death (ICD-9). Geneva, World Health Organization, 1977

20. Strömgren E: The Scandinavian schools of psychiatry. VII World Congress of Psychiatry, PL 46, Vienna, July 11–16, 1983

21. Schneider K: Wesen und Erfassung des Schizophrenen. Zeitschrift für die gesamte Neurologie und Psychiatrie. 99:542–547, 1925

22. Schneider K: Kraepelin und die gegenwärtige Psychiatrie. Fortschritte der Neurologie Psychiatrie 24:1–7, 1956

23. Jaspers K: Strindberg und Van Gogh. Versuch einer pathographyschen Analyse untervergleichender Heranziehung von Swedenborg und Hölderlin. Bern, Bircher, 1922

24. Griesinger W: Die Pathologie und Therapie der psychischen Krankheiten. 4. Auflage, Braunschweig, Wreden, 1876

25. Leonhard K: Die Aufteilung der endogenen Psychosen. Berlin, Akademie Verl, 1959

CHAPTER SIX

Concepts of Schizophrenia After Kraepelin and Bleuler

Charles P. Peters, M.D.

The evolving conceptual history of schizophrenia presents the student of psychopathology with a perplexing and oftentimes contradictory set of descriptive criteria and theoretical tenets. Concurrent diagnostic formulations of the syndrome have reflected clinical, theoretical, and cultural differences.

The purpose of this chapter is threefold. First, the historical evolution of the schizophrenic concept is traced from the earliest 19th century case reports to 20th century empirical research. The psychiatric literature at the turn of the last century is examined for the purpose of understanding the impact of early writers on the evolving concept of schizophrenia. Second, the diverse clinical and theoretical formulations of schizophrenia are delineated, primarily as this split occurred between psychiatrists in the United States and Europe. Finally, the recent convergence of clinical opinion as a function of cross-national research projects and renewed interest in multidimensional diagnostic systems is described.

Historical Foundations: The 19th Century

Investigators in the 19th century first described the psychotic patient in individual case studies. Phillipe Pinel (1), the French physician, laid the groundwork for the modern concept of the major psychoses. Pinel introduced the term *la manie* in his case reports of patients with florid thought disturbance and accompanying affective excess. *La demence* described those patients with pure thought disorder in the absence of gross affective change. Pinel's descriptions of mania and dementia became the dichotomous format around which later formulations of psychosis would converge.

In 1809, the British physician, John Haslam (2), described a group of patients similar to those in Pinel's case studies of dementia. Haslam's patients were neither maniacal or melancholic, but instead demonstrated "a state of complete insanity, unaccompanied by furious or depressing passions."

In 1852, Benedict Morel (3) applied the term *demence praecox* to an adolescent patient, originally bright and active, who gradually became gloomy, silent, and withdrawn. In 1874, Karl Ludwig Kahlbaum (4) described *katatonia*, a syndrome of pathologically changed motor activity accompanied by alternating mutism and frenzied excitement. *Hebephrenia*, a disease of younger patients that resulted in florid psychosis and deteriorating course, was first reported by Ewald Hecker (5) a student of Kahlbaum, in 1871.

The pioneering work of Emil Kraepelin and Eugen Bleuler marked the first consolidation of these diverse syndromes into an integrated system of classification.

Early Conceptualizations: Kraepelin and Bleuler

Kraepelin (1855–1926)

As a student of Wilhelm Wundt in Leipzig, Emil Kraepelin adopted an academic orientation to the emerging field of psychiatry. Encouraged by Wundt to write the *Compendium der Psychiatrie* (6–8), Kraepelin formulated the essential ideas on which the modern concept of schizophrenia was built.

The ensuing revisions of his now famous text depict the evolution of Kraepelin's thinking. In 1893, the 4th edition of the *Compendium of Psychiatry* (7) was published. Dementia praecox, catatonia, and dementia paranoides were grouped together under the heading: "processes of dementing." Although each syndrome was considered distinct from the others, they were grouped together because of shared deterioration in intellectual function.

A reformulation followed in the landmark 1896 edition of his text, in which Kraepelin emphasized two common denominators among this group of psychotic disorders (8). All seemed to demonstrate an early age of onset and a deteriorating clinical course. He reclassified these psychotic syndromes under the heading of dementia praecox.

The diagnostic significance of early age of onset and deteriorating clinical course was further elaborated on in his paper, "The Diagnosis and Prognosis of Dementia Praecox," presented in 1898 to the 29th Congress of Southwestern German Psychiatry in Heidelberg (8a). In this paper, Kraepelin formally delineated the two major psychotic disorders: dementia praecox and manic-depressive illness. Unlike dementia praecox, manic-depressive illness was not confined to an early age of onset, nor did it necessarily entail a poor prognosis.

Although course of illness and prognosis formed the cornerstones of Kraepelin's formulation of dementia praecox, he nonetheless paid considerable attention to phenomenology. Kraepelin noted the presence of such symptoms as hallucinations, delusions, negativism, and stereotyped behavior. Descriptive features were essential ingredients in his early system of classification. In a later edition of his textbook (9), Kraepelin subtyped dementia praecox into 36 major descriptive catagories, each manifesting a distinct constellation of signs and symptoms.

In contrast to Kraepelin, Eugen Bleuler departed from descriptive psychopathology and attempted to specify the underlying processes that were at the core of the behavioral and psychological disturbances in schizophrenia.

Bleuler (1857–1939)

While professor of psychiatry at the University of Zurich and head of the Burghölzli Clinic, Eugen Bleuler concentrated on the further elucidation of the major psychoses. In his 1911 monograph on the subject (10), Bleuler broke with Kraepelin on two critical points. He contended that neither early age of onset nor deteriorating course were pathognomonic or required for the diagnosis of dementia praecox. Instead, Bleuler turned his attention away from descriptive criteria and toward the intrapsychic processes that he believed to be accountable for this group of psychotic disorders.

Bleuler's view of dementia praecox was influenced by the emerging psychoanalytic movement and, in particular, by the writing of Sigmund Freud. Just as Freud had postulated an intrapsychic conflict to be at work in generating the symptom neuroses, Bleuler imagined that a similar "core pathology" could be identified for the psychotic disorders.

Like Kraepelin, Bleuler noted a wide and varying constellation of signs and symptoms among patients bearing the diagnosis of dementia praecox. However, he was more impressed by the shared disturbance in thought processes. Focusing on what he considered to be the "core pathology," Bleuler described the mechanism of "associative splitting." He wrote that a "breaking of associative threads," a disintegration of the cohesive forces connecting one thought to the next, constituted the primary defect among the varied subtypes of dementia praecox. The plethora of symptomatology observed in these patients was secondary to this central disturbance.

Contending that the disorder was neither necessarily of early onset nor deteriorating course, Bleuler abandoned the term *dementia praecox* in 1911 and coined the diagnostic label *schizophrenia*. Bleuler divided the features of schizophrenia into primary and secondary criteria. The associative disturbance was the primary symptom necessary for diagnosis. Disturbances of affect, ambivalence, and autism were secondary to an interaction between the primary associative disturbance and experiential and interpersonal factors. Other phenomena frequently included among the descriptive criteria of schizophrenia, such as hallucinations and delusions, were understandable in relation to the primary defect.

Bleuler's concept of schizophrenia greatly extended the scope of the diagnostic construct. Patients who would have been excluded from Kraepelin's classification system for lack of meeting his stricter criteria were readily assimilated into Bleuler's definition of schizophrenia. Latent, residual, and simple forms of the illness were defined. Each lacked overt signs of psychosis, yet was considered schizophrenic due to evidence of associational thought disturbance.

Polarization of the Concept

As Neale and Oltmanns (11) pointed out in their excellent text, Kraepelin and Bleuler spawned two relatively distinct approaches to the concept of schizophrenia. They differed in their definitions of the disorder and in their analyses of the essential elements of the condition. Kraepelin proposed a narrow and descriptive formulation of schizophrenia that emphasized the longitudinal unfolding of the illness, whereas Bleuler's concept of schizophrenia was theoretically grounded, less descriptive, and more broadly inclusive. European psychiatry embraced the Kraepelinian concept; Bleuler's influence was more apparent in the United States.

The American Concept of Schizophrenia: 1920–1970

Adolf Meyer was founder of the psychobiological school of psychiatry and director of the Henry Phipps Psychiatry Clinic of The Johns Hopkins Hospital from 1909 to 1941. Meyer never subscribed fully to either Kraepelin's or Bleuler's systems of classification. Although Meyer (12, 13) was instrumental in introducing Kraepelin's work in the United States, his ultimate impact was to move American psychiatry away from Kraepelin's narrow descriptive definition of schizophrenia and toward a more broad-based and individualistic view of the disorder. His approach to schizophrenia was more flexible than that of his European colleagues. He did not rely on either specific pathognomonic symptoms or progressive deterioration in making the diagnosis. Meyer believed that the schizophrenic syndrome was the natural result of a life history that could be traced to various physical, social, and psychological forces in the patient's past. He proposed a unique and idiosyncratic basis for each patient's psychiatric illness. Every patient demanded intensive individual study to unravel the essential ingredients of his or her particular illness. No theoretical explanation or standard diagnostic labeling system would substitute.

Harry Stack Sullivan, like Bleuler and Meyer, believed that the schizophrenic patient need not be destined from the outset to unalterable clinical deterioration. Sullivan's interest was in understanding the individual's withdrawal from interpersonal relationships and the emotional and cognitive operations at work in precipitating these reactions. At Sheppard and Enoch Pratt Hospital in Baltimore, Maryland, Sullivan established a special ward for male adolescent patients where he applied modified psychoanalytic principles to the treatment of schizophrenia (14).

Observable behavior played little role in Sullivan's formulation of the syndrome. Instead, he inferred intense anxiety to be the basis of the dissociation of experience in schizophrenia. Sullivan wrote: "I suppose if one had to try to put such things into words, one might say that the schizophrenic suffers an almost unceasing fear of becoming an exceedingly unpleasant form of nothingness by a collapse of the self" (15).

Sullivan's teaching and writing inevitably led to a further broadening of the American concept of schizophrenia. As Schulz (16) pointed out, Sullivan influenced many prominent investigators, including Frieda Fromm-Reichmann, Harold Searles, and Silvano Arieti. Following the lead of Meyer and Sullivan, a number of other influential American psychiatrists further extended the boundaries of the schizophrenic concept.

In 1933, Kasanin (17) described a group of nine patients who had been given the diagnosis of dementia praecox. He observed that each patient demonstrated an acute onset of illness, a rapid recovery, and a predominance of affective symptoms in addition to evidence of thought disorder. These patients engaged in life activities, had relatively good work adjustment, and tended to be more sociable than shy. Depression was noted to have frequently ushered in the acute psychotic symptoms and an identifiable stressor could oftentimes be determined. Kasanin coined the term *schizoaffective psychosis* to categorize these patients who seemed to fall somewhere between Kraepelinean schizophrenia and manic-depressive illness. This term was generally adopted by colleagues to represent a specific schizophrenic subtype.

Zilboorg (18) introduced the term *ambulatory schizophrenia* in 1941. Although individuals with this diagnosis did not meet the strict Kraepelinian criteria, they nonetheless demonstrated clinical characteristics that suggested to Zilboorg a close relationship to schizophrenia. The ambulatory schizophrenic patient manifested oddities of thought, unstable interpersonal relationships, and inability to sustain stable life pursuits. Zilboorg believed that these patients were in the earliest stages of the schizophrenic process.

Hoch and Polatin (19) elaborated on the aforementioned patients when they described the "pseudoneurotic forms of schizophrenia." In keeping with Bleuler's broad concept of schizophrenia, Hoch and Polatin maintained that they were looking at a schizophrenic subtype. They argued that although these patients frequently lacked the more overt signs of psychosis, on closer examination the clinician could elicit the cognitive and emotional disorganization characteristic of the disorder. Diffuse free-floating anxiety, multiple neurotic symptoms, and diverse and perverse sexual practices comprised the salient features noted by Hoch and Polatin. Based on the formulations of Kasanin (17), Zilboorg (18), and Hoch and Polatin, many patients who might otherwise have been considered bipolar, severely neurotic, or borderline were diagnosed under the schizophrenic group of disorders.

From 1920 to 1970, the American concept of schizophrenia grew ever more encompassing and less readily definable. A host of subcategories referred to patients whose psychosis was of short duration, sometimes subtle and at other times completely inapparent.

The concept of schizophrenia in the United States had reached its most dilute form in the American Psychiatric Association's (20) *Diagnostic and Statistical Manual of Mental Disorders, 2nd edition* (DSM-II), published in 1968. DSM-II defined psychosis based on severity of functional impairment rather than on the presence or absence of particular symptoms. A patient was considered psychotic when mental functioning was "sufficiently impaired to interfere grossly with the capacity to meet the ordinary demands of life." The presence of thought disorder, mood disturbance, and behavioral features were noted. However, little elaboration of each symptom complex was provided.

DSM-II provided the barest guidelines for the clinical diagnosis of schizophrenia and relied heavily on the clinician's ability to infer pathology and interpret subtle if not imperceptible hints of underlying thought disturbance. DSM-II represented the broadest interpretation of the schizophrenic concept in American psychiatry and marked the point of greatest divergence from the notion of schizophrenia held by psychiatrists in other parts of the world.

The European Concept of Schizophrenia: 1920–1970

In Europe, Kraepelin's emphasis on descriptive criteria and the natural course of the illness predominated. Clinicians and research psychiatrists paid greater attention to prognosis and observable phenomena than to inferred intrapsychic processes.

In 1939, the Norwegian investigator Langfeldt (21), introduced the concept of "schizophreniform psychosis" to describe patients who evidenced good premorbid adjustment, an acute onset of illness, and a traumatic event almost immediately preceding the psychotic episode. Signs of confusion and affective disturbance during the course of the psychosis were also common.

According to Stone (22), Langfeldt distinguished schizophreniform psychosis from Kraepelinian schizophrenia. Schizophreniform psychosis was considered a distinct syndrome. By contrast, American contemporaries were broadening their concept of schizophrenia and routinely included this population of patients among the schizophrenic subtypes.

The perpetuation of the descriptive school of psychiatry in Europe is well illustrated by Kurt Schneider's (23) 11 first-rank symptoms that were considered pathognomonic of schizophrenia. While acknowledging the significance of the natural course of the illness, he believed that clinical manifestations should take precedence over all other criteria in making the diagnosis.

Schneider's criteria are divided into three broad groups: 1) hallucinatory, 2) delusional, and 3) evidences of disturbance in ego boundary. Hallucinatory experiences include voices speaking the patient's thoughts aloud, the patient experiencing him- or herself as the subject of voices talking aloud, and an awareness of voices commenting on the patient's activity. Delusional symptoms usually involve the patient applying a highly personalized meaning to a normal perception. Simple ideas of persecution or grandiosity were not given great diagnostic weight. Instead, the tendency to attribute special personal significance to a routine innocuous perception was considered to be of exceptional diagnostic importance. Deficits of ego boundary were reflected in the patient's belief in alien control of feelings, impulses, and actions.

First-rank symptoms are not pathognomonic of schizophrenia. As Pope and Lipinski (24) pointed out, 15% to 25% of patients with major affective disorder will at some point in their illness satisfy some if not all of Schneider's criteria. However, this finding does not lessen the significance of Schneider's contribution to the evolution of the schizophrenic concept since the first-rank symptoms further refined a diagnostic system that was descriptively based with minimal reliance on inferential data.

The *British Glossary of Mental Disorders*, published in the same year as DSM-II, adhered to the Kraepelinian model (25). Psychosis and schizophrenia are comprehensively defined. Hallucinations and delusions are described in great detail and follow Schneider's first-rank symptoms quite closely. The nature of the thought disorder is elucidated, and specific reference is made to thought blocking, elliptical and obscure thinking, and thought withdrawal. The elements of affective change are also presented in depth.

DSM-II and the British glossary presented two of the most widely adopted definitions of schizophrenia. With their appearance in 1968, American and European psychiatry had reached the point of greatest divergence in their conceptualizations of this disorder. The United States–United Kingdom Cross-National Project (26) drew attention to the widening gulf between the broad, theoretical approach to the concept of schizophrenia in the United States and the narrow, descriptive definition popular in Europe.

The United States–United Kingdom Cross-National Project

The Cross-National Project for the Study of the Diagnosis of Mental Disorders in the United States and the United Kingdom was undertaken in 1965 to demonstrate cross-national differences in the way psychiatrists make diagnoses and rate psychopathology. That portion of the project focusing on the schizophrenic group of disorders was completed in the period 1965–1970.

Schizophrenic patients were drawn from consecutive admissions to public mental hospitals in New York and London. "Hospital" psychiatrists at each location were responsible for evaluating patients according to indigenous diagnostic criteria. "Project" psychiatrists interviewed the index patients and administered a standardized mental-state interview within 48 to 72 hours of admission. The project interview consisted of 700 items that covered a wide range of current psychiatric symptoms and abnormalities of thinking, speech, and behavior. Project psychiatrists made a diagnosis according to the *International Classification of Diseases* (ICD) (27) of the World Health Organization and the accompanying *British Glossary of Mental Disorders*.

The most significant finding of the project was that the American psychiatrists applied the diagnosis of schizophrenia to a much wider variety of clinical conditions than did their British colleagues. Project psychiatrists found no significant cross-national differences in the number of schizophrenic patients in New York and London. When these same samples of patients were compared on the basis of diagnoses made by hospital psychiatrists, a dramatic preponderance of schizophrenic diagnoses was found in the New York group as opposed to the London group. Since the criteria for project diagnosis of schizophrenia was identical at all project sites, it followed that the criteria for hospital diagnosis were not consistent in the two cities.

Analysis of the data revealed that the New York criteria were considerably more inclusive than either the London criteria or the diagnostic system employed by the project staff. Furthermore, the hospital studies showed that transatlantic disagreements about the diagnosis of schizophrenia were concentrated on certain kinds of patients. The greatest disagreement was over patients whose main complaints were motoric retardation, depressed mood, and anxiety. In London, most of these patients received a diagnosis of affective disorder by hospital staff; in New York, hospital staff freely used the schizophrenic label to diagnose these cases. Another area of significant divergence was in the diagnosis of patients considered manic-depressive, manic type, by the project psychiatrists. These cases were almost invariably labeled schizophrenic on the United States side of the study. Thus the Americans' concept of schizophrenia was shown to be consistently broader than that of either the project staff or their British colleagues.

World Health Organization International Pilot Study of Schizophrenia

The World Health Organization (28) sponsored the International Pilot Study of Schizophrenia (IPSS) in 1966. In addition to gaining cross-cultural data on the schizophrenic syndrome, the study hoped to yield a set of universally acceptable behavioral referents that could form the basis for an international system of diagnosis.

Table 6-1. IPSS prominant features of schizophrenia

Feature	Patients (%)
Lack of insight	97
Auditory hallucinations	74
Verbal hallucinations	70
Ideas of reference	70
Delusions of reference	70
Suspiciousness	66
Flat affect	66
Voices speaking to patient	65
Delusional mood	64
Delusions of persecution	64
Inadequate description of problem	64
Thought alienation	52
Thoughts spoken aloud	50

Note. IPSS = International Pilot Study of Schizophrenia.
Source. Summarized from World Health Organization (28).

Field research centers were established in nine countries: England, the United States, the Soviet Union, China, Colombia, Czechoslovakia, Denmark, India, and Nigeria. Psychiatrists from each participating center were assembled for training in eight instruments to be used in collecting data. The primary assessment instrument was the Present State Examination (PSE) (29).

Patients were initially screened to rule out those patients outside the age of risk for schizophrenia and those who had signs of organicity, drug abuse, or mental retardation. The only criterion for inclusion in the study was the presence of typical signs of psychosis. Altogether, 1,202 patients were evaluated. Using clinician diagnosis and a computer-based assessment program, patients were divided into groups with similar symptomatology. Of the 10 groups generated, 3 contained core schizophrenic patients as determined by consensus diagnosis.

The predominant behavioral features of the least ambiguous group of schizophrenic patients are listed in Table 6-1. Twelve features appeared in this core group more than 50% of the time. Lack of insight, auditory hallucinations, verbal hallucinations, ideas of reference, and delusions of reference were among the most common symptoms reported. Although these symptoms were shared by the majority of the schizophrenic patients being studied, there was no evidence that they were unique to schizophrenia.

Using the IPSS data, Carpenter et al. (30) addressed the task of generating discriminative features useful in the diagnosis of schizophrenia. These investigators first contrasted the IPSS schizophrenic and nonschizophrenic patients on each of the PSE's 443 items; 69 variables were found to dis-

Table 6-2. Carpenter's criteria for schizophrenia

Restricted
Poor insight
Hearing one's thoughts aloud
Early morning awakening ($-$)
Poor rapport
Depressed facies ($-$)
Elation ($-$)
Widespread delusions
Incoherent speech
Unreliable information
Bizarre delusions
Nihilistic delusions

Source. Summarized from Carpenter et al. (30).

criminate between the groups. Discriminant function analysis was applied using these 69 variables. The equation that best discriminated schizophrenia from nonschizophrenia was found to contain 12 variables (Table 6-2).

The Carpenter criteria constitute a flexible system for diagnosis, in that sensitivity and specificity of diagnosis vary with the number of criteria required to generate the diagnosis. The IPSS criteria represented a first step toward returning to a concept of schizophrenia in the United States that substituted specific descriptive criteria for inferred intrapsychic processes.

Research Diagnostic Criteria

The research based diagnostic systems of John Feighner and Robert Spitzer further refined the American concept of schizophrenia. Feighner's criteria (31) focused attention back to Kraepelin's original tenet: that age of onset and chronicity of illness were essential elements to the diagnosis of schizophrenia (Table 6-3). Feighner's system required a duration of illness of at least 6 months and onset before age 40. With these criteria, the acute syndrome no longer qualified as a subtype of schizophrenia. Feighner also required the absence of depressive or manic symptoms sufficient to qualify for probable or certain affective disorder. As a result, Kasanin's (17) schizoaffective schizophrenia could no longer be so readily included under the schizophrenic rubric.

Like the Carpenter IPSS diagnostic system, Feighner's criteria led American psychiatry another step away from the Bleulerian notion of schizophrenia. After drifting apart for more than half a century, the American and European concepts of schizophrenia were again approaching one another. The culmination of this realignment is most evident in the publication of Spitzer et al.'s (32) Research Diagnostic Criteria (RDC) in 1978 (Table 6-4). The RDC is intended to exclude patients with major affective disorder and many borderline-type patients. Like the IPSS and Feighner's criteria,

Table 6-3.   Feighner's criteria for schizophrenia

A. Both of the following are required:
   1. A chronic illness with at least 6 months' duration without return to premorbid level of adjustment
   2. Absence of depressive or manic symptoms sufficient to qualify for probable or certain affective disorder

B. One of the following:
   1. Delusions or hallucinations without confusion
   2. Incoherent verbal communication

C. Three of the following:
   1. Single
   2. Onset of illness before age 40
   3. Poor premorbid social or occupational adjustment
   4. Family history of schizophrenia
   5. No alcohol or drug abuse for 1 year prior to onset of illness

Source.   Summarized from Feighner et al. (31).

Table 6-4.   Research Diagnostic Criteria

A. Two of the following for "definite," one for "probable." Not due to drug or alcohol abuse:
   1) Thought broadcast, insertion, withdrawal
   2) Delusions of control, influence
   3) Nonpersecutory delusions for at least 1 week
   4) Delusions of any type with hallucinations for at least 1 week
   5) Auditory hallucinations (defined in manual)
   6) Nonaffective verbal hallucinations
   7) Continuous hallucinations for several days, or intermittent for at least 1 month
   8) Formal thought disorder accompanied by:
      a) blunted or inappropriate affect, or
      b) delusions, or
      c) hallucinations, or
      d) grossly disorganized behavior

B. Either 1 or 2:
   1) Current period of illness of at least 2 weeks
   2) Previous period of illness of at least 2 weeks, during which subject has met the criteria, and, residual signs of illness remain

C. Neither manic or depressive syndrome during the active period of illness to such a degree that it constituted a prominent component of the syndrome.

Note.   Course and clinical subtype are further defined.
Source.   Summarized from Spitzer et al. (32).

Table 6-5. DSM-III criteria for schizophrenia

A. At least one of the following:
1) Bizarre delusions
2) Somatic, grandiose, religious, or nihilistic delusions, or other nonpersecutory delusions
3) Persecutory or jealous delusions if accompanied by hallucinations
4) Auditory or verbal hallucinations with ongoing commentary or conversation
5) Other nonaffective auditory hallucinations
6) Formal thought disorder with one of the following:
   a) blunted affect
   b) delusions or hallucinations
   c) catatonic or other gross motor disturbance

B. Deterioration from previous level of function

C. Duration of episode of at least 6 months (including prodrome and residual stages)

D. Absence of full affective syndrome

E. Onset before age 45 (not required in DSM-III-R [40])

F. Not due to organic mental disorder or mental retardation

Source. Summarized from American Psychiatric Association (37).

---

the RDC forces the clinician to consider duration of illness and the presence of depression or mania before generating a diagnosis.

The appearance of a diagnostic system based on presenting symptomatology, age of onset, clinical course, and specific exclusion criteria formally introduced American psychiatry to a multiaxial approach to diagnosis.

Multiaxial Systems of Diagnosis

A multiaxial system of diagnosis defines several dimensions relevant to diagnosis. The axes or dimensions of the illness being described can include behavioral features, course of the disorder, social and occupational function, biological markers, and so on. Each patient is described in terms of all axes. Grinker and Holzman (33), Helmchen (34), Van Praag (35), and Bellak and Loeb (36) had all considered such features in their descriptions of schizophrenia. Helmchen and Van Praag emphasized the need to consider etiology and clinical course in addition to presenting symptoms. Bellak stressed the need to assess genetic endowment, family constellation, and possible predisposing organic factors.

A modified multiaxial approach was used by the American Psychiatric Association (37) in the revision of DSM-III published in 1980 (Table 6-5). Reflecting the growing interest in developing an incisive and reliable set of criteria for the diagnosis of schizophrenia and other disorders, this diagnostic system defined five axes: 1) the syndrome, 2) the personality disorder, 3) associated physical illness, 4) psychosocial stressors, and 5) the level of function in the last year. The syndrome axis contained information not only about symptomatology but also about course of illness, age of onset, and concurrent and secondary syndromes.

The introduction to American psychiatry of a comprehensive multiaxial diagnostic system marked a clear shift toward a Kraepelinian approach to schizophrenia. The use of specific descriptive criteria and attention to the natural course of the illness sharply reduced the ranks of patients once readily diagnosed as schizophrenic according to the American definition of the disorder. The American concept of schizophrenia had come full circle to rest firmly on the principles of diagnosis espoused 80 years earlier by Emil Kraepelin.

Conclusion

In this chapter, I have traced the evolution of the concept of schizophrenia since the early formulations of Kraepelin and Bleuler. Their influence on the emerging psychiatry in the United States and in Europe was described and the impact of their contributions on later investigators reviewed. These two concepts of schizophrenia reached a point of greatest divergence with the publication of DSM-II and the *British Glossary of Mental Disorders* in 1968. The United States–United Kingdom Cross-National Project clearly demonstrated the tendency of American and British psychiatrists to diagnose schizophrenia according to markedly different criteria. The findings of the IPSS led to the development of core symptom criteria for inclusion into a system of diagnosis. This was followed by the incorporation of criteria relevant to the natural course of the illness. The multiaxial approach to diagnosis that emerged in the 1970s and early 1980s is perhaps the closest we have come to incorporating empirical clinical studies into a comprehensive, valid, and reliable system of conceptualizing and diagnosing schizophrenia.

References

1. Pinel P: Traite medico-philosophique sur l'alienation mentale, ou la manie. Paris, Richard, Caille et Ravier, 1801
2. Haslam J: Observations on Madness and Melancholy, 2nd Edition. London, Hayden, 1809
3. Morel BA: Etudes cliniques: Traite theorique et practique des maladies mentales. Paris, Masson, 1852
4. Kahlbaum KL: Die Katatonie oder das Spannungsirresein. Berlin, Hirschwald, 1874
5. Hecker E: Die hebephrenie. Archiv fur pathologische anatomie und physiologie und linische medizin 52:394–429, 1871
6. Kraepelin E: Compendium der Psychiatrie. Leipzig, Abel, 1883
7. Kraepelin E: Compendium der Psychiatrie. Leipzig, Meiner, 1893

8. Kraepelin E: Compendium der Psychiatrie. Leipzig, Barth, 1896
8a. Kraepelin E: The diagnosis and prognosis of dementia praecox. Paper presented to the 29th Congress of Southwestern German Psychiatry, Heidelberg, 1898
9. Kraepelin E: Textbook of Psychiatry. Edinburgh, Livingstone, 1919
10. Bleuler E: Dementia Praecox or the Group of Schizophrenias (1911). Translated by Zinken J. New York, International Universities Press, 1950
11. Neale JM, Oltmanns TF: Schizophrenia. New York, John Wiley, 1980
12. Meyer A: The dynamic interpretation of dementia praecox. Am J Psychiatry 21:385–403, 1910
13. Meyer A: Fundamental conceptions of dementia praecox, in Collected Papers of Adolf Meyer, Vol. 2. Edited by Winters EE. Baltimore, MD, Johns Hopkins Press, 1950, p 432
14. Sullivan HS: The modified psychoanalytic treatment of schizophrenia. Am J Psychiatry 11:519–540, 1931
15. Sullivan HS: Tentative criteria of malignancy in schizophrenia. Am J Psychiatry 7:759–782, 1928
16. Schulz C: Schizophrenia: psychoanalytic views, in International Encyclopedia of Psychiatry, Psychology, Psychoanalysis, and Neurology, Vol 10. Edited by Wolman BB. New York, Van Nostrand Reinhold, 1977, pp 48–55
17. Kasanin J: The acute schizoaffective psychoses. Am J Psychiatry 13:97–123, 1933
18. Zilboorg G: Ambulatory schizophrenias. Psychiatry 4:149–155, 1941
19. Hoch PH, Polatin P: Pseudoneurotic forms of schizophrenia. Psychiatr Q, 23:248–276, 1949
20. American Psychiatric Association: Diagnostic and Statistical Manual of Mental Disorders, 2nd Edition. Washington, DC, American Psychiatric Association, 1968
21. Langfeldt G: The Schizophreniform State. Copenhagen, Munksgaard, 1939
22. Stone M: The Borderline Syndromes. New York, McGraw-Hill, 1980
23. Schneider K: Clinical Psychopathology. New York, Grune & Stratton, 1959
24. Pope HG, Lipinski JF: Diagnosis in schizophrenia and manic depressive illness. Arch Gen Psychiatry 35:811–828, 1978
25. Neale JM, Oltsmanns TF: Schizophrenia. New York, John Wiley, 1980
26. Professional staff of the U.S.–U.K. Cross-National Project: The diagnosis and psychopathology of schizophrenia in New York and London. Schizophr Bull 11:80–102, 1974
27. World Health Organization: Manual of the International Statistical Classification of Diseases, Injuries and Causes of Death (ICD-8). Geneva, World Health Organization, 1967
28. World Health Organization: The International Pilot Study of Schizophrenia. Geneva, World Health Organization, 1973
29. Wing JK, Cooper JE, Sartorius N: The Measurement and Classification of Psychiatric Symptoms. New York, Cambridge University Press, 1974
30. Carpenter WT, Strauss JS, Bartko JJ: Uses of signs and symptoms for the identification of schizophrenic patients. Schizophr Bull 11:37–49, 1974
31. Feighner JP, Robins E, Guze SB, et al: Diagnostic criteria for use in psychiatric research. Arch Gen Psychiatry 26:57–63, 1972
32. Spitzer RL, Endicott J, Robins E: Research Diagnostic Criteria (RDC) for a Selected Group of Functional Disorders. New York, Biometrics Research, 1978

33. Grinker RR Sr, Holzman PS: Schizophrenic pathology in young adults. Arch Gen Psychiatry 28:168–175, 1973
34. Helmchen H: Schizophrenia: Diagnostic concepts in the I.C.D.-8, in British Journal of Psychiatry Special Publication No. 10: Studies of Schizophrenia. Lader, MH. Ashford, Kent, Headley Bros, 1975
35. Van Praag HM: About the impossible concept of schizophrenia. Compr Psychiatry 17:481–497, 1976
36. Bellak L, Loeb L: The Schizophrenic Syndrome. New York, Grune & Stratton, 1969
37. American Psychiatric Association: Diagnostic and Statistical Manual of Mental Disorders, 3rd Edition. Washington, DC, American Psychiatric Association, 1980
38. American Psychiatric Association: Diagnostic and Statistical Manual of Mental Disorders, 3rd Edition, Revised. Washington, DC, American Psychiatric Association, 1987

CHAPTER SEVEN

The Historical Background of the Concept of Childhood Schizophrenia

Lauretta Bender, M.D.

Early History

During the 18th and 19th centuries there were occasional anecdotal or single-case reports of children described as mad, insane, mentally deranged, or hysterical (comparable to adults). In his 1867 textbook, Maudsley (1) included a chapter on children's mental disorders. In 1896, Kraepelin's (2) publication on dementia praecox stated that 3.5% of adults had clinical signs traced back to early childhood. In 1908, De Sanctis (3) described several children he called "dementia precocissimo."

After 1911 Bleuler's (4) concepts of schizophrenia became accepted. He stated that "with relative accurate case histories, one can trace back the illness in childhood even to the first years of life in at least 5% of cases and we know of no difference between this infantile form and the other forms of the disease" (p. 241).

Recent History and Follow-Up Studies

Through the first third of the 20th century, increasing numbers of reports of series of cases of schizophrenic children came from Germany (5), Switzerland (6), Great Britain (7), Russia (8, 9), and the United States (10).

In 1933, Howard Potter (11) reported 6 schizophrenic prepubertal chil-

dren, naming symptoms of retraction of interest in the environment, der-
eistic thinking and acting, thought disturbances, defect in emotional rapport
and affect, and defect in motility and behavior. Four years later, Potter and
H. R. Klein (12) made a follow-up report on these 6 children and added 8
additional children, all patients on the Children's Service of the New York
Psychiatric Institute, with the same diagnosis. Thirty years after the original
study, in 1966, a final follow-up study was made by S. Bennett and Klein
(13). Only 1 of the 14 patients was ever able to leave the hospital (in 1954)
and was maintained in a dependent state in the community with a diagnosis
of dementia praecox. Two were not located. Two died in the hospital at
ages of 29 and 31 years, diagnosed as having dementia praecox. Eleven
were in mental hospitals, indistinguishable from other adult schizophrenic
patients diagnosed either hebephrenic or catatonic.

Similar reports have come from many parts of the world: Holland (14),
Spain (15), France (16), Germany (17), Switzerland (18), the United States
(19, 20), Sweden (21), and England (22). These studies started in the 1940s
and continued into the 1960s and 1970s. Such reports would seem to show
that childhood schizophrenia develops into adult schizophrenia. There are
also more recent reports (23, 24) indicating the same conclusion.

The early issues were concerned with the diagnostic criteria for schizophrenia in childhood, whether the symptoms were the same as in adults.
If not, was childhood schizophrenia still the same as in adults, and did
childhood schizophrenia continue into adulthood? Did the illness arise from
brain disease or damage or was it inherited; or was it caused by social or
psychological factors—for example, Frieda Fromm-Reichmann's (25) "schizophrenogenic mother"?

Freud's Influence

New issues arose from Freud (26) and his followers in Europe and from
Adolph Meyer (27) and his followers in America, especially Leo Kanner
(28). Freud's influence came from his teaching that adult neuroses, psychoses, and personality development were determined by early childhood
experiences; his concept of the unconscious mental repression of early childhood experiences; and his acceptance of constitutional disorders in perception, especially of reality, as an ego function. Melanie Klein (7) an Austrian-
turned-British child psychoanalyst, recognized and attempted therapy on
young schizophrenic children, 4 and 5 years of age, in the 1920s. She said
that schizophrenia in childhood was more common than realized and it
should be one of the key functions of a child analyst to find, recognize, and
treat such children. Later she and Anna Freud (29) agreed that schizophrenic
children were unanalyzable because of an inability to play, to impersonate,
to recognize reality, to relate or form a transference to therapists, and to
concentrate, and because of their excessive anxiety. Both adhered to the
Freudian view of cause. Klein spoke more specifically of a psychotic position

in early infancy, which she saw as a point of fixation for anxiety and defenses against psychosis; she also spoke of a depressive position in infancy as a fixation point for depressive anxiety and defenses. Other important child analysts such as Anna Marie Weil (30) of the United States and D. W. Winnicott (31) of England, especially of the "ego psychology school," contributed significantly, First, however, came the contributions of Leo Kanner.

Leo Kanner

Leo Kanner, working at Johns Hopkins Hospital, was influenced by Adolph Meyer. In 1935 Kanner's (28) textbook *Child Psychiatry* was published. It has gone through four editions and 17 printings to 1979. Meyer (32) wrote the preface to the first edition, where he referred to his concept of a psychobiological psychiatry. In his description of childhood schizophrenia, Kanner (28) adhered to Meyer's (33) concept of schizophrenia as an ergasia caused by constitutional factors and life experiences with genetic dynamic factor in development. Constitutional factors were recognized as inborn but not hereditary. Ergasia he saw as a failure or an adequate adaptation or "working through."

Kanner (34) originated the concept of early infantile autism, using a term from Bleuler (4) who saw autism as one of the most important symptoms of schizophrenia in the adult. Throughout the 35 years that Kanner was concerned with infantile autism, he tried to abide with the Meyerian concept that constitution and life experiences were the cause, and decisively returned to it in his last writing on the subject (34). Nevertheless, he contributed enough material in his writings to cause an extensive worldwide following who saw autism as a purely psychologically determined condition. Kanner described the intelligent, obsessive, cold, "refrigerator" parents and emphasized the unique "sui generis" nature or "discrete integrity" of the syndrome of early infantile autism while also saying that these children came into the world with an innate physical and intellectual handicap. He said the combination of extreme aloneness, obsessiveness for sameness, stereotyping activity, and noncommunicative language brought the total picture into relationship to some of the basic schizophrenic phenomena. He differentiated it from childhood schizophrenia by virtue of a detachment present no later than the first year of life. At one point, he said that infantile autism is one of the schizophrenias of Bleuler. Kanner's last words on the subject were: "Constitution and life experiences have confused these children, making normal relationships impossible and driving them to withdraw into schizophrenic behavior" (34, p. 707).

Although Kanner protested that he never intended to describe early infantile autism as a purely psychogenic condition due to the failure of parents to give the child the love and attention needed, this concept, quoting Kanner, has been widespread. Later the term *schizophrenogenic mother* was added and accredited to Frieda Fromm-Reichmann (25) in 1948. There developed a dualism between organic and functional or nature and nurture. Many followers to this day see the parents, especially the mothers, as the sole cause not only of autism but of all types of childhood psychoses, schizophrenia, and neuroses. These include Bettelheim (35), Szurek (36), Blau (37), and Despert (38), as well as many others. Some emphasize deprivation, especially total social emotional deprivation, such as occurs in institutionalized infants, citing Bowlby's (39, 40) studies (although he, himself, did not believe this). Others—such as Wynne (41) and Ruesch and Bateson (42)— have seen all schizophrenias, including infantile autism, as due to a difficulty in communication between the parent and the child.

Margaret Mahler

Margaret Mahler (43, 44) a child analyst of the ego psychology school, contributed from the early 1950s her concept of the symbiotic psychosis in the young child from the second to the fifth year, thus developing later than autism. She saw autism, symbiotic psychoses, and adult schizophrenia as the same illness but with onset at different ages and with different clinical expressions. She saw the essential pictures of symbioses in the "hallucinatory or delusional, somatopsychic, omnipresent fusion with the representation of the mother and, in particular, the delusion of a common boundary with the mother." She said: "The ego regresses in this way when there is a psychotic disorganization in individuation with organismic anxiety." As an ego psychologist, she spoke of an innate defect in perception with an inability to utilize the mothering agent for homeostasis or development of the body image, which creates the pathogenic mother-child relation. She also said that although constitutional in origin, it was also probably hereditary.

Bellevue Studies

Going back to the early 1930s at Bellevue Hospital in New York, Paul Schilder and Lauretta Bender with many associates "viewed"—as Fish and Ritvo (45) said in 1979—"perceptual maturation as inextricably bound up with neurological development of postural control, vestibular functions and motility." Schilder (46) had already emphasized the evidence for biological factors in schizophrenia in the postural control of motility; in the physical dependence reflected into the psyche, the disorder in body image (47), and therefore in self-identity; and also in the organistic anxiety.

In Gesell's (48) 1945 study, *The Embryology of Behavior*, he showed the inherent maturation in the embryo of homeostasis of all internal functions, of the patterning of sleep and states of consciousness, of the patterning of respiration from which speech and language develop, and of the vestibular functions from which the earliest sensation of gravity arises, relating the body to the outer world and to spatial relations. Thus there developed a sense of reality as well as determining the tone of the body, and of posture and motility, which also must maturate. Disturbances in maturation were observed as "soft neurological" signs, as described by Schilder (46), not due to structural pathology but to developmental disorders.

At Bellevue, we developed a definition of childhood schizophrenia as a psychoneurobiologic entity determined by heredity, precipitated often by the stress of a perinatal organic insult with a maturational lag in all areas of functioning, characterized by an embryonic plasticity and revealing different patterns in different periods in life with early infantile autism, symbiotic psychoses, and childhood, adolescent, and adult schizophrenias (49). An important observation was the occurrence of spontaneous remissions—often facilitated by treatments in girls in latency and in boys in puberty—in about half the cases, often followed later by recurrence. Organismic anxiety leads to neurotic defenses sometimes further destructive to the personality, but also often of constructive healing value. Some of the Bellevue workers—Rabinovitch (50) and Helme (see 51)—used the term *dysmaturation*. Clemens Benda (52) spoke of "maturational dysrhythmia." Fish and Ritvo (45) used the term *pan developmental retardation*.

The Bellevue group was able to study 200 schizophrenic children in whom the diagnosis was confirmed later by other medical agencies or hospitals or physicians in 95% of the patients. Follow-up studies averaging 35 years confirmed that schizophrenic children became schizophrenic adults. Hereditary data were found comparable to Kallman's, and about half of the Bellevue children, from 3 to 12 years old on first admission, had histories of onset with autistic features before 2 years of age (20, 53).

In the late 1940s, the concept of plasticity (54) as a characteristic of the schizophrenic pathology in children was developed at Bellevue. The concept is derived from embryology. It refers to primitive undetermined and undifferentiated patterning. In schizophrenic children, it refers especially to those areas of functions, most recently acquired and most actively evolving in human evolution, and characteristic of those brain functions most specifically human. Plasticity is the basis of maturational lags and is observed especially in language, thought processes, cognitive functioning, and orientation in space and time.

Plasticity accounts also for the lack of conceptual boundaries in schizophrenia, as well as the unlimited depths to which schizophrenic patients can deteriorate or heights of giftedness and abstractedness that some may reach (55). Anxiety is the response of the child to the schizophrenic pathology and also leads to neurotic defenses that further complicate the varieties of clinical pictures or personality patterns in schizophrenic children.

There has been considerable research exploring biological deviations in the developmental pattern of schizophrenic children. The vestibular disturbances have been explored in the early perception of gravity, which lead to perception of the world of reality and space and become a model for all perceptions. A variety of research in other perceptual areas has resulted. Vestibular disorders also affect muscular tone and eye movements, extending to studies on the cerebellum (56–59). Motility, postures, mannerisms, and primitive whirling have been investigated (60–62). Homeostasis, biochemistry (63), autonomic functions, rapid eye movement, sleep patterns, and electroencephalograms (64) have all revealed disorders suggestive of maturational lags or pan developmental retardation. Language disorders have been studied, at first because they were so prominent (65, 66) but also because of the implications of biological development (67).

Genetic Studies

Kallman and Roth (68) conducted hereditary studies on childhood schizophrenic twins, confirming a similar incidence to their adult twin studies, not only for inheritance of schizophrenic disorders, but also for the capacity to perform defenses against it (69).

American researchers from the National Institute of Mental Health, Rosenthal and Ketty (70), combined with F. Schulsinger to study in Denmark adopted-out children of schizophrenic parents and nonschizophrenic parents. Their persuasive genetic studies confirmed the inheritance of schizophrenia and emphasized the importance of the stressor-diathesis concept so that it was said that a genetic predisposition is a necessary condition for the development of schizophrenia in adults. They emphasized that environmental factors were still important, especially in the form of stress to precipitate a breakdown or decompensation. They also noted a similar inheritance of other mental illnesses, which they referred to as the schizophrenia spectrum. These studies applied to childhood as well as the adult course of life.

Similar incidence figures for inheritance of schizophrenia in the family members of 100 schizophrenic children from the Bellevue follow-up studies were found (20). Both the schizophrenic children who started with autism and those that did not had on an average 2.1 mentally ill relatives per patient. The children with symbiotic psychoses had more, 2.8 mentally ill relatives per patient, in comparison to the autistic children without symbioses, where the number was 1.8

English Research

In England, the British working party organized by Mildred Creak (22) seemed to consider all childhood psychoses as schizophrenia, with the possibility of different origin such as brain disease. Nine categories of symptoms were defined: 1) gross and sustained impairment of emotional relationships with people; 2) apparent unawareness of one's own personal identity to a degree inappropriate for one's age; 3) pathologic preoccupations with particular objects or certain characteristics of them without regard to their accepted function; 4) sustained resistance to change in the environment and a striving to retain or restore sameness; 5) abnormal perceptual experience in the absence of discernible organic abnormality; 6) acute, excessive, and seemingly illogical anxiety as a frequent phenomenon; 7) speech either lost, or never acquired, or showing failure to develop beyond a level appropriate to an earlier age; 8) distortion of motility patterns; and 9) a background of serious retardation in which islets of normal, near normal, or exceptional intellectual function or skill may appear.

D. W. Winnicott (31), an English child analyst, spoke of schizophrenia as a reversal in maturation where very primitive defenses were brought into play and organized because of environmental abnormalities or deficiencies, at the stage of maximal dependence.

M. Rutter (71, 72), an English child psychiatrist working at Maudsley Hospital, has considered autism as merely a specific behavior problem in early childhood, reacting to many causes. He has considered *childhood schizophrenia* an inappropriate term for the psychotic disorders of childhood, thus denying all forms of childhood schizophrenia.

DSM-III

Published in 1980 the American Psychiatric Association's (73) DSM-III, a multiaxial system, does not recognize childhood schizophrenia. The classification of adult schizophrenia may be used for children, provided all of the diagnostic criteria are present (e.g., formal thought disorders, hallucinations, delusions). For childhood, there is a classification called pervasive developmental disorders, which includes infantile autism and childhood onset of pervasive developmental disorders. No relationship of any of these disorders to each other or to adult schizophrenia is recognized.

Infantile autism is described as having an onset before 30 months and exhibiting a lack of responsiveness to other people, defects in language development, peculiar speech, and bizarre responses to the environment (such as resistance to change and peculiar interest in or attachment to selective animate or inanimate objects).

Childhood onset of pervasive developmental disorders occurs between 30 months and 12 years, showing impairment in social relationships, lack of affective responsiveness and empathy, clinging and asociability, and at least three of the following symptoms: 1) anxiety, 2) oddities in motor movements, 3) abnormalities in speech, 4) disturbed sensitivity to sensory stimuli, 5) self-mutilation, and 6) absence of delusions, hallucinations, and thought incoherence, as in schizophrenia.

The diagnostic criteria for autism and childhood schizophrenia in DSM-III were drawn largely from Rutter's (71, 74) work.

During childhood (i.e., 30 months to 12 years of age), the term *atypical childhood psychosis* is used in place of schizophrenia with many of the same diagnostic criteria that could be used in schizophrenia such as the nine criteria of the British working party (22, 75).

The Nature–Nurture Considerations

The last 15 years have seen a flood of research referred to as "more sophisticated biological and phenomenological." Several reviews (67, 76) have listed approximately 1,500 references, most of which were said to have applied to autism. The problems explored are listed as classification and diagnosis, in relation to other disorders; demographies; parental characteristics; genetics; intelligence; language; perceptual processes; behavioral characteristics; neurobiologic, biochemical, and pharmacologic aspects; behavioral educational treatment; prognosis; and theoretical considerations. There has been a strong emphasis on research methodology and criticism of earlier work because of methodological deficiencies. This statement from one of the reviews is typical: "This decade's research led to the now generally accepted decision that infantile autism is a type of developmental disorder accompanied by severe and, to a large extent, permanent intellectual and behavioral deficit." Any relationship to any developmental disorders as childhood schizophrenia is said to be unproven.

Another group of investigators has also written extensive reviews in favor of the concept that autism and childhood schizophrenia are the same and may be the forerunners of adult schizophrenia, which runs a life course (19, 22–24, 33, 45, 49, 65, 77–97).

Barbara Fish

Barbara Fish (45) has been most prominent in demonstrating the course of autistic infants at risk (by birth from schizophrenic mothers) whom she has followed for 25 years (84), as well as month-old infants seen at an earlier date in well-baby clinics (recognized because of the characteristic biological features).

She has also carefully reviewed an extensive bibliography, often including the same references as the previous reviewers. She has shown the evidence for the inheritance of schizophrenia as reported from the studies in Denmark on adoptive children (70), and from twin studies (68, 98), and other reports from studies of patient series (99).

Genetics alone, of course, is not enough; there are individuals in schizophrenic families who are found to have some of the biological signs but are not psychotic. Stress has been postulated by Rosenthal and Ketty (70) as also necessary. In infants and children, the stress appears to be organic— that is, damage to the brain (prenatal, natal, or postnatal) or an illness in early childhood or later (100).

Biological Factors

Fish reviewed the course of schizophrenia from infancy (autism) to childhood and adolescence and adulthood. She made especially clear the evidence and studies on the neurobiologic factors in schizophrenia as we had emphasized them at Bellevue and wrote on the biological antecedents of the psychoses in children (101).

A statement by Cohen and Shaywitz (102) in the preface to a special issue of the *Journal of Autism and Development Disorders* on biological research in autism is significant: "Autism would appear to be an ideal candidate for biological study. Its appearance during the first months of life, pervasive impact on development and life-long duration suggest the presence of a critical central nervous system dysfunction" (p. 103).

The biological factors include disorganization or dysrhythmias in all of the vital functions of the autonomic nervous system, such as respiratory (103), gastrointestinal, vestibular, and muscle tone. Coeliacs disease is common in schizophrenic children (104, 105). The question as to whether sudden infant death, due to failure in the respiratory function, might not occur more often in autistic infants has been explored by Wright and Hubbard (106). Soft neurologic signs have been observed in schizophrenic children, implying developmental deviations in neurologic maturation, which result in immature motility patterns such as whirling, displayed in the tonic neck reflexes, first studied by Hoff and Schilder (107) and followed by other studies (60, 61, 108).

Vestibular dysfunction in schizophrenia was first noted by Schilder (109) and pursued by him and the Bellevue group and others (59, 110, 111). As I have said earlier: "If one wishes to explain the disorders and symptoms in schizophrenic children by reference to one mechanism in the body, one could best choose the vestibular apparatus" (53, p. 449). Levy et al. (57) reviewed the vestibular dysfunctions and made important contributions.

Immature patterning in respiration has also led to investigations for a possible explanation for sudden infant deaths (106).

The immaturity in all these areas of functioning was anticipated by Gesell (48), who also described it as unpatterned.

Cerebral Cortical Factors

In the last 20 years, significant studies concerning hemispheric dominance in relationship to autism and schizophrenia have put emphasis in right cortical functioning in schizophrenia or dysfunction in the left cortex (112). Wexler (113) provides broader discussion with a review of the literature. Evidence from various areas of research concur on this hypothesis of a specific left hemispheric dysfunction in early childhood autism and child and adult psychoses.

Dawson (114, 115) and Hauser et al. (116) used the electroencephalogram in their research. Using computerized tomography of the brain, Hier et al. (117) also revealed reversed asymmetry of the brain, indicating a dysfunction of the right cortex and the use of the left cortex, thus explaining the abnormal language development in autism. They emphasized the reversal of the left-right asymmetry of the parieto–occipital region and noted that its presence was also found in dyslexic patients, who also have abnormal language development. Piran et al. (118) investigated patterns of motoric laterality and eye preference in young adults and reached the same conclusion. Blackstock (112) made some confirmatory studies on audition and found that autistic children listened mostly with the left ear and preferred musical rather than verbal stimulation, indicating the right cerebral area functioned best for autistic children. Neuropsychological studies done by Dawson et al. (115) showed that autistic subjects showed a pattern of deficit on the sensory-motor, perceptual, and cognitive measures indicative of greater left than right hemisphere dysfunction.

Since the left hemispheric dysfunction in autism has been demonstrated in newborns by Wittelson and Pallie (119), it would appear to be at least congenital and perhaps genetic. This and other evidence also indicate that autism and schizophrenia as well as the reversal of the hemispheric laterality are not secondary to brain damage but part of a single disorder.

Wechsler and Jaros (120), of the Bellevue research team, have shown that schizophrenic children often presented a different psychological pattern on the Wechsler Intelligence Scale for Children than did nonschizophrenic children. These signs included a difference of 16 or more intelligence quotient points between the verbal score and performance score, in either direction. This is a useful sign. There are three additional sets of variances between specified subtests that were significant also to Wechsler, but not as useful for a psychiatrist.

As I have said elsewhere:

> There is no beginning or end to childhood schizophrenia—no alpha and omega—in that sense. The roots of schizophrenia are far back in phylogeny. Only those individuals who are a part of the stream of schizophrenic inheritance are vulnerable or "at risk" to the disorder. It may be expressed in the personality and in the biological traits of many individuals *who are not decompensated*. Thus we find many parents and relatives of schizophrenic children, often gifted, admirable, creative, and with every other possible normal trait or personality characteristic. . . . My own way is to emphasize an embryologic plastic undifferentiated patterning in the maturation of all human biological and psychological functions. When decompensated, it leads to illness; otherwise, it removes (though not completely) the boundaries, the ceiling and the floor, for human capacities to develop, function, and create. This may be an evolutionary phenomenon. In this sense, there is an alpha and omega of schizophrenia indicating infinitude. (121, pp. 117–118).

References

1. Maudsley H: Physiology and Pathology of the Mind. London, 1867
2. Kraepelin E: Dementia Praecox (1896). Translated by Livingston E, Livingston S. Chicago, IL, Chicago Medical Book, 1919
3. De Sanctis S: Demential Praecocissima der frueheren Kindersalters. Folia Neuro-

Biologica 2:9, 1908 (Reprinted in Howells JG [ed] Modern in Perspectives International Child Psychiatry. New York, Brunner/Mazel, 1971, pp 590–610)
4. Bleuler E: Dementia Praecox or the Group of Schizophrenias (1911). Translated by Zinkin J. New York, International Universities Press, 1950
5. Homburger A: Verlesungen uber Psychopathologie der Kindersalters. Berlin, Springer, 1926
6. Tramer M: Die Entwicklungslinie eines Psychotischen Kindes. Schweiz Arch Neurol Psychiatr 27:383, 1931 (Translated by Brunch H, Cottington F. Nervous Child 1:232, 1942)
7. Klein M: The Psychoanalysis of Children. Translated by Strachey A. London, Hogarth Press, 1937
8. Ushakov GK: Symptomology de Initial der, kindesalter, beginnenders, Schizophrenie. Psychiatr Neurol Med Psychol 2:41–47, 1965
9. Ushakov GK: Trends in the investigation of clinical problems in child psychiatry, in Modern Perspectives in International Child Psychiatry. Edited by Howells JG. New York, Brunner/Mazel, 1967, p 375
10. Alexander HCB: Insanity in children. Alien Neurol 14:408 and 15:27, 1893–1894
11. Potter HW: Schizophrenia in children. Am J Psychiatry 12:1253, 1933
12. Potter HW, Klein HR: An evaluation of the treatment of problem children as determined by a follow-up study. Am J Psychiatry 17:681–689, 1937
13. Bennett S, Klein HR: Childhood schizophrenia: 30 years later. Am J Psychiatry 122:1121–1124, 1966
14. Van Krevelen DA: The psychopathology of autistic psychopathy. Acta Paedopsychiat 29:22, 1962
15. Lorento de no R: Vestibular-ocular reflex arc. Arch. Neur. Psychiat. 30:245, 1933
16. Lebovici S: Developments in psychoanalytic theory as applied to children, in Modern Perspectives in International Child Psychiatry. Edited by Howells JG. New York, Brunner/Mazel, 1969, p 200
17. Stutte H: Die prognose der Schizophrenien des Kinde und Jugendalters. Proceedings of the 2nd International Congress on Psychiatry 1:328, 1957
18. Tramer M: Schizoid psychopathy or schizophrenia. Acta Paedo Psychiatr 29:136, 1961
19. Bender L: The life course of schizophrenic children. Biol Psychiatry 2:165–172, 1970
20. Bender L, Faretra G: The relationship between childhood schizophrenia and adult schizophrenia, in Genetic Factors in Schizophrenia. Edited by Kaplan AR. 1972
21. Annell A: Follow-up study on psychotic children. Acta Psychiatr Scand 39:235, 1963
22. Creak EM: Childhood psychoses: a review of 100 cases. Br J Psychiatry 109:84–89, 1963
23. Howells JG, Guirguis WR: Childhood schizophrenia 20 years later. Arch Gen Psychiatry 41:123–128, 1984
24. Petty LK, Ornitz EM, Michelman JD, et al: Autistic children who become schizophrenic. Arch Gen Psychiatry 41:129–135, 1984
25. Fromm-Reichmann F: Notes on the treatment of schizophrenia by psychoanalytic psychotherapy. Psychiatry 11:263, 1948

26. Freud, S: Three essays on the theory of sexuality (1905), in The Standard Edition of the Complete Psychological Works of Sigmund Freud, Vol 7. Translated and edited by Strachey J. London, Hogarth Press, 1957, pp 135–243
27. Meyer A: Constructive formulation of schizophrenia. Am J Psychiatry 1:355–364, 1922
28. Kanner L: Child Psychiatry (1935). Springfield, IL, Charles C Thomas, 1979
29. Freud A: Normality and Pathology in Childhood. New York, International Universities Press, 1965
30. Weil AP: Clinical data and dynamic considerations in cases of childhood schizophrenia. Am J Orthopsychiatry 23:518–529, 1953
31. Winnicott DW: The Maturational Process and the Facilitating Environment, in Collected Papers, 1957–1963. New York, International Universities Press, 1965
32. Meyer A: Preface, in Child Psychiatry. (1935). Edited by Kanner L. Springfield, IL, Charles C Thomas, 1979
33. Meyer A: Psychobiology: a Science of Man. Edited by Winters E, Bowers A. Springfield, IL, Charles C Thomas, 1973
34. Kanner L: Child Psychiatry, 4th Edition. Springfield, IL, Charles C Thomas, 1979
35. Bettelheim B: Love Is Not Enough. Glencoe, NY, Free Press, 1950
36. Szurek SA: Childhood Schizophrenia Symposium, 1955: psychotic episodes and psychotic maldevelopment. Am J Orthopsychiatry 25:519–543, 1956
37. Blau A: Childhood schizophrenia. Journal of the American Academy of Child Psychiatry 1:225, 1962
38. Despert L: Schizophrenia in Children. Psychiatr Q 12:366, 1938
39. Bowlby J: Maternal Care and Mental Health. Geneva, World Health Organization, 1951
40. Bowlby J: Ethological approach to research in child development. Br J Med Psychol 30:320, 1957
41. Wynne LC: Current concepts about schizophrenics and family relationships. J Nerv Ment Dis 169:82–89, 1981
42. Ruesch J, Bateson G: Communication: the Social Matrix of Psychiatry. New York, WW Norton, 1951
43. Mahler MS. On child psychoses and schizophrenia, autistic and symbiotic infantile psychoses. Psychoanal Study Child 7:286, 1952
44. Mahler MS: On early infantile psychoses, the symbiotic and autistic syndromes. Journal of the American Academy of Child Psychiatry 4:554, 1965
45. Fish B, Ritvo ER: Psychoses in childhood, in Basic Handbook of Child Psychiatry, Vol 2. Edited by Noshpitz JO. New York, Basic Books, 1979, pp 249–304
46. Schilder P: The psychology of schizophrenia. Psychoanal Rev 26:380, 1936
47. Schilder P: The Image and Appearance of the Human Body (1935). New York, International Universities Press, 1950
48. Gesell A: Embryology of Behavior. New York, Harper, 1945
49. Bender L: The concept of plasticity in childhood schizophrenia, in Modern Perspectives in International Child Psychiatry. Edited by Howells JG. New York, Brunner/Mazel, 1969, pp 649–684

50. Rabinovitch R: Observations on the differential study of severely disturbed children. Am J Orthopsychiatry 22:230, 1952
51. Bender L, Helme WH: A quantitative test of theory and diagnostic indicators of childhood schizophrenia. Arch Neurol Psychiatry 70:413, 1953
52. Benda C: Childhood schizophrenia, autism, and Heller's disease, in Mental Retardation. Edited by Bowman PW. New York, Grune & Stratton, 1960
53. Bender L: The life course of children with schizophrenia. Am J Psychiatry 30:783–786, 1973
54. Bender L: The concept of plasticity in childhood schizophrenia, in Psychopathology of Schizophrenia. Edited by Hoch P, Zubin J. New York, Grune & Stratton, 1966
55. Bender L: The creative process in psychopathological art. The Arts in Psychotherapy 8:3–14, 1981
56. Holzman PS: Smooth-pursuit eye movements in schizophrenia, in Biology of the Major Psychoses: a Comparative Analysis. Edited by Freedman DX. New York, Raven, 1975, pp 217–218
57. Levy DL, Holzman PS, Proctor LR: Vestibular dysfunctions and psychopathology. Schizophr Bull 9:383–438, 1983
58. Lipton RB, Levy DL, Holzman PS: Eye movement dysfunctions in psychiatric patients: a review. Schizophr Bull 9:19–32, 1983
59. Colbert EG, Koegler RR, Markham CH: Vestibular dysfunction in childhood schizophrenia. Arch Gen Psychiatry 1:600–617, 1959
60. Silver AA: Postural and righting responses in childhood schizophrenia. Psychiatr Q 29:272, 1952
61. Teicher JD: Preliminary survey of motility in children. J Nerv Ment Dis 99:272, 1941
62. Koegler RK, Colbert TG: Childhood schizophrenia. JAMA 171:1045, 1959
63. Sankar DVS, Cates N, Broer P, et al: Biochemical parameters in childhood schizophrenia autism and growth. Recent Advances in Biological Psychiatry 5:76, 1963
64. Hutt SJ, Hutt CA: A behavioral and EEG study of children with autism. J Psychiatr Res 3:181, 1965
65. Kanner L: Irrelevant and metaphorical language in early infantile autism. Am J Psychiatry 103:242–246, 1946
66. Cobrinik L: An exploratory study of speech in seventy disturbed schizophrenic children. Psychiatr Q 40: 1966
67. DeMeyer MK, Hingtgen JU, Jackson RK: Infantile autism: review of a decade of research. Schizophr Bull 7:388–451, 1981
68. Kallman FJ, Roth B: Genetic aspects of preadolescent schizophrenia. Am J Psychiatry 112:599, 1956
69. Kallman FJ: The Genetics of Schizophrenia. New York, Augustin, 1938
70. Rosenthal D, Ketty SS (eds): The Transmission of Schizophrenia, Elmsford, NY, Pergamon, 1968
71. Rutter M: Classification and categorization in child psychiatry. J Child Psychol Psychiatry 6:71, 1965
72. Rutter M: Childhood schizophrenia reconsidered. Journal of Autism and Childhood Schizophrenia 2:315, 1972
73. American Psychiatric Association: Diagnostic and Statistical Manual of Mental

Disorders, 3rd Edition. Washington, DC, American Psychiatric Association, 1980

74. Rutter M: The development of infantile autism. Psychol Med 4:147–163, 1974

75. Creak EM: Schizophrenic syndrome in childhood: further progress report of working party. Dev Med Child Neurol 4:530–534, 1964

76. Rutter M, Schopler E (eds): Autism: A Reappraisal of Concepts and Treatment, New York, Plenum, 1978

77. Bender L: Childhood Schizophrenia. Am J. Orthopsychiatry 17:40–56, 1947

78. Bender L: A career of clinical research in child psychiatry, in Explorations in Child Psychiatry. Edited by Anthony EJ. New York, Plenum, 1975, pp 419–462

79. Campbell M, Hardesty AS, Breuer H, et al: Childhood psychosis in prospective: a follow up. Journal of the American Academy of Child Psychiatry 17:14, 1978

80. Faretra G: Lauretta Bender on autism: a review. Child Psychiatry Hum Dev 10:118–129, 1979

81. Fish B: The detection of schizophrenia in infancy. J Nerv Ment Dis 125:1–24, 1957

82. Fish B: Involvement of the central nervous system in infants with schizophrenia. Arch Neurol 2:115–121, 1960

83. Fish B: Contributions of developmental research to a theory of schizophrenia, in Exceptional Infants, Studies in Abnormalities. Edited by Helmuth J. New York, Brunner/Mazel, 1971

84. Fish B: Infants at risk for schizophrenia: developmental deviations from birth to 10 years. Journal of the American Academy of Child Psychiatry 15:62–82, 1976

85. Fish B: Neurobiologic antecedents of schizophrenic children. Arch Gen Psychiatry 34:1297–1313, 1977

86. Goldfarb W: Childhood Schizophrenia. Cambridge, MA, Harvard University Press, 1961

87. Goldfarb W: The subclassification of psychotic children, in The Transmission of Schizophrenia. Edited by Rosenthal D, Ketty SS. London, Pergamon, 1968, pp 333–342

88. Kanner L: Problems of nosology and psychodynamics of early infantile autism. Am J Orthopsychiatry 19:416–426, 1949

89. Kanner L: To what extent is early infantile autism determined by constitutional inadequacies? Genetics and Inheritance of Integrated Neurological Psychiatric Patterns 33:378–385, 1953

90. Ornitz EM: Disorders of perception common to early autism and schizophrenia. Compr Psychiatry 10:259–274, 1969

91. Ornitz EM: Childhood autism: a review of the clinical and experimental literature. California Medicine 118:21–47, 1973

92. Ornitz EM: Neurophysiologic studies of autistic children, in Autism, Appraisal and Concepts. New York, Plenum, 1977

93. Ritvo ER, Cantwell D, Johnson E, et al: Social class factors in autism. Journal of Autism and Childhood Schizophrenia 1:297–310, 1971

94. Ritvo ER: Autism, Diagnosis, Current Research and Management. New York, Spectrum, 1976

95. Ritvo ER, Freeman BJ: National Society for Autistic Children: definition of the syndrome of autism. Journal of the American Academy of Child Psychiatry 17:565–576, 1978
96. Shapiro T, Juebner HF, Campbell M: Language behavior in a psychotic child. Journal of Autism and Childhood Schizophrenia 4:71–90, 1974
97. Wing JK: Early Childhood Autism. London, Pergamon, 1966
98. Gottesman II, Shields J: Schizophrenia and Genetics: a Twin Study Vantage Point. New York, Academic, 1972
99. Bender L, Grugett AE: A study of certain epidemiological factors in a group of children with childhood schizophrenia. Am J Orthopsychiatry 26:131–145, 1956
100. Bender L: Diagnostic and therapeutic aspects of childhood schizophrenia, in Mental Retardation. Edited by Bowman PW. New York, Grune & Stratton, 1960
101. Fish B: Biologic antecedents of psychosis in children. Archives of Research in Nervous and Mental Diseases 54:49–80, 1975
102. Cohen DJ, Shaywitz BA: Preface, in Special Issue of Neurobiological Research in Autism. J Autism Dev Disord 12: Whole issue 2, 1980
103. Faretra G, Bender L: Autonomic nervous system responses in hospitalized children treated with LSD and UML. Recent Advances in Biological Psychiatry 7:1, 1965
104. Bender L: Coeliac syndrome in schizophrenia (letter). Psychiatr Q 35:386, 1961
105. Graff H, Handford A: Coeliac syndrome in the case histories of five schizophrenics. Psychiatr Q 35:306, 1961
106. Wright CG, Hubbard DG, Graham JW: Absence of inner otoconio. Ann Otol Rhinol Laryngol 88:779–783, 1979
107. Hoff H, Schilder P: Die Lage Reflexe der Menschen. Berlin, Springer, 1927
108. Bender L, Schilder P: Mannerisms as organic motility syndrome. Confinia Neurologica 3:321–330, 1941
109. Schilder P: The vestibular apparatus in neurosis and psychosis. J Nerv Ment Dis 78:135–164, 1933
110. Fish B, Alpert M: Patterns of neurological development in infants born of schizophrenic mothers. Recent Advances in Biological Psychiatry 5:24, 1963
111. Pollack M, Krieger HP: Oculomotor and postural patterns in schizophrenic children. Arch Neur Psychiat 79:720, 1958
112. Blackstock EG: Cerebral asymmetry and the development of infantile autism. Journal of Autism and Childhood Schizophrenia 8:339–352, 1978
113. Wexler BE: Cerebral laterality and psychiatry: a review of the literature. Am J Psychiatry 137:279–291, 1980
114. Dawson G: Lateralized brain dysfunction in autism: evidence from the Halstead-Reitan Neuropsychological Battery. J Autism Dev Disord 13:269–286, 1983
115. Dawson G, Warrenberg SA, Fuller P: Cerebral lateralization in individuals diagnosed as autistic in childhood. Brain Lang 15:353–368, 1982
116. Hauser SL, DeLong GR, Rosmann P: Pneumographic findings in the infantile autism syndrome. Brain 98:667–688, 1975
117. Hier DB, LeMay M, Rosenberger PB: Autism and unfavorable left-right asymmetry of the brain. J Autism Dev Disord 9:153–159, 1979

118. Piran N, Bigler ED, Cohen D: Motoric laterality and eye dominance suggest unique patterns of cerebral localization in schizophrenia. Arch Gen Psychiatry 39:1006–1010, 1982
119. Wittelsen SF, Pallie A: A left hemisphere specialization for language in the newborn: neurological evidence for symmetry. Brain 96:641–646, 1973
120. Wechsler D, Jaros E: Schizophrenic patterns on the WISC. J Clin Psychol 21:288–291, 1966
121. Bender L: Alpha and omega of childhood schizophrenia. Autism and Childhood Schizophrenia 1:115–118, 1971

CHAPTER EIGHT

The Psychodynamics of Schizophrenia I: Introduction and Psychoanalysis

Michael H. Stone, M.D.

Definitions

Psychoanalytic psychodynamics admits of several overlapping definitions. These have been categorized within four related frames of reference by Lazare et al. (1). The first deals with psychoanalytic models for understanding a patient's fundamental problems. Currently, the greatest reliance is placed on several models: one, whose foundation is Freud's tripartite structural theory of id, ego, and superego (2); another, based primarily on object-relations psychology (3–5); and a third, focusing on the psychology of the self (6). In relation to schizophrenia, the theoretical literature is more voluminous in the first two areas; less so, within the area of self psychology.

Psychodynamics also comprises the study of precipitating events and their dynamic meanings, particularly where these are noxious more on account of their symbolic overtones than because of their actual threat to the individual. For example, a person vulnerable to schizophrenia may withstand an assault with a knife, only to succumb, symptomatologically, on being called a "poof."

Understanding someone's problems as a reflection of a particular developmental crisis constitutes yet another aspect of psychodynamics. The crises deemed relevant to schizophrenia tend to be those peculiar to the earliest phases of life. Some of the analytic writers who have turned their attention to this facet of psychodynamics have been closely associated with child and adolescent psychiatry (7–9).

Finally, the manner in which one's personality style may predispose to vulnerability in the face of certain challenges represents still another branch of psychodynamic investigation. A patient's characteristic defensive posture correlates with, and indeed helps to define, one's intrinsic personality style. Within the domain of schizophrenia, a number of personality types are overrepresented in the premorbid and intermorbid phases of the patients' lives; namely, the paranoid, the schizoid, and the narcissistic (10). A comprehensive psychodynamic approach to schizophrenia attempts to understand these peculiarities as well.

Schools of Thought

Psychoanalysis was born of efforts to treat and to understand ambulatory patients. Freud and his colleagues had little access to psychiatric sanitaria of the sort where Kraepelin and Bleuler did their work. Partly as a result of this, the psychoanalytic movement, in its progress not only as a therapy but as a universal psychology, tended to look at the less serious "neurotic" disorders with central vision. Schizophrenia and manic-depression were glimpsed, by orthodox psychoanalysis, out of the corner of its eye. The classic psychoses have always placed a strain on orthodox metapsychology, one result of which, as we shall see, was the creation of a number of schools of psychoanalytic thought, over and above the modifications within the analytic establishment itself, whose ambition was to fashion a theory and a therapy better suited to the more severe disorders than was the traditional metapsychology.

The "schizophrenia problem" was of course not the only stimulus to the formation of the British object relations school, much of whose impetus was derived from hitherto unresolved issues in the psychology of children. Nevertheless it was an important stimulus, even though the connection between the modern conception of schizophrenia and the "schizoid position" of the Kleinians (e.g., 7, 11, 12) is not always close or clear.

The interpersonal school focuses more closely on schizophrenia and, probably for this reason, is experienced as a more deviant offshoot of the analytic movement than that of Melanie Klein (7) and her followers. Harry Stack Sullivan (13, 14), the founder of this school, worked intensively with schizophrenic inpatients, as have the many adherents of his interpersonal approach, including Fromm-Reichmann (15, 16), Will (17), and Searles (18).

The analogy regarding central versus peripheral vision is applicable to another aspect of the psychoanalytic schools as they evolved and branched off: the orthodox Freudians at the turn of the century paid most attention, as did Freud himself, to the individual and the various psychosexual stages through which one passes during the formative years. To be sure, Freud spoke of the "object" as well, but the role of the "other," the specifics of countertransference, and so on, were not spelled out in as much detail as was devoted to the patient or to the hypothetical "average" person. It soon became apparent that the healthier the subject, the more neutral the analyst could remain. Countertransference could not quite be ignored but it could be left in the shadows. Not so with the more severely ill patients. The significance of the other person, whether it be the parents originally or the analyst in the here and now, looms larger with the schizophrenic patient.

Although each school aspires to completeness as a psychology of the human condition, it would not be too gross an oversimplification to state that the three functional levels of interest to psychoanalysis (19)—the neurotic, the borderline, and the psychotic—are most easily understood within the framework of Freudian structural, object-relational, and interpersonal theories, respectively.

If we follow the evolution of interpersonal theory a bit further, we find one group of investigators (20, 21) who remain true to the spirit of Sullivan in their emphasis on dyadic relationships (mother-child; the analyst and the schizophrenic patient), whereas another opens the shutter wider to encompass the whole family. Bateson and Ruesch (22) and Jackson et al. (23) underlined the importance of the mother in the genesis of the schizophrenia condition; Lidz et al. (24) began to address abnormal patterns of communication in whole families where one member was schizophrenic. At this point, one is no longer in the realm of psychodynamics, as narrowly conceived by the structural theorists, but in the realm of dynamics in the sense of precipitating factors. This work has been carried forward by Goldstein and Jones (25) and by Liberman et al. (26), the latter group having studied the impact of family criticism and overinvolvement ("expressed emotion") on recidivism rates in schizophrenic patients.

Before we examine the nature and the merits of the various dynamic theories mentioned above, the reader should be aware that a number of reviews have already been written, some devoted primarily to the works of Freud and his successors (27–29) and others, such as those of Bellak and Loeb (10), Bryce Boyer (30), and Shapiro (31), broader in their scope.

Psychoanalytic Formulations

Freudian Theory Before 1923

Freud dwelt only briefly on what we now call schizophrenia. Diagnostic criteria were less strict than in our day, nor were the fine points of diagnosis particularly important to Freud in the early years. He sometimes referred to the Kraepelinian term *dementia praecox* and at other times to the more psychoanalytic designation *narcissistic neurosis*. The latter term was still used, as Shapiro (31) pointed out, to cover emotional disorders of whatever severity. Bleuler's (31a) monograph on schizophrenia appeared the same year as Freud's (32) Schreber case, still spoken of by the older term *dementia paranoides*. Schreber's psychosis was understood, via Freud's libido theory, as the end result of massive withdrawal (decathexis) of libido (sexualized energy) from the outside world. Freud's model at this time embodied a closed system (33): the disinvested libido had to go somewhere, and that somewhere was Schreber's own ego. This recathexis of the body-ego was postulated as the basis underlying the paranoid patient's megalomanic (inflated ego) or hypochondriacal (hypercathected body parts) delusions.

The original decathexis of the external object (in Schreber's case, another male) was itself provoked, in Freud's view, by the struggle against an outbreak of homosexual libido, such that the paranoid patient "regresses" (travels backward in the path of psychosexual development) from sublimated homosexuality to the primitive stage of narcissism. Here we are in the midst of a conflict-oriented theory: schizophrenia is pictured as an abnormal psychological state reflecting conflicts of particular form and severity, such as might occur in anyone placed in similar circumstances. The specificity of unacceptable homosexual impulses for the development of paranoid psychoses was given wide credence by Freud's colleagues, most notably, Ferenczi (34). Freud did not claim etiologic significance for his theory concerning Schreber; as Modell mentioned (27), Freud was attempting simply to shed light on the phenomenology of such cases.

It was to become a highly controversial topic among analytic theoreticians whether schizophrenia could be explained (i.e., from an etiologic standpoint) purely as the outcome of conflict, or whether one needed to invoke in addition the notion of an inherent weakness or defect. Such a notion was by no means foreign to Freud: we see it adumbrated in his letter to Fliess, dated January 1, 1896 (35). There he speaks of projection as the "determining element" in paranoia. The repressed affect seems "invariably to return in hallucination of voices" (p. 168). The defense (of the delusions that the paranoid patient elaborates by way of "explaining" the voices) Freud saw as failing, because the ego is deformed in the process: "delusions can be interpreted . . . as a statement of defeat, not as a symptom of secondary defense" (p. 168).

The letter to Fliess, however, harkens back to the period when Freud retained some enthusiasm about the possibility of understanding the psyche through neurophysiologic concepts. By the time of the Schreber case, the balance was tipping, in Freud's theoretical reflections, away from the neurologic and toward the psychological. As another example of the latter, relevant to schizophrenia, there is Freud's distinction in the Schreber article between *paranoia,* where there is still object-investment, with regression to narcissism, and *paraphrenia* (similar to our concept of nuclear schizophrenia), where one saw regression to an autoerotic stage, with even less capacity for involvement with the external world.

An important corollary to these formulations was Freud's (36) conviction that paranoid and paraphrenic patients were unable to form a transference and were thus outside the purview of psychoanalytic treatment. There was some disagreement on this point, a detailed discussion of which would take us too far afield; suffice it to say that some of his colleagues, such as Maeder (37) and Bjerre (38) although accepting the homosexual dynamics of paranoid cases, felt that certain paranoid patients were amenable to analytic treatment. I have alluded to a number of other enthusiastic reports dating from the 1910s elsewhere (39).

Several psychoanalytic pioneers, including Freud, were impressed by the analogy between dreaming and the waking thoughts of the schizophrenic patient. In 1936, Jung (40) wrote of the patient with dementia praecox as resembling a dreamer who is awake. In his paper on the unconscious (41), Freud noticed that similar mechanisms are utilized by both the nonschizophrenic dreamer and the schizophrenic dreamer—namely, displacement, condensation, and a "logic" that gives priority to similarities of sound or location. This is the logic of what Freud was to call primary process. It is not easy to assign this phenomenon (when observed in the schizophrenic patient) to its proper place in the balance between defect and conflict, since it partakes of both. Because of a defect (in the process of repression), the schizophrenic patient fails to keep under wraps many of the murderous, incestuous, and other unacceptable thoughts normally relegated to the "unconscious." About the nature and cause of this apparently constitutional defect, the analysts of this generation could only guess. But they did notice that the abnormal mental phenomena manifested themselves with particular intensity under the impact of strong conflict, such that a psychodynamic as well as a constitutional etiology could be invoked. Thus the paranoid woman treated by Bjerre (38) developed ideas of reference (men in the street were mocking her) just in the aftermath of a romantic disappointment.

The schizophrenic patient's preoccupation with the word at the expense of the thing (or person) signified was understood in the libido theory of this epoch as a retention by the verbal signifier of the object—of its libidinal cathexis, at the same time that the idea of the object (akin to the concept of an inner representation) has lost its cathexis. Actually, Freud saw the schizophrenic patient's overinvolvement (hypercathexis) of the verbal idea as a step in the process of restitution; that is, delusion formation, as part of the attempt to regain contact with the world.

Still other dynamic aspects of schizophrenia came under scrutiny in the years surrounding World War I: the localization of a fixation point that might be relevant to this condition was attempted by Abraham (42). A young man with "simple" schizophrenia exhibited such prominent "oral" symptoms (an inability to wean himself from milk, a penchant for quashing the urge to masturbate by drinking some milk) as to lead Abraham to postulate for this and similar cases the primacy of the "oral erotogenic zone" (p. 256). It is of interest, parenthetically, that Abraham mentioned the presence of several other simple schizophrenic patients among the relatives of this patient. Rudin's (43) monograph on the hereditary influences in schizophrenia appeared the same year as Abraham's article; it had little influence on the evolving psychoanalytic conceptions of schizophrenic etiology, since dialogue between the analytic-based and the hospital-based psychiatric communities was as yet almost nonexistent. As for Abraham's emphasis on the oral phase, his remarks were echoed by Nunberg (44), who conceptualized the libidinal conflict in a case of schizophrenia as a sequence involving introjection of a (desired but unacceptable) homosexual object, followed by projection (onto the analyst, much as Schreber had projected his unacceptable strivings onto Dr. Flechsig), with subsequent "regression to the oral phase."

It should become clear to the modern reader, whether familiar with the language of libido theory or not, that the analytic pioneers, faced with the extreme primitivity of the (decompensated) schizophrenic patient's thought and behavior, assigned this condition to the earliest (oral) segment of the psychosexual continuum. They analogized the schizophrenic patient to infants or to dreamers. In addition, to the extent that they embraced, almost exclusively, psychogenic hypotheses concerning *causation,* the analytic pioneers assumed that the intrafamilial traumata suffered by those who eventually succumbed to schizophrenia must have been exceptionally severe.

This primitivity is implied in the remarks by Tausk (45), whose paper on the "influencing machine" sought to explicate the persecutory delusions of a patient with paranoid schizophrenia. Parts of the patient's body were projected onto the environment, as were his various emotional states and sensations. The latter now appear to come from outside the self; specifically, from the influencing machine, similar in all respects to the infernal machine of which Haslam's patient complained (46). Tausk's patient served to highlight a phenomenon characteristic of the schizophrenic patient: the lack of ego boundary. Although this would seem to be the expression of yet another constitutional defect, Tausk strove to capture in it libidinal terms, drawing attention to an apparent regression to a most primitive stage of (object-less) primary narcissism, akin to the situation in earliest development where the infant presumably makes no distinction between self and other. Indeed, psychoanalysts after Tausk pay considerable attention to ego-boundary problems in schizophrenic patients, who demonstrate again and again either confusion between self and other or psychological fusion of self and the other. This, too, is understood in dynamic terms—as, for example, a last-ditch effort to ward off the feeling of annihilation (47), as might be engendered by a thorough-going maternal rejection. As we shall see, the more one relied on psychodynamic (in contrast to defective-constitutional) formulations, the more one felt constrained to hypothesize traumatic mother-child relationships as alone capable of explaining the primitivity of schizophrenic mental life. Speaking of influencing machines, mother was to become for a time the *deus-*, or rather, the *diabolus-ex-machina* of the psychodynamic theoretician. Before we examine this stage in the unfolding of dynamic theories, however, we must first review the changes and elaborations introduced by the promulgation of structural, tripartite theory (2).

Freudian Theory After 1923

The compartmentalization of mental life into the three major components (id, ego, and superego) in Freud's (2) structural theory of 1923 was most readily applicable to normal psychology and to the psychology of neurotic persons, who behave as though torn by various conflicts but are relatively free of significant constitutional defects. The neurotic symptoms in turn, could be explained fairly easily, within the framework of tripartite theory, as the products of conflicts either within one of the three systems (e.g., ego) or between systems (e.g., ego versus superego). The Gordian knot of schizophrenia did not suddenly unravel with the elucidation of this theory: one was still left with the question of severity. Why was the schizophrenic patient's reaction so maladaptive and overwhelming in the face of this or that conflict? Again one was left having to invoke the schizophrenic patient's special sensitivity or introversion, which are constitutional abnormalities, unless one was willing (as many analysts of this era were) to postulate extreme forces (in the form of parental cruelty, rejection, or misuse) as having been operative in the early histories of such patients.

Typically, psychodynamic explanations of this era resemble in many ways those elaborated by Abraham (42) and Freud in the 1910s, only with a refurbishing of the concepts so as to be more in conformity with structural theory and with the dynamics of the Oedipus complex. Robie (48), for example, discussed two cases of schizophrenic patients whom he felt became ill under the impact of strong homosexual impulses: "When a person possessing an introverted personality is subject to perverse homosexual cravings, one of the possible reactions thereto is in certain cases, a psychosis" (p. 471). These patients were men who, in their adolescent years, had been approached and perhaps sexually molested by older homosexual men. The delusional material was filled with references to fear of wanting to perform fellatio, fear of semenlike tastes in the mouth, and so on. One man had blatant incestuous fantasies toward his mother. Robie's theoretical stance, apart from the mention of "sensitivity," was, characteristically for this era, purely psychological. One of the patients was considered to have been at first "psychoneurotic . . . showing a marked mother fixation and homosexuality [in fantasy, not in practice, Ed.], in whom a regression has now taken place to the state of dementia praecox" (p. 478). From a dynamic standpoint, Robie saw schizophrenia as dominated by a combination of homosexual and incestuous cravings and precipitated by a conflict between the perverse cravings and the conscious ideals of the patient. The sensitive or introverted type was deemed vulnerable because of the greater difficulty in such persons in forming heterosexual contacts.

The concept of reality, one's position vis-à-vis reality, and one's ability to test reality become increasingly important in theoretical formulations about the dynamics of various conditions; *neurosis* is no longer used as a universal designation for a mental illness, being held in reserve now for cases showing preservation of contact with reality. Freud (49) characterized neurosis now as stemming from conflict between id and ego (i.e., between one's basic drives and one's sense of the practical), whereas psychosis reflects a "disturbance in the relationship between the ego and the outer world" (p. 149). Freud (49) wrote of the schizophrenic patient's "affective hebetude" (p. 151), resulting from loss of all participation in the external world. This point was emphasized shortly thereafter by Hesnard (50), who felt the theories of the organic school were probably valid as well, but in need of amplification by analytic metapsychology. Hesnard spoke of a schizophrenic end stage where one witnesses the

> crumbling away of outward-directed affective mechanisms, in the wake of defective utilization of instinctual drive, whence the indifference to the world, the nullification of social feeling and simultaneous turning toward satisfactions yielded by the self, such as masturbation . . . and regressive preoccupation with excrement. (p. 726, my translation)

Abraham (51) expressed a less gloomy view in claiming that the schizophrenic patient does not regress so far as to preclude relatedness to others and does not withdraw so completely as to render analytic therapy impossible.

In the decades that followed, the theoreticians most closely allied with Freud made rather minor revisions in the analytic psychology of schizophrenia, mostly along the lines of the emerging ego psychology spearheaded by Hartmann. Federn, besides underlining once again the similarity of dream thought to schizophrenic thought (52), went on to suggest that schizophrenia was ushered in not so much by a break with reality (Freud's viewpoint) as with the creation of a false reality resulting from rupture of the ego boundary (53). Federn did not see delusion as "restitutive."

Katan's (54) formulations remain primarily within the realm of the psychological, as he went on to suggest that the essence of the schizophrenic condition is, rather than an expression of homosexual defense against Oedipal-incestuous wishes, an expression of a "constitutional bisexuality"; the boy's attachment to his mother is not seen as repressed (as in certain neurotics) but simply lost through never having been adequately cathected. Elsewhere, Katan (55) speculated that the schizophrenic patient (using Schreber as his model) is saddled with a strong unconscious wish for femininity, exaggerating castration fear, the retreat from which results in a break with reality. Why this should be the "result" and what occurs in female schizophrenic patients (presumably something similar but with opposite gender valence) is not made clear.

Hartmann (56) applied his concept of *neutralized* aggressive and sexual energy to schizophrenia as well as to the neuroses: the schizophrenic patient, in his view, suffers from a diminished ability to neutralize aggression. This in effect invokes a defect concept, although Hartmann's language is otherwise kept strictly within the bounds of libido theory, as is customary with orthodox analytic theoreticians. Hartmann hoped to explain schizophrenic symptoms as manifestations of excess unneutralized aggressive energy, exerting its deleterious impact either on the self or on the outside world.

Jacobson's (57) contributions are more challenging. Although she also entertained the notion of excess unneutralized aggression, she felt this derived, in contrast to Hartmann's view, from the schizophrenic patient's diminished libidinal drive (i.e., the same end result but from a somewhat different source). Later, however, she was to claim, in a more sweeping departure from orthodox dynamics, that in schizophrenia one witnesses actually the disintegration of tripartite structure (4), a point emphasized also by Kernberg (5). Finally, Jacobson was to contrast the energic situation in the melancholic patient—whose "destructive drive" is all "absorbed" by the superego—with that of the schizophrenic patient—whose superego is "defective," such that the surplus of hostility "breaks through" (an intrasystemic problem, within the ego), engendering symptoms (58).

Jacobson's point about the sadistic superego of the schizophrenic patient is in line with the earlier impression of Laforgue (59), who expressed this view originally, in the context of his metapsychological statement about the genesis of schizophrenia. In an article that foreshadowed the theoretical positions adopted by Melanie Klein (7) and her followers, Laforgue (60) speculated that, in response to defective mothering in the oral (weaning) period, the schizophrenic-to-be child generates fantasies of a good-caretaker mother and of a perfectionistic mother. The image of the real mother is kept out of view ("scotomatized"). The child is unable to tolerate future frustrations and remains fixated at an oral–sadistic stage. A sense of worthlessness develops, out of an inability to live up to the mother's expectations, rage over which engenders a fantasy of "killing" the mother via the child's withdrawing from life and a devaluation of people in general (by a depersonalization of them, a fantasied turning of the child's oppressors into feces).

The controversy concerning the etiologic significance of conflicts and traumatic events versus constitutional weakness was addressed anew by Paul Schilder (61). He argued for a synthetic approach, stating that "the psychical is also at the same time a biological factor" (p. 281, my translation). Schilder felt the fixation point in schizophrenia was in the narcissistic realm, although he admitted "we do not know which experiences correspond with which fixation points" (p. 281, my translation). He criticized the tendency to create static abstractions of supposed psychodynamic precursors to schizophrenia, as though one could speak of certain "primary symptoms that, by some mysterious mechanism wander out from the brain and into the soul" (p. 282, my translation). Regarding specific dynamics, nevertheless, Schilder, like many of his predecessors, was impressed by the frequency with which homosexual fantasies, and irresolvable conflicts set in motion by these fantasies, unleashed the tendency to overt schizophrenic symptoms. Clues to the existence of such fantasies were often embedded in the strange verbal expressions of the schizophrenic patients, whose symbolism could ultimately be comprehended (62) by the psychoanalytic method.

Later, Schilder (63) took analytic theoreticians to task for assuming that because schizophrenia could be understood psychologically, it could somehow be cured. The perennial optimist Adolf Meyer came under especially severe attack. For Schilder, as for many European psychiatrists of the day, whose roots in medicine and neurology were more deeply placed than those in analytic psychology, schizophrenia was an irreversible organic disease whose appearance was often colored, but whose origins were not explained, by particular psychodynamics. The common dynamic explanations were seen as banal by Schilder, who felt they had no causal significance except "insofar as they provoke earlier conflicts of a deeper character" (p. 392). Instead, "the schizophrenic psychosis is a continuous interplay between steps forward and an adaptation to love objects on a higher level . . . and a helpless sinking back into deeper libidinous levels again" (p. 391).

More Recent Freudian Formulations

Theoretical statements on the origins of schizophrenia were still couched in structural language decades after Freud's (2) paper, although attention shifts away from symbolism and content analysis to ego psychology and the analysis of form. Eissler (64) faulted Rosen (65) for considering id impulses as the instigators of schizophrenia, "overlooking that it is the ego's way of functioning which makes a patient a schizophrenic" (p. 152). Although it appears casuistical on the surface, this distinction carried important treatment implications. As Eissler mentioned, one cannot speak of having begun a psychoanalysis with a schizophrenic patient until one has gained some insight into the patient's specific ego deficit, even though one is all too aware of the "long list of his pregenital impulses." Eissler accepted Freud's original premise that there were three phases to the schizophrenic illness (withdrawal, internal elaboration, and restitution), although the phases might appear, according to Eissler, not always in strict sequence but all in a jumble. Discussing this in energic terms, he suggested that "libido may have been withdrawn from part of reality, but other parts . . . may have escaped the process of delibidinization" (p. 153) (i.e., the process of having emotional investment withdrawn). Eissler still pictured delusions and hallucinations as resulting from the "absorption by the visual or auditory apparatus or by thinking" (p. 154) of the narcissistic libido supposedly freed during the schizophrenic patient's loss of interest in (i.e., this "delibidinization" of) the external world. As to the nature-nurture question, Eissler took a position less pessimistic than Schilder's: "the question of whether a schizophrenic patient suffers from a curable disorder is still moot" (p. 151).

Wexler's (66) article from the same year as Eissler's (64) (i.e., 1951) is quite pessimistic in tone regarding the curability of the schizophrenic psychosis via the analytic method, even though the latter is useful in shedding light on central dynamics. Wexler's case concerned a woman with considerable guilt over sexual impulses (she condemned nuns and priests for playing with themselves, an urge she despised in herself as well), which led him to postulate a "primitive, archaic and devastatingly punitive super-ego" (p. 225) as a key factor underlying schizophrenic disorganization. Wexler advised against employment of the standard analytic method with schizophrenic patients, because of the absence of a reasonable ego, an ego that needs not to be dissected further and laid bare but rebuilt and resurrected. The superego abnormality mentioned above justified a theoretical modification, in Wexler's view, to the effect that schizophrenia involved more than a mere withdrawal of cathexes from external objects. Wexler ascribed the punitive superego to the internalization, by the schizophrenic patient, of a "cold, unloving, hostile mother"—the paradigm, as it seemed to Wexler, of the hostile "internal objects" that eventually take up residence in the patient's mind. Bychowski (67) was to make a similar point the following year. This specter of the "schizophrenogenic mother" was to haunt psychoanalytic circles, not only the orthodox Freudians but even more so, as we shall see, the Sullivanians, until very recent times. Federn (68), for example, saw poor mothering as the cause of the schizophrenic patient's faulty self-object differentiation. Those who worked directly with children came sooner to adopt a different view, one that took constitutional abnormalities more readily into account, than was the case with office-based analysts (such as Kohut [6]), whose experience with the primitive mental life of children, or of schizophrenic patients, was relatively meager. As Mahler (9) cautioned, the worst mother with a constitutionally healthy baby might possibly provoke a psychosis, whereas the best mother with the worst (i.e., constitutionally most vulnerable) baby could not protect it against an eventual psychotic decompensation.

Schizophrenia seemed to harken back to so early a phase in the developmental histories of those who exhibit the condition that establishment of the proper sequence of events and assignment of priority to the various etiologic factors became a bewildering task. Is there a cognitive defect that disturbs the process of internalization (of the parental images, for example)? Or do faulty internal objects create distortions in the schizophrenic patient's inner world that subsequently hamper not only relationships with others, but the process of thought itself? Did the faulty internal objects stem from faulty parents properly enregistered by an intact nervous system (a bent key pressed into good wax), or from "good-enough" parents misperceived by a neurophysiologic apparatus that functioned defectively (a good key pressed into bad wax)? Bak (69) felt that unsatisfactory mother-child relationships heightened aggression and led to ego brittleness in the schizophrenic patient. In a similar fashion, Bloch (70) favored the notion of the noxious parent(s) whose "infanticidal desires" supposedly play an important role in the genesis of the schizophrenic patient's feelings of worthlessness. Rapaport (71) was impressed by the possibility that the disturbed reality testing of the schizophrenic patient reflected faulty internal representations, such that what was perceived (in the external world) could only be compared to memory traces that did not correspond to conventional reality (themselves derived from interaction with truly atypical, unconventional caretakers).

The emphasis in Rapaport's work on internalized objects and their vicissitudes places him in the center of psychoanalytic tradition. Arlow and Brenner (72) are two more recent representatives of this tradition, whose nature they helped clarify in their remark about Freud and his predecessors:

> Kahlbaum emphasized motor phenomena in schizophrenia; Kraepelin, the progressive course ending in dementia; and Bleuler, the thought disorder and affective disturbance,. . . . [whereas] The feature of psychosis which Freud decided is of principal importance is the change in the patient's relationship with the persons and other objects of the world about him. (p. 146)

Arlow and Brenner sided with Abraham (51) in viewing the schizophrenic patient as not so uninvolved with the external world (as Freud claimed) as to prevent a transference from occurring. Furthermore, they took the position that delusions, hallucinations, and hypochondriacal symptoms result from conflict and defenses. In relation to a case illustration concerning a schizophrenic woman, they stated: "the anxiety and guilt feelings associated with her highly ambivalent attitude toward her mother produced an alteration of her ability to test reality which resulted in an actual hallucination" (p. 176). Elsewhere, making clear again their conviction about the causal significance of certain psychic phenomena, and about the applicability of tripartite theory, Arlow and Brenner wrote: "Thus delusions and hallucinations . . . can be understood as the result of more or less complex interplay among id, ego and superego" (p. 177). If psychosis resulted merely from a shift of cathexis from object representations to the self, as Freud originally argued, then all psychotic patients should pass through a phase of megalomania. Arlow and Brenner found this hypothesis incompatible with their observation that certain (melancholic) patients instead feel worthless . . . "as though narcissistic libido had been pathologically depleted rather than . . . increased" (p. 170). At the end of their chapter on psychosis, these authors made clear their adherence to a continuum hypothesis reminiscent of Glover's (73) comment that "we are all larval psychotics and have been so since age two. . . . there is no more a sharp line of division between what is to be called psychotic and what we call neurotic than there is between the neurotic and the normal" (p. 178). The yardstick is the degree of disturbance in the various ego functions.

In a more recent formulation, Wexler (74) reiterated his view, opposite to that of Arlow and Brenner (72), of deficit as the key factor in schizophrenogenesis, adding new material concerning the vulnerability of the schizophrenic patient to loss of object constancy (as provoked, for example, by separation from the analyst): the disintegration of complex object representations is associated with loss of the sense of identity, intense anxiety, and restitutive efforts. The resultant psychosis, in this schema, represents the impact of specific dynamics (object loss) superimposed on a specific constitutional defect (viz., in the area of cognition and image formation).

In many of the theoretical positions outlined above, the spotlight has been on psychogenic factors. Often they have been elevated to the level of primary etiologic factors. If constitutional elements figure in the equation, they are not mentioned as constituting necessary-though-not-sufficient factors, although this degree of etiologic significance has sometimes been assigned to psychodynamic factors, as we saw in the schema of Arlow and Brenner (72).

A more integrative and balanced view is that adopted by Frosch (75) in his excellent monograph on the psychotic process. He cited a number of his classically trained predecessors (including Hartmann, Mahler, and Jacobson) as espousing a theory where constitutional and dynamic factors are interwoven. He quoted Jacobson (76) as having remarked that "infantile environmental factors . . . may have a paramount pathogenic . . . influence . . . but few psychiatrists doubt that psychoses are based on endogenous, as yet unknown, physiological processes" (p. 104).

As did Freud at the outset, Frosch (75) "accepts our biological givens and interweaves these with psychoanalytic concepts of the psychotic process" (p. 393). He added an insightful note about the reluctance of Arlow and Brenner (72) to give biology its proper credit, as though to do so were to relinquish control over the patient's illness and to succumb to an attitude of helplessness.

Of the many well-reasoned points in Frosch's (75) book, several deserve special attention. One concerns Frosch's postulate of some kind of primitive or basic anxiety as operative in the psychotic person, who reacts catastrophically to certain stressful situations, fearing disintegration and dissolution of the self. Frosch likened his view to that of Sullivan (13, 14), who, as noted below in further detail, also spoke of the schizophrenic patient as in terror of becoming "nothing." This unbearable state, to which the ordinary person remains a stranger except under the most unusual and life-threatening circumstances, has been alluded to by many authors under many headings, such as fear of annihilation (47, 77), fear of fragmentation (78, 79), and organismic distress (9).

The other, amounting to a reexamination of Freud's (32) postulates in the Schreber case, concerns the role of what Frosch (75) called unconscious homosexuality in the dynamics of paranoid conditions (including the paranoid form of schizophrenia). Frosch marshalled convincing evidence to the effect that paranoid persons have often been the helpless victims of chronic humiliation, verbal or physical, by a parent of the same sex. This humiliation, leading to the paranoid constellation, provides its content but does not determine the form: if a paranoid psychosis is to develop, other factors, constitutional factors in particular, must also be present. The point about humiliation had been made earlier by several Sullivanians (16, 21), but was explored more fully by Frosch. The parental cruelty in this situation does not so much foster wishes for actual sexual contact with a person of the same sex, as foster a sense of having been de-sexed (unmanned, in the case of a male child with a sadistic father), which the child comes eventually to equate with "being homosexual." Frosch suggested that a dynamic similar to the one postulated by Freud as applicable to Schreber (the male paranoid who claims, in effect, "I do not love him; *he* loves *me*") may also be operative in certain female paranoid persons with the erotomanic delusion described originally by de Clérambault (80): the patient, in professing her love for— or her being loved by—a man she does not know personally, may also be warding off unconscious homosexual impulses ("I don't love *her*; I love *him*").

The British Object Relations School

Beginning with Melanie Klein, a number of analytic theoreticians in the British Isles began to raise objections to certain areas of inconsistency in Freudian metapsychology. In addition, Klein and her adherents turned their attention to areas of incompleteness in Freud's theoretical framework, particularly in regard to the psychology of developmental phases distinctly earlier than those to which Freud and the pioneer generation of analysts had direct access. Melanie Klein, for example, and later, the former pediatrician, Winnicott (8, 77), had first-hand clinical experience with very young children, in contradistinction to Freud, whose analysis of Little Hans was carried out *à distance* through consultations with the father. The British object relations school, as Klein and her followers have come to be known, effectively pushed back the boundaries within which psychoanalytic psychology remained "operational," toward the earliest phases of infancy, making psychoanalysis a more comprehensive psychology of the human condition than it had been before. The contributions of this school have been reviewed and reappraised elsewhere (5, 28, 31, 81, 82). As with all psychological investigators whose subject defies direct observation beyond a certain point, the Kleinians (and most especially their founder) filled in with speculation what they could not confirm with data. Thus the early "positions" (paranoid-schizoid; depressive) of the infant became, for the Kleinians, an article of faith in much the same way as had "primary narcissism" for the orthodox Freudians. Through a shift in focus to early, "pre-oedipal" phases of development, the British school sought to improve the explanatory powers of analytic psychology in relation to the more deeply disturbed (borderline and psychotic) forms of psychopathology. Ironically, although the Kleinians worked with children, which the first generation of Freudians did not, neither worked to any great extent with hospitalized schizophrenic patients. More ironically still, Sullivan's experience was precisely with these most profoundly disturbed schizophrenic patients, but he had neither the extensive work with neurotic patients as had the Freudians nor the work with children so familiar to Klein and Winnicott. Each major theoretician strove to build a metapsychological edifice grand enough to contain three groups of patients (neurotic, psychotic, and children); each had to rely for his or her building materials on experience with only one group.

As for the nature-nurture controversy, Klein (7) saw aggression as innate, the manifestation of Freud's death instinct. Apart from this, Klein has little to say about constitutional factors specifically, in regard to schizophrenia. Fairbairn (11) and Winnicott (8) emphasized the nurture component even more strongly, considering aggression as engendered by the child's frustrations with a depriving or otherwise noxious environment. In writing about abnormal developments in the pre-oedipal period under the heading of basic fault, Balint (83) acknowledged either component as a potential source of the disturbance:

> The origin of the basic fault may be traced back to a considerable discrepancy in the early formative phases of the individual between his bio-psychological needs and the . . . psychological care . . . available during the relevant times, . . . [the cause of which discrepancy] may be congenital, i.e., the infant's bio-psychological needs may have been too exacting, . . . or may be environmental, such as care that is insufficient, deficient . . . harsh . . . or indifferent. (p. 22)

The views of the British object relations school concerning schizophrenia consist, absent direct experience with hospitalized schizophrenic patients, primarily of analogies with the conditions of very early infancy and with moderately regressed (but for the most part, ambulatory) "schizoid" patients. As Shapiro (83a) mentioned (p. 100), the primary anxiety of the first 3 months of life is "persecutory," in Klein's (7) estimation, owing to the infant's efforts to project the death instinct onto the breast (the original "object"), which is then experienced, presumably, as "bad" and persecutory. This happens, in the Kleinian model, even under the best of circumstances; an ineffectual mother only exaggerates this tendency. The next stage is characterized by "splitting," with a tendency to idealize the good object and to deny the bad. The writers of this school emphasize object relations and deemphasize libido; as Fairbairn (11) claimed in his original revision of analytic theory, the infant is primarily object seeking. Fairbairn saw the erotogenic zones of the earlier Freudian psychology merely as the paths for object relatedness peculiar to this or that stage of development.

The splitting, seen as a normal phenomenon during this intermediate stage of infancy, can, according to Kleinian theory, become exaggerated under the impact of negative rearing patterns (viz., a nongratifying mother). As we saw, Balint (83) could also accept overintense innate needs as a predisposing factor. Whichever way it comes about, one is then in the realm of pathologic splitting, which, in turn (81) may lead to ego weakness, defective reality perception, and distrust (with subsequent impairment in object relations). An abnormal degree of splitting during the "paranoid-schizoid" phase is seen as the root cause of "schizoid" personality. The latter term is not understood by the Kleinians as a personality disorder with a certain constellation of traits (shyness, aloofness), as it is in modern nosographic terminology, such as in DSM-III (84). Rather, the schizoid person is one who exhibits the pathologic form of splitting to an intense degree. It is a condition diagnosed via inferences about defense mechanisms—a different level of abstraction than the observational one on which diagnosis customarily rests.

Those with schizoid personality, in the Kleinian sense, are considered as more prone to full-fledged schizophrenic decompensation than are persons exhibiting other patterns of defense. For Fairbairn (11), there was a continuum between schizophrenia and the schizoid state (with something akin to our "schizotypal personality" in between), the particular regions of which were never very clearly delineated. Although the dynamics of schizophrenia were also not spelled out in detail by Fairbairn, one gathers that he would have implicated the depriving or rejecting mother, interaction with whom leaves the infant prone to ego weakness, to the emergence of "early oral attitudes" (the reemergence of the schizoid position) and to disintegration of the personality. This is a purely psychogenic picture of schizophreno-genesis, one that is (apart from brief asides about excess innate neediness or aggression) characteristic of the British object relations school. Klein (7), in particular, analogized the anxieties of the infant and its supposed defensive patterns to those observed in adult schizophrenic patients. Later, Rosenfeld (85) expounded a similar theory, also paying lip service to an ill-understood "innate" factor. Psychotic parts of the personality may, in Rosenfeld's conception, be split off in early infancy, but may eventually reappear under certain adverse circumstances, producing a schizophrenic psychosis. The allusion to "psychotic parts of the personality," which would be puzzling to a biologically trained psychiatrist, is another reflection of the Kleinian continuum view of psychopathology, according to which all infants start out with these "psychotic" attributes—attributes that theoretically are capable of resurfacing in anyone. In a similar vein, Guntrip (86) spoke of the "schizoid position" as a universal human attribute that happens to relate to feelings of weakness and aloneness—against which we vastly prefer to defend ourselves, via the depressive position, by feeling "bad but strong."

Even as late as 1969 Balint (83) was still concerned with assigning to the (decompensated) schizophrenic patient the proper zone of regression, which he felt was to some "primitive form of an exclusive two-person, symbiotic, relation" (p. 69). Balint saw in this regression an exaggeration of an otherwise normal infant tendency he labeled "ocnophilia," whose etymology suggests a longing to cling. Like Fairbairn (11), Balint pictured the schizoid patient and the schizophrenic patient on a sliding scale, speculating that the schizophrenic patient had regressed to a different level of the "basic fault" (p. 90) than was typical of the better integrated schizoid person. Meanwhile Balint criticized Freud's (36) notion of a "primary narcissism," on the grounds that even the schizophrenic patient 1) regresses "only to a primitive object relation" (i.e., is still, in however primitive a way, psychologically connected to another person) and 2) does not withdraw from the world in its entirety but merely from triangular, oedipal relationships. A somewhat more extreme position was taken by Guntrip (87) for whom the severely schizoid (= schizophrenic?) person exhibited a pronounced split in the libidinal self and took flight from all object relations, seeking (fantasied) safety in the intrauterine environment.

Winnicott's (8) formulations on schizophrenogenesis are similar: for infantile schizophrenia (or "autism") "failure of ego-support" from the mother was seen as the most important, in some instances perhaps the key, contributing factor. "Latent schizophrenia" (a term used earlier by Bleuler and not defined clearly by Winnicott) and schizoid personality were viewed as milder expressions of the same psychogenic factors. Although he acknowledged that "we cannot diagnose psychotic illness by finding primitive mental mechanisms" (p. 135), Winnicott suggested that environmental factors may be a sufficient cause of disorders within the schizoid spectrum: "Failure in the facilitating environment results in developmental faults [cf., Winnicott's term, *false self*, which overlaps with Balint's *basic fault* to a certain extent] in the individual's personality and in the development of the individual's self, and the result is called schizophrenia. Schizophrenic breakdown is the reversal of the maturational process of earliest infancy" (p. 136). Winnicott made another point relevant to the dynamics of schizophrenia, as he analogized the latter to the circumstances of the very young infant: he urged us to think of the baby not so much as a person who gets hungry etc., but as an "immature being who is all the time *on the brink of unthinkable anxiety*" (p. 57). It is the (good-enough) mother who fends off this unthinkable anxiety through the appropriateness of her care. Her failure may precipitate an outbreak of this anxiety (akin to the fear of annihilation mentioned above), the reemergence of which in later life becomes transmogrified into what we know as "schizophrenia."

The thrust of Bion's (88) contributions to the understanding of schizophrenia is in the area of language; he was less concerned with the dynamics (which he accepted as having been elaborated well enough by Klein) than with the matters of phenomenology and therapy. Thus the (schizophrenic) patient "uses words as things or as split-off parts of himself which he pushes forcibly into the analyst" (p. 113). When the analyst becomes identified with his "internal persecutors," the schizophrenic patient is prone to employ language in an idiosyncratic way—as a mode of action for the splitting of his or her object. Here Bion addressed not the dynamics underlying schizophrenic etiology so much as those relevant to the therapeutic encounter, although presumably reflecting some similar interactional pattern from the past. One such pattern is offered, when Bion stated:

> At the onset of the infantile depressive position, elements of verbal thought increase in intensity and depth. In consequence the pains of psychic reality are exacerbated by it and the patient who regresses to the paranoid-schizoid position will, as he does so, turn destructively on his embryonic capacity for verbal thought as one of the elements which have led to the pain. (p. 118)

Here Bion is attempting to explain (and in purely psychological terms), if not the origins of the schizophrenic psychoses, at least the peculiarities of language one sees in this condition, conceptualized by Bion as a kind of private war against the enemy: thought.

Harry Stack Sullivan, the Washington School, and Interpersonal Theorists

It is a paradoxical note in the history of psychoanalytic thought about schizophrenia that the Freudians and Kleinians who rarely worked with hospitalized schizophrenic patients nevertheless elaborated many theories about their dynamics, whereas Sullivan and his followers, who worked intensively with such patients, left us with a large literature on therapy and on countertransference, but only a few pages on psychodynamic explanation.

As Bryce Boyer (30) mentioned, Sullivan did not take into account such matters as were considered central to Freudian theory: infantile sexuality, the Oedipus complex, and the castration conflict. Nor did he offer a systematic presentation of his theories regarding the origins of the schizophrenic condition.

Contrary to what some have expressed about Sullivan's formulations, he did not expound a wholly psychological view of schizophrenogenesis—stating in one of his earliest articles (89): "That there is hereditary predisposition to the schizophrenic dissociation is fairly certain." Sullivan regarded thought disorder as the fundamental clinical attribute of the schizophrenic patient, but had little to say about its origins.

What comes closest to his manifesto on the dynamic forces behind schizophrenic breakdown is found in Sullivan's (90) comments on the need to preserve a sense of self-worth. This is formed from the opinions of others, most especially the intimates in one's family, at whose mercies, tender or otherwise, the child must live his or her early years. Sullivan felt young children were able to sense, through a kind of emotional contagion, a mother's anxiety. Even an infant being held by an insecure or rejecting mother senses this anxiety. One mechanism available to the child for distancing himself or herself from these inchoate perceptions of the mother's rejection or discomfort is to assign all such experiences, via a dissociative mechanism, to a "not-me." In those destined to become schizophrenic, a rather large territory within the landscape of personality is divided off as "not me," leaving a split in the personality. This is a different "split" from the one Bleuler (91) had in mind (affect split from intellect): various aspects of the personality become realigned into a portion that the schizophrenic patient is still willing to acknowledge, and another portion that is disavowed. Here we are dealing merely with a matter of emphasis, since clinicians of whatever school of thought, before Sullivan and after, were fully cognizant of both varieties of splitting in the schizophrenic psyche.

Somewhat similar to the view of Klein (7) and Glover (73), for whom schizophrenia was seen as a point (answering to the earliest stage of postnatal development) along a continuum, is the Sullivanian conception of schizophrenia as a "process." What traditional nosographers recognized as the diagnostic subtypes (e.g., paranoid, catatonic) were seen as stages or reactions that either disappeared or became manifest, in accordance with life events and with the outcome of therapy. Much later, Pao (92), in his effort to synthesize Freudian, ego psychological, and Sullivanian conceptions, depicted five steps he saw as critical in the evolution of schizophrenic illness: 1) the resurfacing of conflicts, 2) the experience of "organismic panic," 3) the loss of the continuous sense of self, 4) the ego's attempt at restitution, and 5) symptom formation. The catatonic, paranoid, hebephrenic, or "simple" schizophrenic symptomatology "may be viewed as the best possible solution attained by a patient at a given time. . . . Each of such symptomatologies is expected to be encountered in any given patient in the course of long-term treatment" (92, p. 399).

Those most directly influenced by Sullivan, especially those who worked with him at Sheppard and Enoch Pratt Hospital, have become known as the Washington, or interpersonal, school. Fromm-Reichmann (15, 16), having been influenced by the orthodox analytic theoreticians before she emigrated to the United States, blended Sullivanian and Freudian ideas in ways that were acceptable to both groups. Her dynamic formulations include belief in the ability of the schizophrenic patient to form transferences and in the impact of the "schizophrenogenic" mother, whose rejection or skewed responses undermine the future schizophrenic patient of his or her ability to tolerate the stresses of ordinary life. Most important among the latter for Fromm-Reichmann were stresses involving closeness with others, which the schizophrenic patient both desired and feared. This notion was to be lifted into the central place in the dynamics of schizophrenia by later adherents of the Washington school, such as Burnham et al. (93) and (as mentioned by Shapiro) Guntrip (12). Burnham's "need-fear" dilemma relates to the individual's dual tendencies toward closeness, relatedness, and identification with others versus withdrawal, separateness, and the feeling of being a distinct person (94). These tendencies—spoken of by Balint (83) as ocnophilia versus philobatism—are exceptionally difficult for the schizophrenic patient to integrate, for whom intimacy and isolation are often intolerable.

In contrast to the Freudians, who compartmentalized development into numerous discrete stages, or to the Kleinians, whose "positions" were fewer in number and less distinct chronologically, the Sullivanian analysts spoke more of pathogenic patterns of interpersonal relatedness. This lends a somewhat vaguer quality to their comments about the sequence of events in the unfolding of the schizophrenic process. This vagueness need not be construed as inaccuracy: a good case could be made that many of the orthodox analysts, in their assignment of schizophrenia to this or that point of regression or fixation, were unrealistically precise. Be this as it may, Searles (95), the foremost contemporary member of the Washington school, put great weight on the schizophrenic mother's low self-esteem and on her tendency to transmit to her child, during the symbiotic phase of development, the same kind of insecurity and propensity to rage and distrust as she presumably was burdened with in response to the faulty caretaking of her own mother. Kernberg (5) demonstrated parallels between the views of Jacobson (76), stressing ". . . excessive prolongation of the symbiotic phase or a defensive regression, in terms of *refusion* of self- and object representations" (p. 102) and the kinds of transferences, seen in schizophrenic patients, as outgrowths of disturbances during this period, to which Searles drew attention (95). Searles also wrote extensively on the schizophrenogenic effects of the mother's mixed messages; specifically, on the manner in which these appear to drive the other "crazy."

Elsewhere, Searles (18) wrote of the pathogenicity of the shifting of family roles, often noted in the histories of schizophrenic patients, that interfere with the development of a consistent and reliable picture of the external world. As an unconscious defense against the tensions inherent in this kind of family, the child (or at least the future schizophrenic person) identifies with the parents in a primitive fashion, at the expense of whatever capacities may have existed originally for mature relatedness and realistic orientation. In this respect, Searles' views resemble those of Bateson and Ruesch (22), whose "double-bind" theory was to gain widespread acceptance as a key dynamic behind schizophrenic development: the polarized double-message of the mother (e.g., "I love you" expressed in a way that conveyed irritation or hatred) leading to unassimilable splits in the mental life of the child and to eventual "craziness."

This focus on the ability of abnormal mothering somehow to "infect" her offspring inescapably with a case of schizophrenia finds its most vehement expression in the work of Jackson et al. (23), who created a veritable taxonomy of schizophrenogenic mothers: the puritanical mother (overcontrolled, nonsensual), the Machiavellian (manipulative, deceitful), and the helpless (anxious, confused). Certain unfavorable patterns of fathering were also cited as relevant: namely, the defeated, the autocratic, and the chaotic.

Despite the differences in their theoretical roots, the Kleinians of the 1950s and 1960s were in accord with the Sullivanians on the issue of the mother's role, as when Balint cited Lewis Hill (96), for whom the mother of the schizophrenic person was typically "conditional" in her love. Hill saw such mothers as able to relate only to the normal outer shell of their children, remaining "impervious to any impressions as to what went on within them" (p. 109). Otto Will (17) expressed a similar viewpoint, in picturing the infancy of the future schizophrenic person as determined by the relationship of intense closeness to the mother and the person's fear of being engulfed. Other adherents of the Washington school, including many who carried out long and intensive analytic therapy with schizophrenic patients at the Chestnut Lodge, also underlined the pathogenic impact of adverse mothering patterns as the dynamic factor of greatest significance. A patient of Staveren (97), for example, spoke of her mother's "corrosiveness"—the mother's way of throttling all protests by oblique blows aimed at the patient's self-esteem—and of the overwhelming anxiety induced in the patient even when she spoke to Staveren of her hateful feelings toward her mother.

Many of the more recent contributors to the field of family dynamics relevant to schizophrenia took the formulations of the Washington school as an important source of inspiration. If the Sullivanians threw the spotlight onto the mother in their search for clues to the genesis of schizophrenia, Lidz and his followers may be said to have widened the spotlight's aperture so as to include the family as a whole. We are now at a far remove from Freudian conceptualizations of fixation and regression when we look at the kinds of factors emphasized by the family dynamicists. Lidz et al. (24) spoke, for example, of deficiencies in parental nurturance, in the family as a social institution integrating the child's development and in transmitting to the child the proper communicative instruments of his or her culture. Various abnormalities in language, communicational, and family-interactional patterns (the schismatic family, the skewed family) have been identified by Lidz's group. For these investigators, abnormal family patterns outweighed, in their schizophrenogenic potential, constitutional factors in the affected individual. Hereditary influences were either repudiated or downplayed, as in Lidz's comment, "The evidence does not bear out the suggestion that the mother has difficulty in mothering the child who becomes schizophrenic because of some inherent unresponsivity or hypersensitivity in the infant. The mother's problems transcend the relationship to the child and usually clearly antedated his birth" (24, p. 335). Earlier, however, Lidz et al. (98) acknowledged that "both genetic and environmental factors may well be involved" (p. 315). A strong relationship between "parental communication deviance and the probability of extended schizophrenia-spectrum disorders" has been implicated by Goldstein and Jones (25, p. 226). Stierlin (99) outlined a number of intrafamilial dynamisms that, apart from specific peculiarities of language (and so on), appear capable of predisposing certain adolescents to schizophrenic breakdown. Stierlin characterized these under the heading of "mission impossible," alluding to the painful and inescapable situation in which these young people may find themselves entrapped. A parent burdened with shame, realistic guilt (over an actual wrongdoing), weakness, or madness may export his or her own intolerable emotion into the child (e.g., via threatening the child with harm if the latter "exposes" the parent). Or, a vulnerable child may become schizophrenic after being endowed with the mission of sparing some family member the mourning of a deceased sibling or parent. Stierlin does not see these "sociogenic" factors as necessarily dominant in the causal hierarchy relevant to schizophrenia, so much as complementary to the biogenic factors stressed in traditional hospital-based psychiatry.

Still another focus is to be found in the writings of Arieti (20, 100). Although Arieti was to protest against the notion of the schizophrenogenic mother (he felt only about one-fourth of schizophrenic persons had truly rejecting or otherwise noxious mothers), he did accept the Sullivanian view that extreme lack of security in the first few years of life played an important (if not primary etiologic) role in setting the state for an eventual schizophrenic breakdown.

Because of a lack of a trusting relationship with the mother, the preschizophrenic person fails to achieve a "sense of communion, becomes distrustful, avoids emotional contact with others" (20, p. 455) and, according to Arieti, suffers a defect in the development of language—specifically in the areas of symbolization and validation through comparison with the impressions of others. Clinically, one sees primitive, solipsistic thought, of the sort Arieti called "paleologic' (cf., Freud's "primary process"). The typical breakdown during adolescence comes about, in Arieti's conception of the illness, not so much through biological changes in the drives (i.e., the hormonal changes of puberty) nor from the related sociogenic factors (cultural pressure to achieve intimacy) as through an exaggeration of the preschizophrenic person's already faulty cognitive mechanisms (such that he or she becomes engulfed in unrealistic and idiosyncratic thoughts). That such cognitive alterations occur is, of course, beyond challenge; what is different about Arieti's formulation is his view of the thought disorder as a primary etiologic factor rather than a mere epiphenomenon of the schizophrenic condition.

References

1. Lazare A, Eisenthal S. Alonso A: Clinical evaluation, in Psychiatry, Vol 1. Edited by Michels R et al. Philadelphia, JB Lippincott, 1985
2. Freud S: The ego and the id (1923), in The Standard Edition of the Complete

Psychological Works of Sigmund Freud, Vol 19. Translated and edited by Strachey J. London, Hogarth Press, 1957, pp 3–63

3. Fairbairn WRD: Endopsychic structure reconsidered in terms of object-relationships. Int J Psychoanal 25:70–93, 1944

4. Jacobson E: The Self and the Object World. New York, International Universities Press, 1964

5. Kernberg OF: Internal World and External Reality. Northvale, NJ, Jason Aronson, 1980

6. Kohut H: Analysis of the Self. New York, International Universities Press, 1971

7. Klein M: Notes on some schizoid mechanisms. Int J Psychoanal 27:99–110, 1946

8. Winnicott DW: The Maturational Processes and the Facilitating Environment. New York, International Universities Press, 1965

9. Mahler MS: On Human Symbiosis and the Vicissitudes of Individuation, Vol 1: Infantile Psychosis. New York, International Universities Press, 1968

10. Bellak L, Loeb L: Psychoanalytic, psychotherapeutic and generally psychodynamic studies, in The Schizophrenic Syndrome. New York, Grune & Stratton, 1969, pp 343–377

11. Fairbairn WRD: An Object-Relations Theory of the Personality. New York, Basic Books, 1952

12. Guntrip H: Schizoid Phenomena, Object-Relations and the Self. New York, International Universities Press, 1969

13. Sullivan HS: The language of schizophrenia, in Language and Thought in Schizophrenia. Edited by Kasanin JS. Berkeley, CA, University of California Press, 1944

14. Sullivan HS: Conceptions of Modern Psychiatry. New York, WW Norton, 1947

15. Fromm-Reichmann F: Notes on the development of treatment of schizophrenics by psychoanalytic psychotherapy. Psychiatry 11:263–273, 1948

16. Fromm-Reichmann F: Basic problems in the psychotherapy of schizophrenia. Psychiatry 21:1–6, 1958

17. Will O: Psychotherapeutics and the schizophrenic reaction. J Nerv Ment Dis 126:109–140, 1958

18. Searles HF: The schizophrenic individual's experience of the world. Psychiatry 2:119–131, 1967

19. Kernberg OF: Borderline personality organization. J Am Psychoanal Assoc 15:641–685, 1967

20. Arieti S: New views on the psychodynamics of schizophrenia. Am J Psychiatry 124:453–466, 1967

21. Szalita AG: Further remarks on the pathogenesis and treatment of schizophrenia. Psychiatry 15:143–150, 1952

22. Bateson G, Ruesch J: Toward a theory of schizophrenia. Behav Sci 1:251–264, 1956

23. Jackson DD, Block JA, Patterson V: Psychiatrists' conceptions of the schizophrenogenic parent. AMA Archives of Neurology and Psychiatry 79:448–459, 1958

24. Lidz T, Fleck S, Cornelison A: Schizophrenia and the Family. New York, International Universities Press, 1965

25. Goldstein MJ, Jones JE: Adolescent and familial precursors of borderline and schizophrenic conditions, in Borderline Personality Disorders. Edited by Hartocollis O. New York, International Universities Press, 1977, pp 213–229

26. Liberman RP, Wallace CJ, Vaughn CE, et al: Social and family factors in the course of schizophrenia, in The Psychotherapy of Schizophrenia. Edited by Strauss JS. New York, Plenum Medical, 1980, pp 21–54

27. Modell A: Some recent psychoanalytic theories of schizophrenia. Psychoanal Rev 43:181–194, 1956

28. Freeman T, Cameron JL, McGhie A: Chronic Schizophrenia. New York, International Universities Press, 1958

29. Gedo JE, Goldberg A: Models of the Mind: A Psychoanalytic Theory. Chicago, IL, University of Chicago Press, 1973

30. Bryce Boyer L: Historical development of psychoanalytic psycho-therapy of the schizophrenias: the followers of Freud, in Psychoanalytic Treatment of Schizophrenic, Borderline and Characterological Disorders. Edited by Bryce Boyer L, Giovacchini P. Northvale, NJ, Jason Aronson, 1980, pp 71–127

31. Shapiro SA: Contemporary Theories of Schizophrenia. New York, McGraw-Hill, 1981

31a. Bleuler E: Dementia Praecox, oder die Grupper der Schizophrenien. Leipzig, F Deuticke, 1911

32. Freud S: Psychoanalytic notes on an autobiographical account of a case of paranoia (dementia paranoides) (1911), in The Standard Edition of the Complete Psychological Works of Sigmund Freud, Vol 12. Translated and edited by Strachey J. London, Hogarth Press, 1957, pp 3–82

33. Von Bertalanffy L: General System Theory. New York, George Braziller, 1968

34. Ferenczi S: Some clinical observations on paranoia and paraphrenia (1914), in Sex and Psychoanalysis. New York, R Brunner, 1958

35. Freud S: The Complete Letters of Sigmund Freud to Wilhelm Fliess. Edited by Masson JM. Cambridge, MA, Harvard University Press, 1985

36. Freud S: On narcissism (1914), in The Standard Edition of the Complete Psychological Works of Sigmund Freud, Vol 14. Translated and edited by Strachey J. London, Hogarth Press, 1957, pp 67–102

37. Maeder A: Psychologische Untersuchungen an Dementia Praecox-Kranken. Jahrbuch fur Psychoanalytische und Psychopathologische Forschung 2:234–245, 1910

38. Bjerre P: Zur Radikalbehandlung der chronischen Paranoia. Jahrbuch fur Psychoanalyse und Psychopathologische Forschung 3:759–847, 1912

39. Stone MH (with Albert H, Forrest D, Arieti S): Treating Schizophrenic Patients. New York, McGraw-Hill, 1983

40. Jung CJ: The Psychology of Dementia Praecox (Monograph 3). New York, Nervous and Mental Disease Publishing, 1936

41. Freud S: The unconscious (1915), in The Standard Edition of the Complete Psychological Works of Sigmund Freud, Vol 14. Translated and edited by Strachey J. London, Hogarth Press, 1957, pp 159–215

42. Abraham K: The first pregenital stage of the libido, in Selected Papers on Psychoanalyses. New York, Brunner/Mazel, 1916, pp 248–279

43. Rudin E: Zur Vererbung und Neuentstehung der Dementia Praecox. Berlin, Springer Verlag, 1916

44. Nunberg H: Der Verlauf des libido Konfliktes in einem Falle von Schizo-phrenia. Internationale Zeitschrift für Psychoanalyse (1919) 7:301–345, 1921
45. Tausk V: On the origin of the influencing machine in schizophrenia. Psychoanal Q 2:519–556, 1933
46. Haslam J: Illustrations of Madness (with a description of the tortures experienced by bomb-bursting, lobster-cracking and lengthening of the brain). London, G Hayden, 1810
47. Little MI: Transference Neurosis and Transference Psychosis. Northvale, NJ, Jason Aronson, 1981
48. Robie TR: The oedipus and homosexual complexes in schizophrenia. Psychiatr Q 1:468–484, 1927
49. Freud S: Neurosis and psychosis (1924), in The Standard Edition of the Complete Psychological Works of Sigmund Freud, Vol 19. Translated and edited by Strachey J. London, Hogarth Press, 1957, pp 149–153
50. Hesnard ALM: La theorie psychoanalytique ou "instinctive" de la schizophrenie. L'Encephale 21:725–726, 1926
51. Abraham K: Short study of the development of the libido viewed in the light of mental disorders (1924), in Selected Papers of Karl Abraham. Edited by Jones E. London, Hogarth Press, 1927, pp 418–501
52. Federn P: Psychoanalysis of psychoses. Psychiatric Q 17:3–19, 246–257, 470–487, 1943
53. Federn P: Ego Psychology and the Psychoses. London, Imago, 1953
54. Katan M: The nonpsychotic part of the personality in schizophrenia. Int J Psychoanal 35:119–128, 1954
55. Katan M: Schreber's hallucination about "little men." Int J Psychoanal 31:32–35, 1950
56. Hartmann H: Contribution to the metapsychology of schizophrenia. Psychoanal Study Child 8:177–197, 1953
57. Jacobson E: Contributions to the metapsychology of psychotic identifications. J Am Psychoanal Assoc 2:239–262, 1954
58. Jacobson E: Problems in the differentiation between schizophrenic and melancholic states of depression, in Psychoanalysis: General Psychology. Edited by Lowenstein R. New York, International Universities Press, 1966, pp 449–518
59. Laforgue R: Contribution a l'etude de le schizophrenie. Evolution Psychiatrique 3:81–96, 1935
60. Laforgue R: Scotomization in schizophrenia. Int J Psychoanal 8:473–478, 1926
61. Schilder P: Psychologie der Schizophrenie vom psychoanalytischen Standpunkt. Zeitschrift fur die Gesamte Neurologie und Psychiatrie 112:279–282, 1928
62. Vigotsky LS: Thought in schizophrenia. Archives of Neurology and Psychiatry 31:1063–1077, 1934
63. Schilder P: The psychology of schizophrenia. Psychoanal Rev 26:380–398, 1939
64. Eissler K: Remarks on the psychoanalysis of schizophrenia. Int J Psychoanal 32:139–156, 1951
65. Rosen JN: The treatment of schizophrenic patients by direct analytic therapy. Psychiatry 21:3–37, 1947

66. Wexler M: Structural problem in schizophrenia: the role of the internal object. Bull Menninger Clin 15:271–234, 1951

67. Bychowski G: Psychotherapy of Psychosis. New York, Grune & Stratton, 1952

68. Federn P: Ego Psychology and the Psychoses. New York, Basic Books, 1952

69. Bak R: The schizophrenic defense against aggression. Int J Psychoanal 35:129–134, 1954

70. Bloch D: Some dynamics of suffering: effect of the wish for infanticide in a case of schizophrenia. Psychoanal Rev 53:531–554

71. Rapaport D: Organization and Pathology of Thought. New York, Columbia University Press, 1951

72. Arlow J, Brenner C: Psychoanalytic Concepts and the Structural Theory. New York, International Universities Press, 1964

73. Glover E: A psychoanalytic approach to the classification of mental disorders. Journal of Mental Science 78:819–842, 1932

74. Wexler M: The evolution of a deficiency view of schizophrenia, in Psychotherapy of Schizophrenia. Edited by Gunderson J, Mosher L. Northvale, NJ, Jason Aronson, 1975, pp 161–174

75. Frosch J: The Psychotic Process. New York, International Universities Press, 1983

76. Jacobson E: Depression: Comparative Studies of Normal, Neurotic and Psychotic Conditions. New York, International Universities Press, 1971

77. Winnicott DW: Transitional objects and transitional phenomena. Int J Psychoanal 34:89–97, 1970

78. Bergeret J: Abrege de Psychologie Pathologique. Paris, Masson, 1975

79. Kernberg OF: Borderline Conditions and Pathological Narcissism. Northvale, NJ, Jason Aronson, 1975

80. de Clérambault G: Les Psychoses Passionelles, in Oeuvre Psychiatrique. Paris, Presse Universitaire de France, 1942

81. Segal H: Introduction to the Work of Melanie Klein. New York, Basic Books, 1973

82. Sutherland JD: The British object-relations theorists. J Am Psychoanal Assoc 28:829–860, 1980

83. Balint M: The Basic Fault. New York, Brunner/Mazel, 1969

83a. Shapiro SA: Contemporary Theories of Schizophrenia. New York, McGraw-Hill, 1981

84. American Psychiatric Association: Diagnostic and Statistical Manual of Mental Disorders, 3rd Edition. Washington, DC, American Psychiatric Association, 1980

85. Rosenfeld H: Notes on the psychopathology of confusional states in chronic schizophrenia. Int J Psychoanal 31:132–137, 1950

86. Guntrip H: The manic-depressive problem in the light of the schizoid process. Int J Psychoanal 43:98–112, 1962

87. Guntrip H: Personality Structure and Human Interaction. New York, International Universities Press, 1961

88. Bion W: Notes on the theory of schizophrenia. Int J Psychoanal 35:113–118, 1954

89. Sullivan HS: Schizophrenia: its conservative and malignant features. Am J Psychiatry 81:77–91, 1924

90. Sullivan HS: Clinical Studies in Psychiatry. New York, WW Norton, 1956
91. Bleuler E: Dementia Praecox, oder die Gruppe der Schizophrenien. Leipzig, Deuticke, 1911
92. Pao PN: On the formation of schizophrenic symptoms. Int J Psychoanal 58:389–401, 1977
93. Burnham D, Gladstone A, Givson R: Schizophrenia and the Need-Fear Dilemma. New York, International Universities Press, 1969
94. Will O: Paranoid development in the concept of the self. Psychiatry 24:76–86, 1961
95. Searles HF: Collected Papers on Schizophrenia. New York, International Universities Press, 1965
96. Hill LB: Psychotherapeutic Intervention in Schizophrenia. Chicago, IL, University of Chicago Press, 1955
97. Staveren H: Suggested specificity of certain dynamisms in a case of schizophrenia. Psychiatry 10:127–135, 1947
98. Lidz T, Cornelison AR, Terry D: Intrafamilial environment of the schizophrenic patient, VI: the transmission of irrationality. Arch Neur Psychiatr 79:305–316, 1958
99. Stierlin H: The transmission of irrationality reconsidered, in The Nature of Schizophrenia. Edited by Wynne LC, Cromwell RL, Matthysse S. New York, John Wiley, 1978, pp 517–525
100. Arieti S: The Interpretation of Schizophrenia, 2nd Edition. New York, Basic Books, 1974

CHAPTER NINE

The Psychodynamics of Schizophrenia II: Other Contributors and Discussion

Michael H. Stone, M.D.

Other Analytic Contributors

There are several other psychoanalytic investigators whose commentary about the psychodynamics of schizophrenia are worthy of attention, but whose affiliations could not be classified under the headings thus far mentioned (in Chapter 8). The most important of these is Rado, whose roots were nourished in the same soil that supported the main trunk of Freudian theory, off of which his oeuvre represents a somewhat peripheral branch. One could in fact refer to the Radovian or adaptational school, were it not that, with respect to schizophrenia, the founder was also its sole member. To Rado belongs the credit of putting forward the notion of the "schizotype," as constituting the phenotypic expression of the hereditary predisposition to a schizophrenic illness. The now widely accepted concept of a schizophrenic spectrum of conditions (1) is adumbrated in Rado's (2) classification of schizotypal variants, spanning the "decompensated" schizotype (in effect, the core schizophrenic), the compensated schizotype (akin to our borderline schizophrenic or to DSM-III's [3] "schizotypal personality"), and the schizoid personality. Fairbairn's (4) classification, as we saw, was similar, but without the emphasis on hereditary factors. Furthermore, Rado advanced the hypothesis that the schizophrenic phenotypes were themselves the derivatives of a genetically determined, central dysregulation of hedonic control, with the net result that the schizotype suffers a defect in the capacity to experience pleasure ("anhedonia"). This defect, in turn, has serious psychological consequences for the schizotype in that the balance between pleasure and frustration during the course of friendships or intimate relationships (which encourages ordinary people to move toward others) becomes tilted toward the negative. The schizotype is exquisitely sensitive to pain in attempts at intimacy but uniquely handicapped in efforts to derive satisfaction.

Bellak, an analyst with a lifelong interest in schizophrenia, demonstrated (like Rado) a receptiveness to data from biologically and genetically oriented researchers. He developed rating scales for the more precise assessment of ego functions, which are routinely found to be severely weakened in schizophrenic patients, for a multiplicity of reasons and in many different combinations. The mixture of organic, hereditary, and psychogenic factors contributing to the "final common pathway" (of manifest schizophrenia) varies from patient to patient: one will show reasonably good abstract thought, Bellak noted, others show the marked eccentricities of "formal thought disorder," along with autistic preoccupations and poor abstracting abilities (5). The particular value of Bellak's contributions lie more in his encyclopedic grasp of the phenomenology of schizophrenia and in his efforts to integrate biological research with analytic intuition than in the area of psychodynamic theory.

McGhie (6) was also interested in the attentional deficit in schizophrenic patients, which, along with a defect in short-term memory, he felt might contribute to the characteristic symptom patterns. Inability to distinguish relevant from irrelevant stimuli represents an abnormality stemming from innate defect rather than from conflict.

The latest contribution of the British analyst Freeman (7) is shorn of the optimism that pervaded many of the earlier theoreticians. He found their formulations (8–11) of little heuristic value, stating that "it is still impossible to identify children and young adolescents who will succumb to a schizophrenic psychosis" (p. 237). Freeman also raised an objection to the tendency on the part of many psychoanalytic writers to apply hypotheses developed from one subtype of schizophrenia across the board to schizophrenic patients of all subtypes. Parenthetically, we might note that the Schreber case, recently reexamined by Grotstein (12), despite its florid and much discussed dynamics (relating to success-avoidance, homosexual conflicts, maternal deprivation, and so on) may not be archetypal for schizophrenia; Schreber, himself, may have been qualitatively different, diagnostically, from the more commonly encountered "praecox" cases, occurring at a much younger age and with a more chronic course than Schreber's. Freeman understood the psychotic identification, seen in remitting forms of schizophrenia, as a defense against a homosexual wish fantasy; identifications seen in the chronic illness may be a defense against loss—the delusional objects serving as "substitutes for real object representations" (p. 240). Although Freeman contended that real object relations are replaced by psychotic identifications at the onset of all schizophrenic psychoses, he has said that the later state of reconstruction, with restoration of the boundary between self and other, does not proceed nearly as effectively in the catatonic-hebephrenic cases as in the paranoid. Clinical recovery is associated, in Freeman's view, with schizophrenic psychoses that "present with manic-depressive features alongside persecutory phenomena" (p. 242). His nosography adheres, in this regard, more to Bleulerian than to contemporary research diagnostic criteria of diagnosis (which would tend to disqualify such cases as truly "schizophrenic"). Freeman also continued the analytic tradition of writing in a causal language about dynamics, as when he stated that "delusions (melancholic or persecutory) are the *result* [emphasis added] of an identification with an object which has been in receipt of the hostile component of ambivalence" (p. 341).

This tendency to ascribe causal significance to dynamic factors is visible also in the contributions of Azima (13), who felt that problems in "orality" (and in object relations dominated by serious disturbances in the early oral phases of development) were central to the pathogenesis of schizophrenia. Memory traces of severe frustrations during the first year and a half of life (i.e., the *oral* phase) persist, in Azima's schema, as a kind of vicious circuit: the "bad introjects," derived from negative experiences with primary caretakers. His recommendations for therapy arise directly out of his theoretical model: Azima advocated replacement of the bad introjects with better ones, built up out of gratifying experiences with a therapist (seen often and over a long period of time).

Azima's recommendations, which extended to such direct gratifications as bottle feeding, serve as a natural bridge in our discussion to the work of Marguerite Sechèhaye (14), the originator of this form of treatment for schizophrenic patients. Sechèhaye's method, "symbolic realization," involved gratification of primitive oral needs by giving her patients something symbolically related to the original craving (e.g., giving an orange rather than milk from the breast), within an intense relationship and in a soothing atmosphere. Sechèhaye assumed that (maternal) frustration of oral needs played an essential role in psychotic breakdown (the patient, Renee, to whom she devoted particular effort, had decompensated during childhood), "since the massive regressions of schizophrenics to elementary levels of affective life lead us to suppose these patients have undergone trauma at this stage, profoundly marking their affective development and driving them to psychosis" (p. 76). Inasmuch as the instinctual needs of the oral period (e.g., for food, soothing, warmth) assert themselves, by definition, in the youngest of infants, Sechèhaye felt that nongratification of these needs would necessarily be more pathogenic than would the subsequent frustration of needs for expansion, power, and sexuality, all of which belong to a later time when the child is "older, stronger and more independent of his mother" (p. 76). Although Sechèhaye tended to underline the nurture as opposed to nature aspects of schizophrenia—as when she wrote of the preschizophrenic infant's ego as "still normal in some sectors, [but] open to invasion by id drives, which the now psychotic ego defends itself through delusion and hallucination" (p. 109)—she acknowledged constitutional factors also. For Sechèhaye, these may express themselves in the general strength or weakness of the drives (an infant with strong drive reacts more vigorously to frustration) or in the form of specific predisposition to schizophrenia. Less severe instances of the latter are seen in the "schizoid constitution" (15), a notion for which she is indebted to Kretschmer (16). Bleuler (15), with whom Sechèhaye studied at the Burghölzli, also spoke of a schizoid constitution, but gave greater weight to psychological factors, which Bleuler felt would alone account for the typical features of autism, introversion, and withdrawal from the external world. It is this view that Sechèhaye came to endorse.

Sechèhaye's preoccupation with the symbol and the process of symbolization reflects an important trend in the French-speaking psychoanalytic community. In a similar way, the strong interest on the part of the French schools in psychic structure (also discernible in Sechèhaye's writing) parallels the British interest in object relations. Both represent attempts to refine Freudian theory so as to encompass in a more meaningful way the various pre-oedipal (borderline and psychotic) conditions. Structure and object relations are themselves interrelated: it is the internalization of object relations that creates mental "structures." These structures are generally spoken of in abstract terms not easily defined, probably because of our having at this time only the most tenuous grasp of what neurophysiologic mechanisms underlie mental structure. Perhaps they are the psychical expression of experiences preserved in long-term memory, via changes in synaptic activation states of cells distributed widely within the neocortex (17). Important memory patterns become "programmed" with special durability by early experience, in a fashion hinted at by Freud (18) and later in Wiener's (19) work on cybernetic feedback mechanisms. A number of French psychoanalysts have drawn attention to the fragility of mental structures in the schizophrenic person and to the ill-defined boundaries between self and non-self (20, 21). The schizophrenic person is susceptible to fragmentation (the antithesis of structure). Utilizing an object relational frame of reference, Bergeret (20) understood paranoid delusions in schizophrenia as reflecting an "intermediary stage, between two extremes, of object-relation, where external objects are not denied so much as not perceived as truly separate; the object is *consubstantial* with the subject and is experienced as belonging to the being or *essence* (of the subject) but not to his *possession*" (p. 169, my translation). The actual need-satisfying external object and its hallucinatory representation are likewise not kept properly separate.

One notes in the French authors a profound interest in the psychological, the symbolical, the semantical, and finally the philosophical. Constitution is left very much in the shadows. Schizophrenia thus becomes understood as something gone awry in the process of symbolization, and this impediment is often placed in the foreground in discussions of etiology. For a thorough presentation of these analytic writers and their views, one should consult Ledoux (22). There the contributions of Lebovici, Widlöcher, and Lacan are elucidated in considerable detail. Elsewhere, I (23) have reviewed some of the ideas on schizophrenogenesis elaborated by Racamier and Andre Green.

A number of contemporary French theoreticians who remain close to Freudian tradition have drawn attention to problems in the process of symbol formation in schizophrenia. Chasseguet-Smirgel (21), in her treatise on the ego ideal, noted that

> as the formation of symbols ultimately constitutes an extension of one's own body into external space, it represents an attempt to regain the cosmic ego. This process is not unrelated to primitive animism and magic; in the schizophrenic one can observe a reappearance of the confusion between the individual's own body and nature. (p. 141)

Further on, she remarked on an interesting dynamic operative in some paranoid persons (and by extension, some paranoid schizophrenic persons); namely, the sense of humiliation that may be provoked by being seen naked. Freud mentioned such exposure as contributing to the origins of paranoid delusions; the theme is of relevance to the dynamism of shame (which Chasseguet-Smirgel related to the ego ideal) versus that of guilt, which relates to the super ego.

In the work of Widlöcher (24) the psychogenesis of psychotic conditons (and their borderline variants) is reevaluated in accordance with structural theory. The core of Widlöcher's theory is expressed in ego psychological terms, but certain conceptions of Winnicott (25) and Melanie Klein (26) are interwoven. As set forth in Ledoux's (22) monograph, Widlöcher's main point consists in the assertion of a "structural kernel" relative to the psychoses, consisting of a defect still more "basic" than that affecting reality testing. Widlöcher wrote of a fundamental lack of identification with reality, stemming from a defect to the ability to preserve the illusion of omnipotence. This vital illusion is preserved under normal circumstances by symbiotic fusion with the mother—here, the good-enough mother of Winnicott (25): "The infant accedes to a proper sense of reality to the extent it will have maintained a sense of omnipotence and incorporated the maternal object, the symbiotic relationship have previously been sufficiently good" (cited by Ledoux [22], my translation). In the psychotic person, Widlöcher found that the "initial matrix of the ego's identificatory system is marred by an *essential fragility* [emphasis added]," (p. 737) one serious consequence of which is that the (prepsychotic individual) is unable to internalize the maternal image adequately. The resulting "psychotic organization" shows several characteristic features: Widlöcher attached special importance to fear of fragmentation and to a predominance of fantasy, shorn of customary censorship because of an "anomaly of imagination that creates a split between the world of fantasy and that of reality" (22, p. 739). This "anomaly" comes close to the notion of a constitutional defect, although Widlöcher did not speak of innate neurophysiologic defect in so many words. In fact, Widlöcher referred much as did Glover (27) and many other Kleinian writers, to a "continuum" between psychosis and borderline states, conceptualized in purely (or at least primarily) psychological terms. Schizophrenia, in this schema, is pictured as residing at one extreme of a continuum relating to a psychotic kernel (or nucleus: Fr. "noyau"), whose traits include fear of fragmentation, a chaotic organization of libidinal development (lacking the usual sequence and hierarchy of oral, anal, and phallic structures), and an intensity of the aggressive drive, which impedes the proper fusion of libidinal and aggressive tendencies. Thus psychosis (and presumably schizophrenia) is seen in terms more complicated than can be neatly ascribed to "orality," according to Widlöcher, for whom causality nevertheless remained a matter of adverse psychological factors whose point of origin lies in the vicissitudes of mother-infant symbiosis.

In the work of Lacan (28) we return to the special interest, noted already in the contributions of Sechèhaye (14) and Chasseguet-Smirgel (21), in the symbolic process and in the deformations of this process encountered in the schizophrenic person. Lacan's comments on the psychodynamics of schizophrenia are not all of a piece, having undergone considerable change from the beginning of his career to the end, some 40 years later. His doctoral thesis (28) was on paranoid psychosis. Little known outside the French-speaking community, the tone of this monograph is Freudian; its treatment of the nature-nurture issue is rather evenhanded for its time. Psychogenic and constitutional theories are reviewed extensively. Having despaired finally, after this meticulous examination, of finding any unitary constitutional underpinning for paranoid forms of psychosis, Lacan decided in favor of "vital conflicts" as the "efficient though non-specific" (p. 346) causes. Paranoid states derive, in Lacan's view, "from very diverse pathogenic routes; they cannot be completely defined either by their content nor by their . . . mechanisms" (p.335). Four primary traits of the paranoid person were singled out: grandiosity, distrust, false judgment, and social inadaptability. In some passages, Lacan made it clear he considered paranoid patients to enjoy a better prognosis than is typical for schizophrenic patients, and hazarded the opinion that these cases may belong to the domain of manic-depression (where a favorable outcome is more the rule). In the concluding portions of his treatise, Lacan offered a psychodynamic model for paranoia that centers on the notion of fixation at the developmental stage relevant to superego formation (a position similar to that of Chasseguet-Smirgel's, since the ego ideal is encompassed in the concept of superego). Lacan stressed sexual conflicts as of particular significance, involving erotization of the anal zone, a tendency to sadomasochism, and (excess) secondary narcissism, all under the influence of what Lacan referred to as the fraternal complex. The latter relates to the themes of repressed homosexuality, persecution, and aggressive as well as self-punitive tendencies. So far we do not discern any remarkable difference between Lacan's metapsychology of paranoia and the theories offered by other psychoanalytic writers of that era (either on "paranoia" or "schizophrenia"—the two states largely overlapping in their usage at this time).

Later, Lacan (cf., Ledoux [22]) was to shift his focus onto linguistical and semiotic issues, about which he wrote in an obscurantist manner (reminiscent of the structuralist-deconstructionist philosopher, Derrida). In some respects he remained close to Freud, as when he formulated the concept of forclusion (rejection of an idea), based on his reading of Freud's (29) Wolf-Man. Traditional psychoanalytic commentary on this celebrated case serve, in Lacan's later writing, as the springboard for theorizing that is far removed from case material (i.e., from the phenomenological) and completely removed from attention to the "defect" side of schizophrenogenesis. The focus is instead on language—specifically, on its signs and the corresponding *signifiants* (the sound-images of the linguistical sign) (e.g., the spoken word *horse*) and *signifiés* (the conceptual component) (e.g., our idea of a horse, which could equally well be summoned by equus, Pferd, and so on). Those who wish to become more familiar with Lacan's oeuvre will find the Bär (30) article and the book by Muller and Richardson (31) illuminating.

A sampling of Lacan's thought, as it pertains to his later conception of psychosis, is offered in the following passage from Ledoux (22, my translation), which includes a brief quotation from Lacan's *Ecrits* (32):

> The defect which lends to psychosis its essential character is to be found in the rejection (*forclusion*) of the Name of the Father in the place of the Other: "For the psychosis to be unleashed, the Name of the Father must become rejected, *verworfen*; that is to say, never acceding to the place of the Other, there to be invoked in symbolic opposition to the Subject" (Lacan, *Ecrits* [32]). One must make it clear that the Name of the Father, this keystone of the symbolic structure, wellspring of the Law, has much to do with the mother, and that what mother does with the Word of the father plays a decisive role in the fate of her child. If mother acknowledges the word of the father, his function as Law, the child will accept the symbolic castration and accede to symbolic Order and to Language. He will have a *name*, a place in the family. In the reverse situation, the child remains prisoner of the imaginary, subjected to a dual relationship. It is this non-attribution on the part of the mother of the paternal function which prevents the child from acceding to the paternal metaphor. The Name of the Father permits the child, in effect, to detach itself from the fusional relation with the mother, with imagination and with conflict. (p. 104)

As Ledoux (22) mentioned, several of the more orthodox contemporary French psychoanalysts, including Andre Green and Laplanche, have taken issue with Lacan because of his tendency to brush aside consideration of affect (so important to traditional Freudian theory) in his preoccupation with the internal representations of linguistical signs.

Critique and Discussion

In the preceding pages I have attempted to present the dynamic formulations of the various analytic schools with as little comment as possible on their merits or shortcomings, as reflected in the light of current knowledge. My hope has been to enable the reader to reevaluate the material, when seen in its historical context, in a relatively unbiased atmosphere. It is only natural that to us, a hundred years after Freud's visit to Charcot in 1885, many of the early analytic theories of schizophrenogenesis appear naive and out-moded—much as ours will, if our species and the term *schizophrenia* both survive, a century from now. With this in mind, we may proceed to a more critical examination of these dynamics and to an attempted updating and integration of what is most useful in all that we have reviewed.

Many of the formulations have continuing relevancy with respect to the content of the schizophrenic person's unusual turns of speech and thought; they also have considerable power as aides in rendering coherent the often arcane symbolism embedded in these mental productions. (This was visible in the Schreber case and, more recently, in the works of Sullivan, Arieti, and Searles [33].) Perhaps their greatest cogency lies in the matter of chro-nology; that is, in making sense of the timing at which breakdown occurs and in enhancing our ability to select out from the welter of possibilities just those intervening variables that are the true precipitants of psychotic decompensation.

But one wants to know the meaning of the alluring similarities between the schizophrenic person's thought and extreme reactions and the ideas and behavior of very small children. Is one in the realm of causation? Of cor-relation? Of coincidence? What is the validity of analytic theory regarding the conjectured early traumata or the points of fixation and regression con-sidered critical to the discussion of schizophrenia? Most pressing of all is the question of root cause of the schizophrenic illness— its "distal etiology," in the language of the geneticists. As a corollary to this, should schizophrenia be understood as a disease entity, or was Meyer (34) more correct when he labeled it a reaction-pattern, or Glover (27) when he spoke of psychosis as the mental accompaniment of regression, under stress, to a particular early phase in the continuum of development? It is precisely in these latter areas that psychoanalytic theory has been unconvincing; at times, misleading.

There are, of course, comparisons to be made between the primitive forms of self- and object representations in children (as outlined by Jacobson [35] and Kernberg [36]) and the abnormalities in self- and object represen-tations encountered in severely disturbed patients. The analogy is not com-plete, however; normal children, in particular, rarely exhibit confusion between reality and make-believe to a degree matching the boundary confusion of the (decompensated) schizophrenic individual. Other differences, where the psychologies of the child and the schizophrenic person do not overlap, have been enumerated by Sass (37) and discussed by Sandler (38), who said: "the capacity to *dis*identify, to impose boundaries is not lost in the adolescent, whereas in the schizophrenic it is" (p. 518). Nor is it necessary for the caretaking figures of childhood to have failed, actively or passively, during the phases deemed relevant to schizophrenia, for eventual schizophrenic breakdown to occur. Strict environmentalists can always introduce the argument that if one knew all the details of early interaction, the traumata would be exposed. This argument is sometimes marshalled in an effort to explain why one child with three or four siblings falls ill, where the rest remain healthy. Within this closed universe there is no rebuttal. Studies of identical twins reared apart (39), however, have demonstrated the eerie similarity not only in overall development, but in the small details of everyday life—of two persons unknown to each other, reared in different homes, alike only in a common genome. Evidence from this source and from others I have reviewed earlier in my "discussion" of genetic influences in the psychoses (40) compel one to acknowledge the primacy of heredofamilial and constitutional factors in the etiology of schizophrenia. Psychodynamic formulations should be reappraised in conformity with these findings, as embodying correlational, but not primary causal, significance in the domain of schizophrenia. Regarding secondary causal implications, the evidence is contradictory. Cross-fostering studies (41) show a risk of developing schizophrenia in children adopted-away from a schizophrenic parent that is comparable to the risk in children born to and reared by a schizophrenic parent. The *paternal* half-siblings (who have not shared the same womb or birth canal) have been shown to succumb as often to schizophrenia as the maternal half-siblings of schizophrenic persons (42).

From this material it would appear that "schizophrenogenic" environments provide neither necessary nor sufficient causes for the clinical stigmata of schizophrenic breakdown (43). On the other side, genetic factors may not be sufficient (or else the incidence of schizophrenia in the co-twins of a schizophrenic monozygotic twin would be 100% instead of the observed 40%). Certain environmental stressors may be at least contributory if not to the innate cognitive defects of schizophrenia, at least to the time of breakdown and to the rate of relapse. Dohrenwend (44) singled out marriage, birth of a first child, loss of a job, and death of a loved one as being strategic "proximal" phenomena "through which stress is transmitted to individuals" (p. 387). Goldstein and Jones (45) found that parental communicational deviance was correlated with extended schizophrenia-spectrum disorders in early adulthood; Sturgeon et al. (46) noted a heightened rate of recidivism in schizophrenic persons exposed to (negative) expressed emotion in their families. At the extremes of the otherwise interacting constitutional and environmental factors, we may see a "good-enough" mother (as in Winnicott's [25] term) fail to shield the child genetically at ultra-high risk from developing schizophrenia, or, we may see a deplorable mother (i.e., "bad enough," one might think, to engender serious psycho-pathology) rear an invulnerable child without any serious psychological consequences to the latter (47). Meissner (48) made a similar point: "There is no substantial evidence to suggest . . . that individuals who lack the ge-netic diathesis . . . would develop (schizophrenia), however pathogenic (the environment)" (p. 628).

If psychoanalytic dynamics are unsatisfactory in explaining the origins of schizophrenia, they do highlight in a cogent manner its phenomenology. This is especially so if we narrow the focus (as we should) to schizophrenia as defined by contemporary, strict criteria: the older and broader definitions of Bleuler (15)—or of Winnicott (25), who spoke of autism, childhood schizophrenia, and adult schizophrenia in the same breath—include too many "false-positives" (manic-depression, in particular) to permit satisfac-tory correlations between dynamics and clinical phenomena. Insufficient attention was paid by *any* of the analytic groups (especially the Sullivanians and the Kleinians) to the Kraepelinian subtypes, as though dynamics ap-plicable to one form of the illness held equally well for other forms. Fur-thermore, much evidence (49) has come to light suggesting that the Kraepelinian schema is itself too broad: what has been traditionally blended together as "paranoid schizophrenia" may represent the coexistence, in extreme form, of two separate processes, one conducing to paranoid states and the other to schizophrenia.

What Freudian theoreticians had to say about the primitive orality of the schizophrenic person, about the tendency to regress to an early "oral" stage, or about the defectiveness of the ego and harshness of the superego seem unexceptionable—as long as one understands these abnormalities as epi-phenomena of the schizophrenic constitution rather than as causes of the eventual psychosis. The same can be said for the fused self- and object representations Jacobson (35) posited as characteristic of the schizophrenic person's inner world. The descriptions of splitting, projective identification, and other primitive defenses (33, 36, 50) appear to capture accurately what the schizophrenic person *does*, although not how the individual got to be the way he or she is. The primitive defenses appear, in fact, to be mani-festations of (innate) defect, later pressed into service as (rather shaky and inadequate) "defenses." The primary-process or paleologic language, de-scribed by Freud (29), Arieti (51), and the French school (especially Lacan [28]), should likewise be viewed as an epiphenomenon, not a cause, of the schizophrenic condition. One has the impression that the "causal factor" singled out as crucial was often the factor reflecting a special interest on the part of the theoretician: for example, language (Arieti [51], Lacan [28]), superego (Jacobson [35]), ego (Eissler [52]), and family schism (Lidz et al. [53]). All these factors are important and interconnected: the problem is not which is *the* factor, but how are the factors related and what are their relative contributions in any given case.

Before we look at these interrelationships and try to assess the place of the various factors in the hierarchy of etiology, it will be useful to shift our attention briefly to some data from neurophysiology that bear on the matter of primary cause. Considerable evidence has accumulated to the effect that core schizophrenic patients exhibit abnormalities in a number of cerebral functions mediated most efficiently (although not exclusively) by the dominant hemisphere (54, 55). The subject has been reviewed extensively by Gruzelier (56, 57), who mentioned abnormalities of hippocampal function, subserving semantic encoding, and, as likely sites of dysfunction, the posterior temporoparietolimbic regions of the left hemisphere and (when dysfunction is severe) the left frontal region (57). Concomitant limitations in *non*dominant hemisphere function may contribute to the characteristic thought disorder of schizophrenic patients. Again, schizophrenic patients may need to be distinguished from paranoid patients: whereas *non*paranoid schizophrenic persons appear to be right- (or nondominant) hemisphere processors, paranoid persons are left-hemisphere processors (49). These regions of the brain in particular appear to serve, as best we can surmise, as the "black box" in which the genotypic aberrations that underlie schizophrenia (and constitute its most distal etiology) are translated into the phenotypic peculiarities we recognize at the clinical level. According to the model I am proposing here, it is to neurophysiologic abnormalities that we must look for our primary cause (literally, the sine qua non) of schizophrenia—abnormalities (particularly of cognition, attention, and other "data-processing modalities) without which we will not encounter schizophrenic psychopathology. Apart from these preexisting central nervous system abnormalities and the vulnerabilities to which they give rise, a patient is not likely to tell us, for example, as did the young man with whom Arieti (58) once worked "I am growing my father's hair!"

Freudian and Kleinian psychodynamic models, in contrast, relate not to the distal etiology of schizophrenia, but to the manifestations of the original genetically induced vulnerability. The causal overtones of the language in which many of these formulations are written should be replaced by the more humble language of correlation and analogy. This need is felt most keenly in relation to Melanie Klein's work, in which schizophrenia is understood in purely psychological terms (as it were, the software) without, as Freeman et al. (59) mentioned, any reference to disturbances in the function of the mental apparatus (i.e., the hardware). Particularly in relation to schizophrenia, libido theory emerges not as the explanation, to which it aspired, but merely as the translation—of one language into a metalanguage at the same level of abstraction. This problem is visible, for instance, in Federn's (60) comment that (the schizophrenic patient's) ego weakness is caused by a "diminished cathexis." More properly, "ego weakness" is a label we affix to the situation where someone's difficulty in remaining deeply involved with others becomes noticeable. Something temporally anterior "causes" these otherwise parallel phenomena. In the case of "diminished cathexis," one causal factor might well be the kind of central hedonic dyscontrol postulated by Rado (2) that robs the schizophrenic individual of pleasure in close relationships.

Some psychodynamic interpretations, although less powerful indicators of cause than was once thought, merit our interest as providing a convenient isomorphism between psychological and neurophysiologic frames of reference. Fromm-Reichmann (9) understood the schizophrenic person as "swamped by unconscious material" (p. 2) that breaks through the barriers of dissociation (whereas neurotic and healthy people succeed in keeping this material dissociated). Her statement maps very closely onto the neurophysiologist's hypothesis concerning inappropriate cross-talk between hemispheres in schizophrenia; the neurologist's right-hemisphere visuospatial-oriented mode of "thinking" resembles the analyst's concepts of primary process and unconscious (61). Fromm-Reichmann's remark also presages contemporary emphasis on the *dis*organization of the "true" schizophrenic individual (i.e., the nonparanoid type) in contrast to the *hyper*organization encountered in the paranoid states (including the prognostically more favorable "paranoid" form of schizophrenia).

With the above points in mind, we are in a position to construct a more comprehensive model of schizophrenogenesis. Here, traditional psychodynamic formulations are integrated with the neurophysiologic data that must now be incorporated as a kind of inseparable companion to any such theory. The schema presented in Figure 9-1 is relevant to a typical schizophrenic decompensation of adolescence. The most distal etiologic factors depicted are the central nervous system defects responsible for hedonic dyscontrol and cognitive impairment; still more distal would be the genic abnormalities underlying these defects. As the latter begin to express themselves in clinical phenomena at various phases of development, the psychoanalytic concepts reviewed in this chapter find their utility. I have chosen concepts from whatever seemed most useful in the different schools of thought. The defects are reflected in the subsequent development of characteristic symptoms, which tend to erupt in the wake of certain key conflicts, such as the one posed in the illustration under the heading of "increased demands to achieve intimacy and generativity." This is the normal task of the adolescent and would be opposed in the pre-schizophrenic individual by inordinate fears of closeness. Defect thus antedates but is influenced by conflict (whereas in neurosis there is, for all intents and purposes, only conflict).

The defects themselves interact to amplify disturbances in relationships. The vulnerable young pre-schizophrenic person not only is hampered by a diminished capacity to experience keen pleasure in intimacy, but is (typically) also hampered by faulty mechanisms for "reading" the expressions

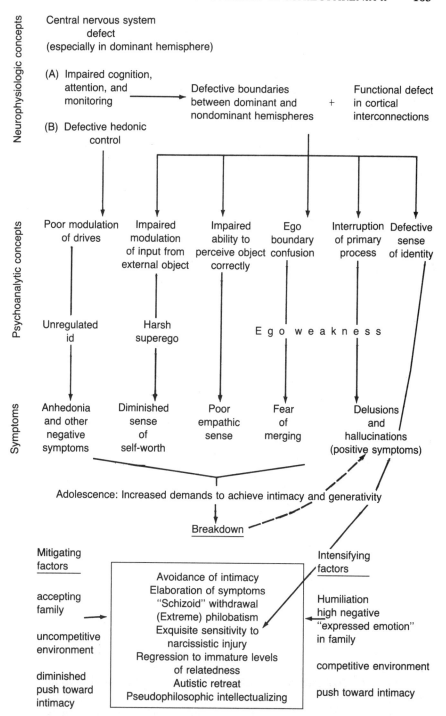

Figure 9-1. An integration of neurophysiologic and psychodynamic factors

and intentions of other people and by a tendency to say the wrong thing and react in an inappropriate manner that alienates other people. This misreading of others is perhaps best understood in terms of Magaro's (49) dichotomy; namely, that paranoid persons rely on conceptual processes without adequate constraint by perceptual data, whereas (nonparanoid) schizophrenic persons rely on perceptual data without adequate categorization from conceptual processes. The superiority of the latter in problem solving may underlie the often more favorable outcome of paranoid patients.

Worse still, the schizophrenic person's ego-boundary defect (62) is of a sort that predisposes to worry about "merging" with anyone he or she would get close to such that, beyond the limits of tolerance, a sense of one's own identity would be lost. The hormonal changes of adolescence, pressure from peers, and pressure from the family all conspire to overwhelm the individual's capacities, and thus breakdown occurs. The precipitant is often a taunt about one's *identity* (you're ugly, you're skinny, you're a "fag"), something a healthier person could shrug off, by virtue of the self-assuredness concerning self-worth, which the pre-schizophrenic individual generally lacks.

These events may be accompanied by the outbreak of the symptoms we customarily associate with schizophrenia. Whether the "positive" symptoms (e.g., hallucinations, delusions) or the "negative" symptoms (e.g., anhedonia, affect constriction, impoverishment of thought) predominate probably depends on the interplay of various constitutional factors. Evidence has been accumulating that the negative symptoms correlate with frontal lobe hypofunction (63). This "hypofrontality" may even be the expression of an abormally high rate of pruning of axonal connections in the frontal lobes of future schizophrenic persons (64). Since this process is well advanced in adolescent schizophrenic persons, Hoffman (64) speculated that schizophrenic breakdown, which tends to manifest itself in this age range, may actually have more to do with this neuroanatomical abnormality than with the psychological stresses of puberty.

At the clinical level we see, however, this may be a regression to simpler, more primitive states of the developing schizophrenic individual's own development—states that are reminiscent of, share some features of, but are not identical to, normal childhood. Gedo and Goldberg's (65) hierarchical model is relevant here.

Ideally, the model itself should be rendered "dynamic," as it cannot be on paper, in such a manner as to account for various combinations of influences, present at different strengths or levels of intensity. To take but one example, the homosexual conflict of the paranoid schizophrenic patient has been the object of considerable psychoanalytic interest since the Schreber (12) case. The contributory factors to this conflict are not always the same. In some patients who become manifestly psychotic, one will elicit the history of repeated humiliation by the same-sexed parent, to which Frosch (66) drew attention. (In Figure 9-1, I have listed such humiliation among the intensifying factors, heightening the likelihood of psychosis.) But there are other pre-schizophrenic individuals who become psychotic (e.g., in late adolescence), even within the context of a warm and accepting family. Perhaps the genetic loading has been especially severe (67). In any event, the mere age-related push toward intimacy may suffice as the precipitant—of a florid delusional system involving homosexual symbolism. In this situation, the psychodynamic may not be attraction to a male so much as dread of the female—seen as desirable in her own right, but terrifying, as the symbol of *every other* task about which the schizophrenic individual feels incompetent. For the "schizotype" (2), it is disconcerting enough (because of problems in empathy) just to become close to another person. But heterosexuality carries with it the possibilities—threats, as they would be experienced by the schizotype—of marriage and children, whose maintenance obligates one to work consistently and successfully. The schizotype requires no abuse from his family to become panicky at the prospect of performing in all these areas. He senses he will fail; if he is a particularly vulnerable schizotype, he will escape this failure by withdrawal and psychosis. He will tend to remain withdrawn and in poor emotional contact with others, until, after midlife, he reaches an age when life no longer expects him to perform well in those sectors of life where he is especially handicapped. Meantime, the schizophrenic person may, thanks to his concrete way of thinking, "conclude" he is homosexual, because he notices himself backing away from closeness with the opposite sex. This form of overinclusive reasoning is particularly apt to occur in patients with strong paranoid trends. The reduction of frontal-lobe axonal connectivity of which Hoffman (64) spoke may underlie this tendency toward oversimplified, "paranoid" thinking. The tendency may develop, of course, even in schizophrenic persons whose fantasy life is exclusively heterosexual. From the standpoint of psychoeconomics, it is preferable to face humiliation only on the *one* front (of faulty gender identity) than on half a dozen fronts simultaneously (inability to resonate emotionally with a spouse, to work competently, to deal with one's children and so on).

The model I have outlined here will, it is hoped, put in better perspective the genesis and evolution of schizophrenic illness (whether of the "pure" type or commingled with the paranoid process). It is important to recognize that schizophrenia begins with constitutional defect. In all likelihood, we are actually dealing with genetic heterogeneity, implying that any one of several varieties of "defect" may give rise to clinical pictures close enough to our archetype of "schizophrenia" that we are comfortable calling all of them schizophrenia at the gross clinical level. Sometimes the illness may be set in motion even without the adverse patterns of family interaction invoked by the more narrowly conceived dynamic formulations of the past. Although she may make the hospital course stormier and the recovery more precarious in one of her vulnerable children, the "double-binding" mother does not "make" one schizophrenic.

Some of the confusion in earlier psychodynamic schemata relative to schizophrenia was the inevitable consequence of confusion in the realm of diagnosis. Statements concerning regression to early oral stages, to fusion of self- and object images may be more valid for psychosis of any form than for schizophrenia per se. Schizophrenic individuals diagnosed as such in Bleuler's time who went on to exhibit a favorable outcome often turned out to have manic-depression when rediagnosed by contemporary criteria (68). If the schizophrenic process and the paranoid process are orthogonal, and neurophysiologically distinguishable (49), then these concepts should be addressed separately in any attempts to analyze their evolution from a dynamic perspective. As we have noted, this has to some extent already been attempted. The British school, for example, tends to assign the regression in schizophrenia to an earlier stage than that in paranoia; the defensive patterns of the paranoid person (who relies on projection and projective identification) and the schizophrenic person also appear dissimilar. Paranoid psychoses often have a later onset and show more advanced development cognitively and emotionally (49) than nonparanoid schizophrenia. These differences become less visible in the combined state: paranoid schizophrenia. Psychodynamic theories derived from experience with one diagnostic subgroup may not be applicable to other subgroups within the broad domain of functional psychosis. Some of the literature on dynamics of schizophrenia grew out of the hypotheses set forth in the Schreber (12) case, yet Schreber, reexamined in the light of current nosology, may represent a predominantly paranoid illness that passed transitorily (and relatively late) through a "paranoid schizophrenic" episode—without his originally having had a core (and nonparanoid) schizophrenia. Similarly, the Wolf-Man (29) may have been borderline with respect to manic-depressive illness rather than to a schizophrenic illness. Psychodynamic theory ought to be modified not only to account for the different phases of early development to which nonparanoid, in contrast to paranoid, schizophrenic patients appear to have regressed (some authors have already adjusted for this, intuitively), but greater emphasis should be placed on the fundamental difference between the normal fusion of self and object in the normal infant and the disorganization and eccentricity of the internalization process that is peculiar to the schizophrenic individual. Regression in schizophrenia is not to a normal past stage but to an abnormal primitive state only roughly comparable to certain stages of normal development.

Psychodynamics represents inferences a step removed from the clinical observation on which they are based. The many theories reviewed here and the abstract nature of the material may give the reader the impression that ours has been an academic pursuit. It has not. There is an equilibrium between theory and therapy, even where the connections between the one and the other seem tenuous. Early Freudian dynamics of schizophrenia were such as to spur false hopes (not in Freud, to be sure, but in his followers) of its curability. The theory of the schizophrenogenic mother laid a heavy burden of guilt on a generation of mothers, only a few of whom were blameworthy—and then not of causing but of aggravating a schizophrenic condition. It is time now for psychoanalysis to refine further the psychodynamic model Freud fashioned a century ago in his integrated psychobiological view of psychosis. There is a need to assimilate the newest data from the neurophysiologic and psychogenetic sectors. New psychodynamic formulations should rely insofar as possible on what is testable rather than on what is speculative, should address themselves to strict definitions both of schizophrenia and of paranoia, and should be woven together out of the best material from all the various schools of thought. This is the necessary first step in fashioning a more humane, more effective, and more realistic treatment for our most challenging group of patients.

References

1. Kety SS, Rosenthal D, Wender PH, et al: Mental illness in the biological and adoptive families of adopted schizophrenics, in Transmission of Schizophrenia. Edited by Rosenthal D, Kety S. Oxford, Pergamon, 1968, pp 345–362
2. Rado S: Psychoanalysis of Behavior: Collected Papers. New York, Grune & Stratton, 1956
3. American Psychiatric Association: Diagnostic and Statistical Manual of Mental Disorders, 3rd Edition. Washington, DC, American Psychiatric Association, 1980
4. Fairbairn WRD: An Object-Relations Theory of the Personality. New York, Basic Books, 1952
5. Bellak L, Loeb L: Psychoanalytic, psychotherapeutic and generally psychodynamic studies, in The Schizophrenic Syndrome. New York, Grune & Stratton, 1969, pp 343–377
6. McGhie A: Psychological studies of schizophrenia. Br J Med Psychol 39:281–288, 1966
7. Freeman T: Nosography and theory of the schizophrenias. Int J Psychoanal 66:237–243, 1985
8. Hill LB: Psychotherapeutic Intervention in Schizophrenia. Chicago, IL, University of Chicago Press, 1955, pp 108–109
9. Fromm-Reichmann F: Basic problems in the psychotherapy of schizophrenia. Psychiatry 21:1–6, 1958
10. Segal H: Psychoanalytical approach to the treatment of schizophrenia, in Studies of Schizophrenia. Br J Psychiatry, Special Publication No. 10. Edited by Lader MH. Ashford, Kent, Headley Brothers, 1975, pp 94–97
11. Will O: Psychotherapeutics and the schizophrenic reaction. J Nerv Ment Dis 126:109–140, 1958
12. Grotstein JS: The Schreber Case revisited: schizophrenia as a disorder of self-regulation and of interactional regulation. Yale J Biol Med 58:299–314, 1985
13. Azima H: Object relations therapy of schizophrenic states, in Psychotherapy of Schizophrenic and Manic Depressive States. Edited by Azima H, Glueck B, Jr. Washington, DC, American Psychiatric Association, 1963
14. Sechèhaye M: Symbolic Realization. New York, Grune & Stratton, 1956

15. Bleuler E: Dementia Praecox, oder die Gruppe der Schizophrenien. Leipzig, Deuticke, 1911
16. Kretschmer E: Korperbau und Charakter. Berlin, Springer Verlag, 1922
17. McClelland JL. Rumelhart DE: Parallel Distributed Processing. Cambridge, MA, MIT Press, 1986
18. Freud S: Project for a scientific psychology (1895), in The Standard Edition of the Complete Psychological Works of Sigmund Freud, Vol 1. Translated and edited by Strachey J. London, Hogarth Press, 1957, pp 295–343
19. Wiener N: Cybernetics. New York, John Wiley, 1948
20. Bergeret J: Abrégé de Psychologie Pathologique. Paris, Masson, 1975
21. Chasseguet-Smirgel J: The Ego Ideal. Translated by Barrows P. New York, WW Norton, 1984
22. Ledoux MH: Conceptions Psychoanalytiques de la Psychose Infantile. Paris, Presses Universitaires, 1984
23. Stone MH (with Albert H, Forrest D, Arieti S): Treating Schizophrenic Patients. New York, McGraw-Hill, 1983
24. Widlöcher D: Etude psychologique des etats prepsychotiques. Rev de Neuropsychiatrie Infantile, 21:735–744, 1973
25. Winnicott DW: The Maturational Processes and the Facilitating Environment. New York, International Universities Press, 1965
26. Klein M: Love, Guilt and Reparation and other works 1921–1945. New York, Dell, 1975
27. Glover E: A psychoanalytic approach to the classification of mental disorders. Journal of Mental Science 78:819–842, 1932
28. Lacan J: De la Psychose Paranoiaque dans ses Rapports avec la Personnalite (1932). Paris, Editions du Seu, 1975
29. Freud S: From the history of an infantile neurosis in The Standard Edition of the Complete Psychological Works of Sigmund Freud, Vol 17. Translated and edited by Strachey J. London, Hogarth Press, 1957, pp 7–122
30. Bär E: Understanding Lacan. Psychoanalysis and Contemporary Science 3:473–544, 1974
31. Muller JP, Richardson WJ: Lacan and Language. New York, International Universities Press, 1982
32. Lacan J: Ecrits: A Selection. New York, WW Norton, 1977
33. Searles HF: Collected Papers on Schizophrenia. New York, International Universities Press, 1965
34. Meyer A: The Collected Papers, Vol 3. Baltimore, MD, Johns Hopkins University Press, 1951, pp 302–304
35. Jacobson E: The Self and the Object World. New York, International Universities Press, 1964
36. Kernberg OF: Borderline Conditions and Pathological Narcissism. Northvale, NJ, Jason Aronson, 1975
37. Sass LA: Time, space and symbol. Psychoanalysis and Contemporary Thought 8:45–85, 1985
38. Sandler J (with Freud A): The Analysis of Defense: The Ego and the Mechanisms of Defense Revisited. New York, International Universities Press, 1985
39. Juel-Nielsen N: Individual and Environment: Monozygotic Twins Reared Apart. New York, International Universities Press, 1980

40. Stone MH: The Borderline Syndromes. New York, McGraw-Hill, 1980
41. Wender PH, Rosenthal D, Kety SS, et al: Cross-fostering: a research strategy for clarifying the role of genetic and experiential factors in the etiology of schizophrenia. Arch Gen Psychiatry 30:121–128, 1974
42. Kety SS, Rosenthal D, Wender PH, et al: Mental illness in the biological and adoptive families of adopted individuals who have become schizophrenic, in Genetic Research in Psychiatry. Edited by Fieve RR, Rosenthal D, Brill H. Baltimore, MD, Johns Hopkins University Press, 1975, pp 147–165
43. Gottesman II, Shields J: Schizophrenia: The Epigenetic Puzzle. Cambridge, Cambridge University Press, 1982
44. Dohrenwend BP: Sociocultural and sociopsychological factors in the genesis of mental disorders. J Health Soc Behav 16:365–392, 1975
45. Goldstein MJ, Jones JE: Adolescent and familial precursors of borderline and schizophrenic conditions, in Borderline Personality Disorders. Edited by Hartocollis P. New York, International Universities Press, 1977, pp 213–229
46. Sturgeon D, Turpin G, Kuipers L, et al: Psychophysiological responses of schizophrenic patients to high and low expressed emotion relatives: a follow-up study. Br J Psychiatry 145:62–69, 1984
47. Anthony EJ: The developmental precursors of schizophrenia, in Transmission of Schizophrenia. Edited by Rosenthal D, Kety SS. Oxford, Pergamon, 1968, pp 293–316
48. Meissner WW: The schizophrenic and paranoid process. Schizophr Bull 7:611–631, 1981
49. Magaro PA: The paranoid and the schizophrenic: the case for distinct cognitive style. Schizophr Bull 7:632–661, 1981
50. Rosenfeld H: Notes on the psychopathology of confusional states in chronic schizophrenia. Int J Psychoanal 31:132–137, 1950
51. Arieti S: The Interpretation of Schizophrenia, 2nd Edition. New York, Basic Books, 1974
52. Eissler K: Remarks on the psychoanalysis of schizophrenia. Int J Psychoanal 32:139–156, 1951
53. Lidz T, Fleck S, Cornelison A: Schizophrenia and the Family. New York, International Universities Press, 1965
54. Gur RE: Left hemisphere dysfunction and left hemisphere overactivation in schizophrenia. J Abnorm Psychol 87:226–238, 1978
55. Flor-Henry P, Yeudall LT: Neuropsychological investigation of schizophrenia and manic-depressive psychoses, in Hemisphere Asymmetries of Function in Psychopathology. Edited by Gruzelier JH, Flor-Henry P. Amsterdam, Elsevier, 1979, pp 341–362
56. Gruzelier J: Hemispheric imbalances masquerading as paranoid and non-paranoid syndromes? Schizophr Bull 7:662–673, 1981
57. Gruzelier JH: A critical assessment and integration of lateral asymmetries in schizophrenia, in Hemisyndromes. Edited by Myslobodsky MS. New York, Academic, 1983
58. Arieti S: The concept of schizophrenia, in The Schizophrenic Reactions. Edited by Cancro R. New York, Brunner/Mazel, 1970, pp 25–40
59. Freeman T, Cameron JL, McGhie A: Chronic Schizophrenia. New York, International Universities Press, 1958

60. Federn P: Ego Psychology and the Psychoses. London, Imago, 1953
61. Stone MH: Dreams, free-association and the non-dominant hemisphere. J Am Acad Psychoanal 5:255–284, 1977
62. Tausk V: On the origin of the influencing machine in schizophrenia (1919). Psychoanal Q 2:519–556, 1933
63. Weinberger DR, Berman KF, Zec RF: Physiological dysfunction of the dorsolateral prefrontal cortex in schizophrenia, I: regional cerebral blood flow evidence. Arch Gen Psychiatry 43:114–124, 1986
64. Hoffman R: Computer simulations of neural information processing and the schizophrenia-mania dichotomy. Arch Gen Psychiatry 44:178–188, 1987
65. Gedo JE, Goldberg A: Models of the Mind: A Psychoanalytic Theory. Chicago, IL, University of Chicago Press, 1973
66. Frosch J: The Psychotic Process. New York, International Universities Press, 1983
67. Matthysse SW, Kidd K: Estimating the genetic contribution to schizophrenia. Am J Psychiatry 133:185–191, 1976
68. Vaillant GE: Manic-depressive heredity and remission in schizophrenia. Br J Psychiatry 109:746–749, 1963

CHAPTER TEN

Family Psychopathology and Schizophrenia

John G. Howells, M.D.

In the last three decades the family approach movement in psychiatry has gathered momentum and has developed into three distinct areas: family psychiatry, family therapy, and family and schizophrenia. These three approaches came together for the first time at a symposium on the family at the Third World Congress of Psychiatry at Montreal in 1961.

The original definition of family psychiatry is found in the first book devoted to it (1), based on the work at the Institute of Family Psychiatry from 1949 to 1959. It reads as follows:

Family psychiatry is a clinical approach by which a child, an adolescent or an adult, referred from a family because of emotional disorder, is regarded as an indication of family psychopathology. This concept leads to the employment of procedures for investigating the psychodynamics of the whole family in its social and cultural setting and to offering treatment on a family basis. In family psychiatry, a family is not regarded merely as a background to be modified to help the presenting patient alone. Family psychiatry accepts the family itself as the patient, the presenting member being viewed as a sign of family psychopathology. The family itself is the therapeutic target. (p. 4)

In family therapy, the emphasis is on psychotherapy in a family setting. Family therapy had its origins in the work of the late Nathan Ackerman in New York in the 1930s, whose first paper, "The Unity of the Family" (2), was published in 1938 in a pediatric, rather than a psychiatric, journal.

Ackerman and Kempster (3) envisioned family therapy as an approach to the link between disorders of family living and the disorders of individual members of the family. Their technique called for dynamically oriented therapeutic interviews of the family, based on the assumption that a person's emotional difficulties stemmed from disturbances in the overall interaction of all the family members. The family was the setting for treatment of this person; the individual was the therapeutic target.

The third element in the above definitions, family dynamics and schizophrenia, is considered in this chapter, which will focus attention on the four most important schools of thought. These schools initiated study of this field, and they still influence opinion today. A more detailed account is given elsewhere (4, 5).

Problem of Definition

Schizophrenia constitutes a long-recognized disorder with the most fascinating complex of symptoms in the whole of medicine. Yet international authorities do not agree about its definition, its incidence, or its etiology.

That there is no agreement about its definition constitutes one of the greatest barriers to the formulation of investigations on it and to the comparison of research work going on in different countries—as the work on family psychopathology and schizophrenia will also demonstrate. Traditional European psychiatry bases its definition on the descriptive work of the German psychiatrists (6, 7); to them the syndrome manifests a complex of symptoms that makes it unmistakable in most instances. In some European centers, usually with a dynamic orientation, and in the United States, the definition is widened to include many patients who would not conform to the strict criteria of the German psychiatrists. In an attempt to bring order into definition, the Norwegian psychiatrist Langfeldt (8) proposes a classification of psychoses based on two types: process and nonprocess psychoses. Process psychosis covers the organic endogenous type; nonprocess psychosis covers the remainder. Stephens and Astrup (9, 10) have shown that process psychosis is accompanied by a poor prognosis. It would seem that nonprocess psychosis includes the graver types of emotional illness (neurosis) manifesting well-marked abnormal behavior. Abnormal behavior can arise from a number of causes: toxic, endocrinal, emotional, and schizophrenic. In some quarters, unfortunately, abnormal behavior is always assumed to be due to schizophrenic processes, despite the fact that some of the most alarming behavior is seen in agitated emotional states. Schizophrenia and emotional illness should not be confused, otherwise the definition of schizophrenia will be greatly widened and embrace nonschizophrenic abnormal behavior. Sometimes symptomatology overlaps; for example, that dyspnea of anemia overlaps with dyspnea of cancer of the chest does not make anemia and cancer of the chest into two identical conditions. Similarly, some of the symptomatology of severe emotional states (e.g., withdrawal) overlaps with the symptoms of schizophrenia, but this does not make schizophrenia and emotional illness into identical conditions.

Differing definitions of schizophrenia constitute one of the reasons for the disparities in estimations of the incidence of the condition. In Europe, where a definition akin to the process definition of Langfeldt (8) is employed, the condition is uncommon. For example, English studies (11–13) point to the low incidence of schizophrenia. In some countries, the condition is diagnosed much more frequently than this.

Definitions of the condition and thus more accurate studies of incidence would gain from the isolation of the etiologic factor or factors in this condition. Many formulations are put forward: genetic, constitutional, endocrinal, neuropathologic, biochemical, toxic, and psychological. The latter has hitherto been confined to formulations based on individual psychopathology. It was natural that, with the increasing interest in the family, its psychopathology should be explored as a possible fundamental etiologic factor. However, work here may be frustrated for the same reasons as operate in other fields, and one of the most cogent is the failure to arrive at an agreed definition of the condition. Criteria employed in its definition should be clearly stated in every case.

Criteria for Judgment

Some common criteria for establishing the value of each school of thought must be enunciated at the start. The following parameters of judgment are used:

1. Is the condition under study indubitably schizophrenia?
2. Is the anomaly in family functioning definable by precise criteria?
3. Does the anomaly cause schizophrenia or is it only associated with it? In other words, is a definite link established between the anomaly and schizophrenia? When the anomaly is present, is schizophrenia produced? When the anomaly is removed, will the schizophrenia be ameliorated?
4. Is this anomaly always present in the family when one of its members is schizophrenic? A representative sample of schizophrenic persons must be studied.
5. Is this anomaly present in the families of schizophrenic persons by chance? Controlled studies must be used to match groups of healthy patients, neurotic patients, and schizophrenic patients.
6. Does the hypothesis satisfy a characteristic feature of the illness: its onset in adolescence?

A striking feature of most of the literature on this subject is the lack of clear concepts. Ironically, it seems experts on communication frequently find it difficult to communicate. Intellectualization, based on a modicum of fact, flourishes. The danger of such vagueness is that it may be interpreted as a cloak for ignorance and the formulations ignored. An even greater danger is that we may assume knowledge when there is none, and elevate the work to the status of conviction.

In putting forward the various viewpoints of the proponents, care has been exercised even to the employment of paraphrase when in doubt. The main studies here are those of Bowen, Wynne, Lidz, and the Palo Alto group.

Bowen

Bowen's (14) view is that the schizophrenic psychosis of a patient is a symptom manifesting an acute process involving a triad of the family. The family unit is regarded as a single organism, and the patient is seen as that part of the family organism through which the overt symptoms of psychosis are expressed. The initial focus of the study was on the mother-patient relationship, and the hypothesis was later extended to regard the psychosis in the patient as a symptom of the total family problem. This coincided with developing "family psychotherapy" as a new plan of treatment.

Bowen has come to regard schizophrenia as a process that requires three or more generations to develop. A constant finding in his families was a marked emotional distance between the parents. Bowen referred to this as "emotional divorce." Both parents are equally immature. One denies the immaturity and functions with a facade of overadequacy, whereas the other accentuates the immaturity and functions with a facade of inadequacy. There are some constantly recurring situations that accompany the overadequate-inadequate reciprocity, among which is the domination-submission issue. On personal issues, especially those requiring decisions that affect both parents, the one who makes the decision becomes the overadequate one and the other becomes the inadequate one.

One of the outstanding characteristics of the family is the inability of the parents to make decisions. For the mother, pregnancy becomes a constant frustration between "promise of fulfillment" and a "threat that it could not be true." A significant shift in the husband-wife relationship begins when the wife first knows that she is pregnant. At this point, she becomes more emotionally invested in the unborn child than in her husband.

The mother-child relationship become the most active and intense relationship in the family. The term *intense* describes an ambivalent relationship in which the thoughts of both, whether positive or negative, are largely invested in each other. The mother makes two main demands on the patient, the more forcible of which is the emotional demand that the patient remain helpless. This is conveyed in subtle, forceful ways that are out of conscious awareness. The other is the overt, verbalized, "hammered home" demand that the patient become a gifted and mature person. Bowen described two levels of process between the mother and the patient. Much of the emotional demand that the patient remain a child is conveyed on an action level and out of conscious awareness of either mother or patient. The verbal level is usually a direct contradiction to the action level. In this reciprocal functioning, Bowen sees similarities between it, Wynne's "pseudomutuality," and Jackson's "complementarity."

The subject of the mother's concern about the patient and the focus of her "picking on" the patient are the same as her own feelings of inadequacy about herself. The term *projection* refers to the all-pervasive mechanism in the mother-child relationship. According to Bowen, the mother can function more adequately by ascribing to her child certain aspects of herself, which the child accepts. This is of crucial importance in the area of the mother's immaturity. The mother then "mothers" in the child the helplessness, which is her own projected feeling, with her adequate self. Thus a situation that begins as a feeling in the mother becomes a reality in the child. The projection occurs also on the levels of physical illness, a mechanism in which the soma of one person reciprocates with the psyche of another person and an anxiety in one person becomes a physical illness in another. The somatic reciprocation often includes definite physical pathology.

The child, Bowen believes, is involved in the same two levels of process as the mother, except that the mother actively initiates her emotional and verbal demands, and the child is more involved in responding to the mother's demands than in initiating his or her own. In this process, Bowen can see similarity with Bateson's "double-bind" hypothesis. The response of the patient to the mother's demands varies with the degree of functional helplessness of the patient and the functional strength of the mother. Bowen leans strongly to the belief that the essential process is confined to the father-mother-patient triad, rather than to the whole family.

When the child's self is devoted to "being for the mother," Bowen holds, the child loses the capacity of "being for himself." Bowen stressed the function of "being helpless," rather then the fixed "is helpless" viewpoint. The process in which the child begins to "be for the mother" results in an arrest in the child's psychological growth.

The rapid growth of the child at adolescence interferes with the functioning equilibrium of the interdependent triad. There is an increasing anxiety in all three members, and the growth process repeatedly upsets the equilibrium while the emotional process attempts to restore it. Conscious verbal expressions demand that the child be more grown up. The course from adolescence to acute psychosis is one in which the child changes from a helpless child to a poorly functioning adult to a helpless patient. Once free of the mother, the child faces outside relationships without a self of his or her own. The psychosis represents an unsuccessful attempt to adapt the severe psychological impairment to the demands of adult functioning. It represents a disruption of the symbiotic attachment to the mother and a collapse of the long-term interdependent father-mother-patient triad.

The patient need not develop a psychosis. According to Bowen, unresolved, symbiotic attachments to the mother vary from the very mild to the very intense, the mild one causes little impairment, and schizophrenic psychosis develops among those with the most intense unresolved attachment. The psychotic collapse is seen as a failed effort at resolution.

Bowen's work also led to formulations about the therapy of schizophrenic patients. It could also be seen that when the father was encouraged to be less inadequate and to be a husband in a fuller sense, the emotional divorce disappeared and the patient lost the symbiotic relationship with the mother. The closer emotionally the parents were to one another, the greater the patient's improvement.

The work just outlined will be briefly discussed in the light of the six criteria put forward in the introduction.

1. A precise definition of schizophrenia, which would win universal acceptance, is not found in the work.
2. The anomaly in family functioning is clearly expressed, but it is far from being a simple or discrete concept.
3. A link between the anomaly and schizophrenia is not too clearly established. Indeed, the anomaly need not cause schizophrenia; it is a matter of degree of anomaly. There are no experiments on the artificial production of the anomaly and thus of schizophrenia. It is claimed, however, that attenuating the anomaly by treatment aimed at increasing the father's participation may improve the patient.
4. It is not known whether the sample was representative of all schizophrenic persons. The pattern seemed consistent for the group studied, however.
5. It is not known if the anomaly is present by chance alone, because no control groups were employed and studied.
6. An explanation is offered for the age of onset in adolescence: the unsuccessful attempt by the patient to adapt his or her severe psychological impairment to the demands of adult functioning.

Wynne

Wynne and his colleagues (15–21) concentrated mainly on schizophrenic illness in which the onset of psychosis occurred acutely in late adolescence or early adulthood. They considered that the universal necessity for dealing with both the problems of relation and identity leads to three main solutions: mutuality, nonmutuality, and pseudomutuality.

Each person brings to the relations of genuine mutuality a sense of his or her own meaningful, positively valued identity. Out of the experience of participation together, mutual recognition of identity develops, including a growing recognition of each other's potentialities and capacities.

Many interpersonal relations are characterized by nonmutuality. The interchange of customer and salesclerk, for example, does not ordinarily involve, beyond the purchase of merchandise, a strong investment in excluding noncomplementarity or in exploring what the relationship has to offer to either person.

Pseudomutuality is a miscarried solution of widespread occurrence. This kind of relatedness, in an especially intense and enduring form, contributes significantly to the family experience of people who later—if other factors are also present—develop acute schizophrenic episodes. In pseudomutuality, emotional investment is directed more toward maintaining the sense of reciprocal fulfillment of expectations than toward accurately perceiving changing expectations. The relation that persists cannot be given up, except under very dire or special circumstances, nor be allowed to develop or expand. Thus the pseudomutual relation involves a characteristic dilemma. Divergence is perceived as leading to disruption of the relation, and therefore must be avoided; however, if divergence is avoided, growth of the relation is impossible.

Wynne and his colleagues believed that within the families of individuals who later developed acute schizophrenic episodes, those relations that are openly acknowledged as acceptable have a quality of intense and enduring pseudomutuality. In these families, the predominant prepsychotic picture is that of a fixed organization with a limited number of engulfing roles. Such a family role structure may already be forming in the fantasy life of the parents before the birth of the child, who sometimes is expected to fill some kind of void in the parents' lives. This view holds that noncomplementarity has a more intense and enduring threat in the families of schizophrenic persons than it has in other families in which pseudomutuality may also appear. It also holds that, in the families of potential schizophrenic persons, the intensity and duration of pseudomutuality has led to the development of a particular variety of shared family mechanisms by which deviations from the family role structure are excluded from recognition or are delusionally reinterpreted. The individual family member is not allowed to differentiate his or her personal identity either within or outside the family role structure.

Normally, shared cultural mechanisms and codes facilitate the selection of those aspects of communication to which attention should be paid. In contrast, in schizophrenic relations, the shared mechanisms facilitate a failure in the selection of meaning. It is not simply that divergence is kept out of awareness, but rather that the discriminative perception of those events that might specifically constitute divergence is aborted and blurred.

Pseudomutuality must be maintained at all costs. This leads to the maintenance of stereotyped roles in the families of schizophrenic persons. These roles constrict identity development and contribute to serious crises, including psychosis (16).

According to Wynne and his colleagues, the potential schizophrenic person develops considerable skill and an immense positive investment in fulfilling family complementarity and in saving the family (as well as him- or herself) from the panic of disillusion. However, as the individual approaches chronological adulthood, with the shift or loss of family figures and exposure to new outside relations more seductive or coercive than earlier ones, there comes a time when the family identity can no longer be superimposed on his or her ego identity. Acute schizophrenic panic or disorganization seems to represent an identity crisis in the face of overwhelming guilt and anxiety attendant on moving out of a particular kind of family role structure. Later, pseudomutuality is reestablished, in a chronic state, at a greater psychological distance from the family members, with an increasing guilt and anxiety over subsequent moves toward differentiation, and with heightened autism, loneliness, and emptiness of experience. The psychotic episode as a whole represents a miscarried attempt at attaining individuality. The person succeeds in attaining independence in some ways, but only by withdrawal. In addition, the overt psychosis may have a covert function of giving expression to the family's collective, although disassociated, desires for individuality.

Wynne and his colleagues believed the fragmentation of experience, the identity diffusion, the disturbed modes of perception and communication, and certain other characteristics of the acute reactive schizophrenic personality structure are derived to a significant extent by processes of internalization from characteristics of the family social organization. Thus they have gone on to study the links between family patterns of thought disorder in schizophrenia. They believed that it was possible to differentiate individual forms of thinking and to predict the form of thinking that would develop from the patterns of perceiving, relating, and communicating within the family (17, 18, 20, 21).

Comments on the above work in the light of the six criteria are as follows:

1. No clear definition of schizophrenia emerges.
2. The anomaly in family functioning is less clearly defined than in Bowen's work. The anomaly is diffuse if not separated into a number of unlinked parts. Aspects of it show similarities to the views of Bowen and the Palo Alto group.
3. The direct link between the anomaly and schizophrenia is not clear. There are no experiments in producing the family anomaly and, hence, schizophrenia. The results of family therapy are not precisely stated. From the form of family functioning, however, it is claimed that it is possible to predict the type of schizophrenia.
4. Varieties of the anomaly, it is maintained, are always found in the families of schizophrenic persons, but it is not known whether the group studied is a representative sample of schizophrenic persons.
5. It is said that the parents, not the family, of schizophrenic children, schizophrenic adolescents, and neurotic children can be differentiated. But the method employed is indirect and imprecise—through the Thematic Apperception Test and Rorschach techniques. The findings would

be equally consistent with differing attitudes in parents in different groups of the emotionally ill.

6. An explanation, with similarity to Bowen's view, is offered for the emergence of schizophrenia in adolescence.

Lidz and His Colleagues

Lidz, Fleck, Cornelison, and their Yale colleagues have also been responsible for a number of important studies concerning anomalies in patterns of behavior in the families of schizophrenic persons (22–43). Lidz began his interest in the families of schizophrenic persons in 1949 (44). He studied the histories of 50 patients and found that in only 5 could the patient be considered to have been raised in a reasonably favorable home (i.e., containing two stable and compatible parents until the patient was 18 years old). The overwhelming majority were impeded by multiple deleterious influences, which were chronically present or frequently recurrent. The paternal influence, according to this gross evaluation, was harmful as frequently as the maternal. In 1952 Lidz commenced a series of investigations on the families of 17 patients (45), and Flecke issued a progress report in 1960 (46).

Some of the characteristic forms of family dysfunction related to schizophrenic manifestations that the workers observed were:

1. Failure to form a nuclear family, in that one or both parents remain primarily attached to one of his or her parents or siblings.
2. Family schisms due to parental strife and lack of role reciprocity.
3. Family skewing when one dyadic relationship within it dominates family life at the expense of the needs of other members.
4. A blurring of generation lines in the family, as when one parent competes with children in skewed families, when one parent establishes a special bond with a child, giving substance to the schizophrenic child's claim that he or she is more important to the parent than the spouse, and when continued erotization of a parent–child relationship occurs.
5. A pervasion of the entire family atmosphere with irrational, usually paranoid, ideation.
6. The persistence of conscious incestuous preoccupation and behavior with the group.
7. A sociocultural isolation of the family as a concomitant of the six preceding conditions.
8. A failure to educate toward and facilitate emancipation of the offspring from the family, a further consequence of the first five points.
9. The handicapping of a child's efforts to achieve sexual identity and maturity by the parents' uncertainty about their own sex roles.
10. The presentation to a child of prototypes for identification that are

irreconcilable in a necessary process of consolidating his or her own personality.

Lidz concluded that it is a tenable hypothesis that schizophrenia is a type of maladaption and malintegration due to deficiencies in acquired instrumental techniques in ego structuring, rather than the cause of some process that disrupts the integrative capacity of the brain.

Comments on the six criteria are as follows:

1. Here again, it is not clear that the 17 patients were in fact indubitably schizophrenic individuals.
2. The anomalies of schizophrenic families are several in number, although prominence is given to the child's receiving a confused grounding in linguistic meanings. Even the latter is a broad concept.
3. A clear link between the anomalies present in the family and schizophrenia is not established.
4. Not one anomaly, but one of a number of anomalies, are said always to be present in the families of schizophrenic individuals. The anomalies differ in male and female schizophrenic persons. It is not known if the sample of schizophrenic patients is representative of all schizophrenic individuals.
5. Controlled studies are not employed, and the possibility of the anomalies being present by chance is not excluded.
6. The hypothesis does not adequately explain the emergence of schizophrenia in adolescence.

The Palo Alto Group

In 1952 a group of workers commenced a 10-year research project at Palo Alto. From this work, one element—the "double-bind" hypothesis—has received a great deal of attention. The workers themselves, however, regard it as part of a general communicational approach to a wide range of human behavior, including schizophrenia (47–53). They are particularly concerned with the incongruity in communication. It may be useful to repeat here the definition of a double bind from the original paper on the project (47):

The necessary ingredients for a double-bind situation, as we see it, are:

1. Two or more persons. Of these, we designate one, for purposes of our definition, as the "victim." We do not assume that the double bind is inflicted by the mother alone, but that it may be done either by mother alone or by some combination of mother, father and/or siblings.
2. Repeated experience. We assume that the double bind is a recurrent theme in the experience of the victim. Our hypothesis does not invoke a single traumatic experience, but such repeated experience that the double-bind structure comes to be an habitual expectation.

3. A primary negative injunction. This may have either of two forms: (a) "do not do so and so, or I will punish you"; (b) "if you do not do so and so, I will punish you." Here we select a context of learning based on avoidance of punishment rather than a context of reward seeking. There is perhaps no formal reason for this selection. We assume that the punishment may be either the withdrawal of love or the expression of hate or anger—or most devastating—the kind of abandonment that results from the parent's expression of extreme helplessness.

4. A secondary injunction conflicting with the first at a more abstract level, and like the first enforced by punishments or signals which threaten survival. This secondary injunction is more difficult to describe than the primary for two reasons. First, the secondary injunction is commonly communicated to the child by nonverbal means. Posture, gesture, tone of voice, meaningful action, and the implications concealed in verbal comment may all be used to convey this more abstract message. Second, the secondary injunction may impinge upon any element of the primary prohibition. Verbalization of the secondary injunction may, therefore, include a wide variety of forms; for example, "Do not see this as punishment"; "Do not see me as the punishing agent"; "Do not submit to my prohibitions"; "Do not think of what you must not do"; "Do not question my love of which the primary prohibition is (or is not) an example"; and so on. Other examples become possible when the double bind is inflicted not by one individual but by two. For example, one parent may negate at a more abstract level the injunctions of the other.

5. A tertiary negative injunction prohibiting the victim from escaping from the field. In a formal sense, it is perhaps unnecessary to list this injunction as a separate item since the reinforcement at the other two levels involves a threat to survival, and if the double binds are imposed during infancy, escape is naturally impossible. However, it seems that in some cases the escape from the field is made impossible by certain devices which are not purely negative, e.g., capricious promises of love, and the like.

6. Finally, the complete set of ingredients is no longer necessary when the victim has learned to perceive his universe in double-bind patterns. Almost any part of a double-bind sequence may then be sufficient to precipitate panic or rage. The pattern of conflicting injunctions may even be taken over by hallucinatory voices.

The Palo Alto workers conceived the family situation of the schizophrenic individual as follows:

1. A child whose mother becomes anxious and withdrawn if the child responds to her as a loving mother. That is, the child's very existence has a special meaning to the mother, which arouses her anxiety and hostility when she is in danger of intimate contact with the child.

2. A mother to whom feelings of anxiety and hostility toward the child are not acceptable, and whose ways of denying them is to express overt loving behavior to persuade the child to respond to her as a loving mother and to withdraw from him if he does not. "Loving behavior" does not necessarily imply "affection"; it can, for example, be set in a framework of doing the proper thing, instilling "goodness," and the like.

3. The absence of anyone in the family, such as the strong and insightful father, who can intervene in the relationship between the mother and child and support the child in the face of the contradictions involved.

In this situation, the mother of a schizophrenic child will be simultaneously expressing two orders of message. If the mother begins to feel affectionate and is close to her child, she begins to feel endangered and must withdraw from the child. She cannot accept this hostile set, however, and must simulate affection and closeness with the child to deny it. The child must not discriminate accurately between orders of message, in this case the difference between the expression of simulated feelings (one logical type) and real feelings (another logical type). As a result, the child must systematically distort his or her percept of metacommunicative signals. It is essential to appreciate that the double-bind situation is responsible for the inner conflicts of logical typings.

The Palo Alto workers give an example. The mother might say; "Go to bed; you're very tired. I want you to get your sleep." This overtly loving statement is intended to deny a feeling that could be verbalized as: "Get out of my sight because I'm sick of you." This means that the child must deceive him- or herself about his or her own internal state to support the mother in her deception. To survive with her, the child must falsely discriminate his or her own internal messages, thus upsetting the logical typing, as well as falsely discriminate the messages of others. The child is punished for discriminating accurately what the mother is expressing and is punished for discriminating inaccurately—thus caught in a double-bind situation. It is hypothesized that the child continually subjected to this situation develops a psychosis. A psychosis seems a way of dealing with double-bind situations by overcoming their inhibiting and controlling effect.

At first the double bind was studied in relation to a two-party situation, but was later extended to involve a three-party case: mother, father, and child. The parents and schizophrenic child formed a special triadic system in the larger family unit. Psychotic behavior, seen as an attempt to adapt to double-bind situations, was viewed as a sequence of messages that infringed a set of prohibitions that are qualified as not infringing them. The only way an individual could achieve this was by qualifying incongruently all levels of his or her communication. At a later stage, the interest of the workers focused on the many manifestations of incongruent communications in the family.

At the end of 10 years of research, the group agreed on a statement about the double bind (48):

1. The double bind is a class of sequences that appear when phenomena are examined with a concept of levels of communication.
2. In schizophrenia the double bind is a necessary but not sufficient condition in explaining etiology and, conversely, is an inevitable by-product of schizophrenic communication.

3. Empirical study and theoretical description of individuals and families should, for this type of analysis, emphasize observable communication, behavior, and relationship contexts rather than focusing upon the perception or affective states of individuals.

4. The most useful way to phrase double-bind description is not in terms of a binder and a victim, but in terms of people caught up in an ongoing system that produces conflicting definitions of the relationship and consequent subjective distress. In its attempts to deal with the complexities of multilevel patterns in human communications systems, the research group prefers an emphasis upon circular systems of inter-personal relations to a more conventional emphasis upon the behavior of individuals alone or single sequences in the interaction. (p. 157)

Comments on the six criteria are as follows:

1. Yet again, the workers must be able to satisfy psychiatric opinion that they are indubitably studying schizophrenic patients.

2. At first the anomaly of family functioning was isolated as the double-bind hypothesis. However, later this concept was greatly broadened to include incongruent communication and to involve a system or pattern of relating.

3. The direct link between the broad and recent description of anomalies and the onset of schizophrenia is far from clear. This applies even to the narrower concept of the double bind. The results of the treatment of schizophrenic patients by the manipulation of the family anomalies are not sufficiently clear to make a reliable judgment possible.

4. The workers imply that the double bind is a necessary but not sufficient condition to cause schizophrenia. Furthermore, they add that the double-bind situation may result from schizophrenia. It is not known whether the sample employed is a true representative sample of schizophrenic persons as a whole.

5. The anomalies could be present by chance in the families of schizophrenic persons. Controlled studies are not employed. The double-bind situation, for instance, is very common in everyday life. It is also clear that in addition to manifesting or producing double-bind situations, the parents who do this also have a number of other qualities that may be disturbing to the children. It could be argued that these other qualities within the parents are equally significant in producing schizophrenia.

6. Convincing reasons for the development of the illness in adolescence are not given.

A Critical Assessment of Family Dynamics in the Etiology of Schizophrenia

The four main studies reviewed here can be assessed in the light of the six criteria put forward earlier.

First, none of the studies offers a clear definition of schizophrenia by which the subjects under study were selected and that could find unquestioned acceptance by psychiatrists. Visitors from Europe and the United States attending clinics in the other's areas must be impressed with the wide differences in establishing criteria for the diagnosis of schizophrenia. To the writer, the careful criteria for the diagnosis of schizophrenia based on European psychiatry would be met only by a fraction of the patients seen under treatment as being schizophrenic in family-oriented centers in the United States. The remainder, although having a severe degree of pathology, appear to be severely emotionally ill but not schizophrenic. Thus, should this view be substantiated, the findings of studies on these patients would be relevant to emotional illness, but not to schizophrenia. It is essential to have agreement about the criteria for the diagnosis of schizophrenia before findings can be compared and deductions made from the studies.

Second, the anomalies of family functioning said to be associated with the production of schizophrenia in a family member are not always a single, simple, discrete concept. Sometimes they are broad, are sometimes fragmented into a number of parts, and are sometimes several in number. There is general broad agreement that defects of interpersonal communication are involved. But the authorities do not agree on the precise nature of the significant anomalies of communication, and the greater the number of conflicting theories, the more likely they are all to be wrong. Also, the defects of communication noted may, of course, result from the illness and not be the cause of it. In the main, the workers concentrate on one anomaly and take little account of many other coexisting anomalies that may be present. These coexisting anomalies might be equally significant in causing schizophrenia.

Third, regarding the relationship between the anomaly of family functioning and schizophrenia, no direct link is well established in any of the studies. In no instance is the anomaly experimentally produced in order to cause schizophrenia. The results of treatment to relieve the schizophrenia through removal of the anomaly are not convincing.

Fourth, in terms of the existence of an anomaly, most of the workers claim that the anomaly noted is always present in the families of the schizophrenic patients studied. Some maintain, however, that its presence varies with the sex of the schizophrenic person. However, it is not demonstrated that a representative sample of schizophrenic patients is under study.

Fifth, the possibility that the anomalies exist by chance alone is not excluded in any of the studies by adequate controls. Should the English epidemiologic studies (11–13) be correct, approximately one-third of the general population is significantly emotionally disturbed. Should schizophrenic persons come from a representative group of families of the population at large, then in one-third of families of a schizophrenic person, family psychopathology will be found by chance alone. Furthermore, disturbed families are less likely to cope with schizophrenic members, and thus institutionalized schizophrenic persons will be present from such families in greater numbers (i.e., a selection factor may also be operating). It may be true that the psychopathologic mechanisms described in the families of schizophrenic persons may also be found in nonschizophrenic families. Emotional divorce, immaturity, inadequacy, ambivalence, projection, pseudomutuality, stereotyped roles, family schisms, family skews, parental strife, family isolation, distortion of meaning, the double bind, unloving parents, incongruent communication, and mystification are elements found in nonschizophrenic families. Control studies will say to what extent. Experience with problem families would suggest that all pathologic mechanisms are more manifest in severely emotionally disturbed families but do not necessarily give rise to schizophrenia.

Sixth, one may ask why schizophrenia appears in late adolescence, even though family trauma has been bearing on a sensitive organism for a number of years. Some answers are offered. According to Bowen, there is a clash of strength between parent and child in adolescence. According to Wynne, it is a matter of different processes: "disaffiliation" in childhood psychosis and distortion of meaning in adult schizophrenia. Other possibilities remain, however, that are not incompatible with an organic etiology. Many physical conditions are tied to an age of onset.

Additional Comments

As was mentioned earlier, the above six questions are not exhaustive. Further comments can be made.

While it can be argued that the family psychopathology has causal significance for schizophrenia, it can also be held that the presence of schizophrenia causes family psychopathology. It would be strange if such a severe and perplexing disorder did not have some effect on the family state. This must be especially true of childhood psychosis, where one sees the sad disappointment and puzzlement of a mother at the lack of response from her child.

It must be adequately explained why one member of the family develops schizophrenia rather than another, and also why that family member develops schizophrenia rather than some other clinical condition.

Whether the manifest pathology is caused by events within the individual or outside in the family is the essential question. Some workers see processes at work in the family that distort communication, perception, and meaning; an equally large group of workers see distortions resulting from interference with the intracerebral organic machinery of thought and communication (54–56).

Two other possible explanations of the perceptual anomalies are that an underlying constitutional weakness in the individual is released by emotional stress emanating from the family, or that an existing constitutional weakness in a family member provokes a family reaction that may be harmful, but need not necessarily be so. The important and careful study of Pollin et al.

(57) on identical twins may support this view. These possibilities need further exploration.

Finally, I lean toward the view that the anomalies, noted by the workers on family psychopathology reviewed here, are found with additional anomalies in the families of the emotionally ill and, by chance, in the families of schizophrenic persons. These anomalies are not significant in the etiology of schizophrenia, which is probably caused by intracerebral organic factors. The studies, however, are not wasted. Despite their inconclusive nature, the studies undertaken may be the springboard for further conclusive research. Should it ever be established, according to the views of the writer, that the patients under study are not schizophrenic, a great deal will have been learned from these painstaking and ingenious studies about the psychopathology of emotionally disturbed individuals and families.

References

1. Howells JG: Family Psychiatry. Edinburgh, Oliver & Boyd, 1963
2. Ackerman NW: The unity of the family. Archives of Pediatrics 60:51, 1938
3. Ackerman NW, Kempster SW: Family therapy, in Comprehensive Textbook of Psychiatry. Edited by Freedman AM, Kaplan HI. Baltimore, MD, Williams & Wilkins, 1967
4. Howells JG: Family psychopathology and schizophrenia, in Modern Perspectives in World Psychiatry. Edited by Howells JG. New York, Brunner/Mazel, 1971, pp 391–424
5. Howells JG, Guiguis WR: The Family and Schizophrenia. New York, International Universities Press, 1985
6. Kraeplin E: Zur Diagnose und Prognose der Dementia Praecox. Allg Z Psychiat 56:254, 1899
7. Bleuler E: Dementia Praecox oder Gruppe der Schizophrenein, in Handbuch der Psychiatrie. Edited by Aschaffenberg G. Leipzig and Wien, 1911
8. Langfeldt G: The Prognosis in Schizophrenia and the Factors Influencing the Course of the Disease: A Katamnestic Study, Including Individual Re-Examination in 1936. London, Oxford University Press, 1937
9. Stephens JH, Astrup C: Prognosis in 'process' and 'non-process' schizophrenia. Am J Psychiatry 119:945, 1963
10. Stephens JH, Astrup C: Treatment outcome in 'process' and 'non-process' schizophrenics treated by 'A' and 'B' types of therapists. J Nerv Ment Dis 140:449, 1965
11. Pemberton J: Illness in general practice. Br Med J 1:306, 1949
12. Council of the College of General Practitioners: Working party report. Br Med J 2:585, 1958
13. Kessell WIN: Psychiatric morbidity in a London general practice. British Journal of Preventative Social Medicine 14:16, 1960
14. Bowen M: A family concept of schizophrenia, in The Etiology of Schizophrenia. Edited by Jackson D. New York, Basic Books, 1960
15. Morris GO, Wynne LC: Schizophrenic offspring and styles of parental communication. Psychiatry 28:19, 1965

16. Ryckoff I, Day J, Wynne LC: Maintenance of stereotyped roles in the families of schizophrenics. Arch Gen Psychiatry 1:93, 1959
17. Singer MT, Wynne LC: Thought disorder and family relations of schizophrenics, III: methodology using projective techniques. Arch Gen Psychiatry 12:187, 1965
18. Singer MT, Wynne LC: Thought disorder and family relations of schizophrenics, IV: results and implications. Arch Gen Psychiatry 12:201, 1965
19. Wynne LC: Pseudomutuality in the family relations of schizophrenics. Psychiatry 21:205, 1958
20. Wynne LC, Singer MT: Thought disorder and family relations of schizophrenics: a research strategy, in Theory and Practice of Family Psychiatry. Edited by Howells JG. Edinburgh, Oliver & Boyd, 1963, pp 807–819
21. Wynne LC, Singer MT: Thought disorder and family relations of schizophrenics, II: a classification of forms of thinking. Arch Gen Psychiatry 9:199, 1963
22. Cornelison A: Casework interviewing as a research technique in a study of families of schizophrenic patients. Mental Hygiene 44:551, 1960
23. Fleck S: Psychiatric hospitalization as a family experience. Special Treatment Situations 1:29, 1962
24. Fleck S, Cornelison A, Norton N, et al: The intrafamilial environment of the schizophrenic patient, III: interaction between hospital staff and families. Psychiatry 20:343, 1957
25. Fleck S, Freedman DX, Cornelison A, et al: The understanding of symptomatology through the study of family interaction, in Schizophrenia and the Family. Edited by Lidz T, Fleck S, Cornelison A. New York, International Universities Press, 1966
26. Fleck S, Lidz T, Cornelison A, et al: The intrafamilial environment of the schizophrenic patient: incestuous and homosexual problems, in Individual and Familial Dynamics. Edited by Masserman J. New York, Grune & Stratton, 1959
27. Fleck S, Lidz T, Cornelison A: Comparison of parent-child relationships of male and female schizophrenic patients. Arch Gen Psychiatry 8:1, 1963
28. Lidz T: Schizophrenia and the family. Psychiatry 21:21, 1958
29. Lidz T: The relevance of family studies to psychoanalytic theory. J Nerv Ment Dis 135:105, 1962
30. Lidz T, Cornelison A, Fleck S: The limitation of extrafamilial socialization, in Schizophrenia and the Family. Edited by Lidz T, Fleck S, Cornelison A. New York, International Universities Press, 1966
31. Lidz T, Cornelison A, Fleck S, et al: The intrafamilial environment of the schizophrenic patient, I: the father. Psychiatry 20:329, 1957
32. Lidz T, Cornelison A, Fleck S, et al: The intrafamilial environment of the schizophrenic patient, II: marital schism and marital skew. Am J Psychiatry 114:241, 1958
33. Lidz T, Cornelison A, Singer MT, et al: The mothers of schizophrenic patients, in Schizophrenia and the Family. Edited by Lidz T, Fleck S, Cornelison A. New York, International Universities Press, 1966
34. Lidz T, Fleck S, Cornelison A, et al: The intrafamilial environment of the schizophrenic patient, VI: the transmission of irrationality. Archives of Neurology and Psychiatry 79:305, 1958
35. Lidz T, Fleck S: Schizophrenia, human integration and the role of the family, in The Etiology of Schizophrenia. Edited by Jackson D. New York, Basic Books, 1960

36. Lidz T, Fleck S: Family studies and a theory of schizophrenia, in The American Family in Crisis. Des Plaines, IL, Forest Hospital Publications, 1965
37. Lidz T, Fleck S, Alanen Y, et al: Schizophrenic patients and their siblings. Psychiatry 26:1, 1963
38. Lidz T, Fleck S, Cornelison A, et al: The intrafamilial environment of the schizophrenic patient, IV: parental personalities and family interaction. Am J Orthopsychiatry 28:764, 1958
39. Lidz RW, Lidz T: Therapeutic considerations arising from the intense symbiotic needs of schizophrenic patients, in Psychotherapy with Schizophrenics. Edited by Brody EB, Redlich FC. New York, International Universities Press, 1952
40. Lidz T, Schafer S, Fleck S, et al: Ego differentiation and schizophrenic symptom formation in identical twins. J Am Psychoanal Assoc 10:74, 1962
41. Lidz T, Wild C, Schafer S, et al: Thought disorders in the parents of schizophrenic patients: a study of utilizing the object sorting test. J Psychiatr Res 1:193, 1963
42. Rosman B, Wild C, Ricci J, et al: Though disorders in the parents of schizophrenic patients: a further study utilizing the object sorting test. J Psychiatr Res 2:211, 1964
43. Sohler DT, Holzberg J, Fleck S, et al: The prediction of family interaction from a battery of projective tests. Journal of Projective Techniques 21:199, 1957
44. Lidz RW, Lidz T: The family environment of schizophrenic patients. Am J Psychiatry 106:332, 1949
45. Lidz T, Fleck S. Cornelison A: Schizophrenia and the Family. New York, International Universities Press, 1966
46. Fleck S: Family dynamics and origin of schizophrenia. Psychosom Med 22:333, 1960
47. Bateson G, Jackson DD, Haley J, et al: Toward a theory of schizophrenia. Behav Sci 1:251–264, 1956
48. Bateson G, Jackson DD, Haley J, et al: A note on the double bind-1962. Fam Process 2:154, 1963
49. Haley J: The family of the schizophrenic: a model system. American Journal of Nervous and Mental Disease 129:357–374, 1959
50. Haley J: Observation of the family of the schizophrenic. Am J Orthopsychiatry 30:460–467, 1960
51. Jackson DD: The question of family homeostasis. Psychiatr Q (Suppl 31, part 1):79–90, 1957
52. Jackson DD (ed): The Etiology of Schizophrenia. New York, Basic Books, 1960
53. Jackson DD, Weakland JH: Schizophrenic symptoms and family interaction. Arch Gen Psychiatry 1:618–621, 1959
54. McGhie A, Chapman J: Disorders of attention and perception in early schizophrenia. Br J Med Psychol 34:103, 1961
55. Chapman J, McGhie A: A comprehensive study of dysfunction in schizophrenia. Journal of Mental Science. 108:487, 1962
56. McGhie A, Chapman J, Lawson JS: Disturbances in selective attention in schizophrenia. Proc R Soc Lond [Biol] 57:419, 1964
57. Pollin W, Stabenau JR, Tupin J: Family studies with identical twins discordant for schizophrenia. Psychiatry 28:60, 1965

CHAPTER ELEVEN

Psychotherapy of Schizophrenia: 1900–1920

Doris B. Nagel, M.D.

From the beginning of the century until about the mid-1960s there evolved an increasingly significant minority of psychiatrists who practiced with the conviction that an organic disease model for schizophrenia was mistaken and that the syndrome was largely an adaptational problem based on earlier experiences and perhaps some constitutional predisposition. They developed a new type of psychotherapy that aimed at mutual understanding between doctor and patient of the patient's development and of the unconscious conflicts determining his or her symptoms, with the goal of making a healthier form of adaptation possible through abreaction, enhancement of the ego, and conscious choice. Individual psychoanalytic psychotherapy, or interpretative psychiatry, might or might not be accompanied by other forms of psychotherapy, behavior therapy, milieu treatment, family therapy, medication, or other modalities of treatment. These psychiatrists established a rational foundation for their work and attempted to make it increasingly effective, until by the 1950s and 1960s individual intensive psychotherapy of schizophrenia was an acceptable subspecialty among American psychiatrists and there was a rich literature on the subject. In the United States before 1920, the two most influential forerunners in this field were Abraham Arden Brill and Edward J. Kempf, two markedly contrasting

This chapter is based on a presentation delivered at the Regional Meeting of the World Psychiatric Association in New York in November 1981.

characters and intellects, both of whom possessed a passionate therapeutic zeal and devoted a substantial part of their working lives to practicing interpretative psychotherapy with schizophrenic patients.

The European Background

The concepts of *dementia praecox* and *schizophrenia* were originally based on hypotheses of primary organic pathology, which, once known, would largely explain the entire symptom picture and its course over time. Those two diligent observers of asylum patients, Emil Kraepelin in Germany and Eugen Bleuler in Switzerland, prescribed for their patients kindly symptomatic treatments drawn from the medical practice of the times; the forms of psychotherapy recommended were those any medical doctor might utilize to get patients to feel more comfortable during an acute illness, to adapt to a chronic or recurrent condition, and to avoid acute relapse. To Kraepelin or Bleuler, psychotherapy of the disease itself made no more sense than psychotherapy of general paresis or hypothyroidism. As Carl Jung (1) was to recall many years later, in the Burghölzli of 1900–1910, if a patient seemingly recovered through psychotherapy, the diagnosis of schizophrenia had to be changed. Nonetheless, the newly delineated syndrome, comprising patients without gross organic lesions, provided the 20th century with a fresh framework for research and speculation about its nature.

Bleuler was the first academic asylum director to encourage the application of Freud's psychoanalytic theories to hospitalized patients. During the first decade of this century, Zurich's Burghölzli clinic inspired several budding psychotherapists of schizophrenia (2). But despite his interest in psychoanalysis, Bleuler's assumption of a mechanical disruption of associations as the fundamental defect in schizophrenia tended to close the door to psychogenic origin theories and to psychotherapy as a primary mode of treatment. He believed the illness would reveal meaningful complexes, but it was not caused by them (3). Nonetheless, some of his concepts, such as autism and ambivalence, had immense psychodynamic significance and provided an important theoretical foothold for psychotherapeutic thinking. Moreover, his emphasis on a continuum between schizophrenic phenomena and normality fostered a new atmosphere of potential mutuality between doctor and patient.

Bleuler found that the uncovering of emotion-fraught complexes and abreaction did not help his patients, and the slight improvement sometimes seen might be attributable to disguised suggestion. He believed that positive transference, which could be utilized in hysteria, often evolved into pathologic infatuation in schizophrenia, followed by paranoid persecutory delusions that made the treatment unmanageable. Attempts to educate the schizophrenic thinking processes were mostly futile, although "drill" methods could establish simple healthy patterns of living. Intelligent patients particularly could be educated to attain improved self-control despite symptoms (3).

The gifted psychoanalyst Carl Jung went a step further toward a psychotherapeutic orientation than his mentor Bleuler during his early work at the Burghölzli clinic between 1900 and 1909. He drew his inspiration from Freud, whose ideas he ardently supported and spread at that time, while applying the new psychoanalytic theory to hospitalized dementia praecox patients. Although they did not overtly provide a psychotherapeutic orientation, Burghölzi's diagnostic association studies (4) and Jung's influential book on dementia praecox (5) laid out the manner in which unconscious complexes of ideas associated with powerful affects could determine symptoms. Jung decided, moreover, that the irreducible organic element in acute schizophrenia might not be primary. Psychogenetically determined emotional states could generate a metabolic toxin, which in turn produced physiologic alterations and further disruption of personality at times.

Although not admitting it publicly until later, Jung believed the talking cure could work as a primary form of treatment for the condition itself, albeit only in selected patients, enabling the patient to leave the mental disease behind for good (1). From 1903, Jung's technique was to uncover, through the word association test he had devised, the repressed dramatic "story" behind the patient's withdrawal from reality and to seek with the patient a more adaptive resolution of the deeply felt human conflict or dilemma that was unearthed. For Jung this need not be a sexual conflict; it could even consist of overpowering guilt as a result of secretly committed crimes. Jung's theory and methods were interestingly elaborated further in ways that were not widely understood or embraced by psychiatrists of the time.

Kraepelin is usually seen as psychodynamically blind, but his picture of the fundamental difficulties in dementia praecox implied more openings for the psychotherapist than the cognitive theory of Bleuler did. Kraepelin emphasized the reduction of volition and the dulling of feeling for former relationships and pursuits as primary, a picture that corresponded to the importance for psychotherapy of engaging the patient's interest first and foremost.

Kraepelin advised that simple persuasion by a physician possessing "great patience, kindly disposition, and self-control," could sometimes calm excited states when other remedies failed. Open encouragement helped convalescing patients, and discussion of hallucinations and delusions with recovering patients could allow them at least to recognize the symptoms of their own illness (6). But Kraepelin believed that those who were developing psychogenetic theories were building speculative castles in the air, and he dismissed Jung's psychogenetic toxin theory as completely without foundation (7).

The most important contributions underlying the new psychotherapeutic perspective toward schizophrenic patients were, of course, those of Sigmund Freud. In the 1890s he had published cases in which, as in conversion hysteria, certain psychotic symptoms as well seemed to represent psychological defenses determined by unconscious mental conflicts. A temporary or chronic state of hallucinatory wish fulfillment could result from the refusal to accept an unbearable set of events in reality, with repression of both the memory and its affect, and subsequent behavior as though the experience had not occurred (8). Chronic paranoia could be produced by a struggle against the return of repressed memories along with shameful-pleasurable feelings regarding childhood sexual activities, with vague reproaches seeming to issue from others (9). Symptoms that previously seemed simply bizarre now began to make sense, and the physician, with the patient's help, could hope to achieve understanding and possibly assist the conscious resolution of an underlying conflict with permanent strengthening of the ego.

The therapeutic techniques that Freud utilized with hysterical patients could be attempted with patients with dementia praecox as well (10). *The Interpretation of Dreams* (11), once one accepted the explicit analogy between dreaming and psychotic states, provided a brilliantly rich array of instruments for understanding delusions and hallucinations: the role of wish fulfillment, the concept of regression, the distinction between primary and secondary process with the mechanisms of transformation from one to the other, the Oedipus complex, the use of symbolism, and so on. The *Three Essays on the Theory of Sexuality* (12) added a necessary developmental framework within which a therapist could seek the early infantile fixations through whose unconscious persistence symptoms might later break out. Freud's detailed analysis of the case of Schreber (13), although not concerned with treatment, provided a helpful model for looking at paranoid productions. Later, Freud's structural theory would provide still another useful vantage point for the understanding of schizophrenic patients, but even by 1905 the founder of psychoanalysis had provided a solid footing on which psychotherapeutic pioneers could explore the psychotic wilderness in the attempt to guide back out of it a functioning personality. A good discussion of Freud's contribution to a basis for psychoanalytic psychotherapy of schizophrenia can be found elsewhere (14).

Freud's personal antipathy toward human beings who behaved in uncivilized ways and his belief that such patients could not develop a transference discouraged interest in working with them. Nonetheless, a number of his immediate followers gave their attention to these conditions and tried to achieve a psychoanalytic understanding of them, whether or not they were sanguine about treatment. Karl Abraham, Carl Jung, and A. A. Brill (all three of whom counted both Freud and Bleuler among their mentors), Sandor Ferenczi, Paul Federn, Herman Nunberg, Viktor Tausk, and others published important contributions in this field.

The United States

In the United States, the concepts of dementia praecox and schizophrenia became blended and utilized as if they were one. It was Kraepelin's description and classification that were chiefly taught, but a spreading aversion to the implications of the term *dementia praecox* led to early use by many of the designation *schizophrenia* instead. Psychotherapists of schizophrenia ignored or disagreed with the fixed etiologic and prognostic implications of Kraepelin as well as the irreversible cognitive disruption theory of Bleuler, while focussing on the recently formulated diagnostic category whose organic underpinnings, if any, remained to be discovered. They defied Freud's view, too, that the schizophrenic individual could not develop a transference and that the schizophrenic condition represented a final psychological adaptation with which one was not to interfere. The element of inaccessibility might make things difficult, but not impossible for a determined therapist.

In those days, however, it was only a few doctors who sat down with the patients hour after hour to establish a dialogue with them, and most of those who did soon stopped. In the United States, prominent psychiatric teachers and administrators like Adolf Meyer and William Alanson White tended to believe, with the psychotherapists, that schizophrenia was a maladaptation rather than a disease. Utilizing their own psychodynamic knowledge, such as it was, they advised patients and their families and taught and supervised younger physicians. They created unique opportunities for psychoanalytically oriented psychiatrists to study and work with schizophrenic patients, but in the end they obtained little experience themselves in treating psychotic patients directly with psychotherapy. The early reaction of American psychiatrists to psychoanalytic ideas can be found elsewhere (15, 16).

A. A. Brill

A. A. Brill (1874–1948) is known as the first American psychoanalyst, as a founder of the New York Psychoanalytic Society and Institute, as the first translator of Freud's work into English, as the writer of the first American textbook of psychoanalysis, and as a tireless proselytizer for psychoanalysis in the United States. It is less well remembered that he enthusiastically treated any patient who could be kept out of a hospital, and he taught state hospital psychiatrists for many years, generating in them an interest in doing psychotherapeutic work with schizophrenic patients.

An Austrian Jew by birth, Brill immigrated alone and penniless to the United States at age 14 and, pursuing an education with great determination, graduated from Columbia University's medical school in 1903 at the age of 30. The entire psychiatric armamentarium in New York at that time, according to him, consisted of a few nonspecific medications, hydrotherapy, and electrotherapy. There were no physicians specializing in mental treatment, although there was a nonmedical psychotherapy movement gathering momentum in the northeast and competing with physicians for patients. Brill's exposure to psychiatry in medical school consisted of a few lectures about mania, melancholia, paranoia, and general paresis. Illustrative patients were brought in, having been instructed to play their roles to the hilt for the benefit of the students (17).

Working at Central Islip State Hospital in New York from 1903 to 1907,

Brill participated in Adolf Meyer's first series of courses at the Pathological Institute (later Psychiatric Institute) of the New York State Hospitals, where Meyer had embarked on an ambitious program to vitalize the system and to raise its standards for the study and care of patients. Brill read Kraepelin and other European writers recommended by Meyer, and elicited detailed life histories from his patients, occasionally noting puzzling spontaneous recoveries in hospitalized chronic dementia praecox patients. When he wanted to leave the state hospital system for private practice, he determined to learn the best psychotherapeutic methods for treating outpatients. After studying hypnotism, suggestion, persuasion, and reeducation, he went off to Europe in 1907 to seek more effectual methods.

Winding up as one of Bleuler's assistants at Burghölzli for several months, influenced heavily by Jung, meeting Ernest Jones and Sandor Ferenczi, conversing with Freud and becoming his official English translator, he returned to New York as an avid convert to the psychoanalysis of 1908. With him he brought Jung's book on dementia praecox and Freud's hysteria papers, both of which he promptly translated for the benefit of American readers. His psychotherapeutic experiences with patients in Burghölzli had begun to turn him into a therapeutic optimist. He analyzed two dementia praecox patients according to Jung's association test and reported on them at length on his return (18, 19). There are later allusions to one of these patients in Brill's writings, referring to him as having remained well and still in correspondence with Brill. Brill had to be circumspect in referring to him, since the patient can now be identified as a brilliant young man who later became active in the psychoanalytic movement, published papers in the field, and became a key figure in the editing and publishing of Freud's works during the 1920s (20).

Brill modified his technique considerably when working with adult schizophrenic patients. His aims were threefold: 1) to reestablish the patients' contact with reality; 2) to arouse the patients' interest in their own illness, so they would be willing to discuss their hallucinations and delusions; and 3) to help the patients make a socially acceptable adaptation (21).

Diagnosing his patients according to the psychosexual stages of development described by Freud and Abraham, Brill would determine what the patient's infantile fixations were and, over time, would adjust the goals of treatment according to the tenacity of the fixations. Those who could not attain an adult heterosexual adjustment would be helped to sublimate their interests at an earlier stage. After his patients were functioning well, he continued to keep in touch with them indefinitely.

Schizophrenic patients were seen as regressing to an early autoerotic or narcissistic state in which their libido was withdrawn from objects. The patients either remained in their own inner world (chronic schizophrenia) where they could live more peacefully than in an outer world that they could not for any number of reasons tolerate,· or they would attempt to reattach themselves to the external world, transforming it according to the inner struggles that they projected onto it, as in paranoia. It was seen as difficult but not impossible to influence a schizophrenic patient once the detachment from reality had occurred (2).

To achieve rapport, Brill was active. He once gave a young man a reprint of the paper about the successfully treated Burghölzli patient to start the patient talking about his own similar problems. Once he made home visits for months before a patient would come to his office. He believed that almost any patient would eventually develop confidence in the therapist and a passive attachment to him or her.

Brill was open and honest with his patients, challenging their delusions from the start. He deplored the lack of frankness with which most doctors approached the psychotic patient, because it added to the patient's confusion and corrupted the doctor. Nor did the psychoanalytic disciple abandon other approaches if he thought they were serviceable. He educated, hypnotized, persuaded, advised, suggested, admonished, and manipulated the environments of his patients throughout his professional career. His methods were more like those of a contemporary eclectic psychotherapist than of a present day psychoanalyst.

Edward J. Kempf

In contrast to Brill, Edward J. Kempf (1885–1971) was a native American innovator and synthesizer. He grew up as the oldest child in a large Catholic medical family in the Midwest. As an undergraduate at the University of Indiana, his chief mentor was the psychologist Ernest K. Lindley, a former student of G. Stanley Hall and friend of William James and Adolf Meyer. His chief intellectual inspiration came from reading the works of Charles Darwin, whose views on evolution made Kempf relinquish his religious beliefs. Kempf entered Western Reserve Medical School with an intense interest in understanding human evolution through the study of physiology and pathology. Before he graduated in 1910, he had been introduced to Sherrington's and Pavlov's work and methods, which led him to view human activities and the mind in terms of complex integrated sensorimotor reflex circuits. As a medical student, he read about European psychiatric concepts, including Kraepelin's, and assimilated William Alanson White's *Mental Mechanisms* (22) and Freud's *Studies on Hysteria* (10) and *Three Essays on the Theory of Sexuality* (12), both of which Brill had recently translated.

After a disappointing year at the Cleveland State Hospital following graduation, where Kraepelin's classification was used but no one was doing psychotherapeutic work or psychopathologic research, Kempf moved to the Central Hospital for the Insane in Indianapolis in 1912–1913. There he independently developed a system of psychoanalyzing the symptoms of dementia praecox, applying Freud's theory as he understood it from the book on hysteria. His "medical psychological" treatment methods resulted in dismissal from his job, but Ernest Lindley helped him obtain a position under Adolf Meyer in the newly opened Phipps Clinic at Johns Hopkins University in Baltimore. There, too, Kempf came into conflict with his colleagues because (as he later recalled it in a letter dated September 7, 1959 to Burnham [23]) they could not accept his radical view that

> each specific symptom was evidence of a special psychopathological function in the patient that had been caused by special oppressive condemnations by special persons. In other words, the patient had been criticised, shamed, and ridiculed into repressing from consciousness, so as to forget, what had been condemned in himself as shameful, unclean, sinful, and guilty, by someone in his family or other impressive person. (p. 7)

These special persons either had to be analyzed themselves and become collaborators in the patient's treatment or had to be eliminated from the patient's life if the patient was to recover and remain well.

In 1914 Kempf assumed the post of clinical psychiatrist at St. Elizabeths Hospital in Washington, DC, a position newly created by William Alanson White to enable its holder to pursue psychoanalytic research with the large number of psychotic patients there. The period from 1914 until 1920, when Kempf moved to New York City, was an immensely productive one, resulting in several papers and Kempf's two major early books. He was avidly observing, actively theorizing, and intensively treating schizophrenic patients and their families, as well as observing lower primates to compare their sexual behavior with that of humans.

In his first book, *The Autonomic Functions and the Personality* (24), Kempf made a remarkable although premature, synthesis of current knowledge from various fields, particularly evolutionary theory, neurophysiology, reflexology, psychology of emotion, behaviorism, and psychoanalysis. He created a monistic physiologic model of human psychology, giving a central role to the autonomic apparatus and its "segmental cravings." This model was applied to the study, classification, and treatment of psychiatric problems in his finest and most influential work, *Psychopathology* (25), published in 1920.

Kempf's therapeutic methods were consistent with his evolving theoretical model and the psychodynamic classification that he devised. All therapeutic approaches must aim at reducing asocial autonomic cravings (akin to but different from Freud's infantile sexual fixations) or at strengthening the ego so it can control cravings by dominating the final motor pathway to action.

The ego was viewed as a compensatory integration that has evolved so as to allow the organism to maintain physical fitness and to act as a unity. The compensatory status makes it vulnerable to disintegration under various influences such as fatigue, illness, toxins, drugs, and injuries. Therefore, the first principle in treating pernicious dissociation neuroses (as he called schizophrenia) was to eliminate any toxins, or precipitants (including oppressive associates), and to restore the physical strength of the organism. The psychotic or delirious patient must be kept happy and free of causes of fear or anger. If this can be accomplished and there is no organic damage, the prognostic outlook is good. For example, a psychosis in which incestuous cravings are evident should subside in due time when the patient is removed from the stimulating milieu and nursed in a way that satisfies preadolescent cravings. Once the acute psychosis subsides, psychoanalysis may begin. Like Brill, Kempf did not exclude any other methods that might assist recovery as well, and he emphasized the need for an active stance on the part of the therapist.

Although Kempf utilized and incorporated Freud's early thinking into his frame of reference, his therapeutic techniques differed from Freud's in significant ways. He confronted the patient eye to eye and allowed the patient to assume any postural attitude at any time, while those postures were interpreted as readily as if they were verbal communications. Kempf associated the Freudian analyst's position behind a reclining patient with an authoritarian stance, while he preferred a model of brotherly egalitarianism. He proceeded by sympathetic questioning, guiding the patient's attention and interest. An altruistic transference must be developed and maintained. In the context of this rapport, the patient becomes aware of his or her repressed craving and must express it in words without restraining the affect associated with it.

Developmentally, Kempf reasoned, the socialized ego is built around the employment of the speech apparatus, and speech becomes the chief weapon of socialized defense and aggression. If the "hypertense" segment is allowed to control speech, it thereby makes a common adjustment with the tendencies of the other autonomic segments, and the repressed affect is assimilated into the ego.

Kempf's career after 1920 is fascinating to follow, but his later activities and fall into obscurity will not be considered here. His early publications provided a major impetus to Harry Stack Sullivan's work with schizophrenic patients, and *Psychopathology* (25) was widely read. He influenced not only a number of younger practitioners but some of his mentors as well, including Meyer and White.

Both Brill and Kempf reported numerous case studies showing dramatically good results of psychoanalytic psychotherapy with schizophrenic patients, and both reported failures as well. They were fully aware of the time-consuming and difficult nature of the work and the fact that any one therapist could work with relatively few such patients over a lifetime, but both men persisted throughout their lives in their belief that for many patients falling in the category of schizophrenia the so-called disease was, rather, an understandable developmental adaptation capable of change.

Conclusion

We approach the close of the 20th century with increased knowledge about human beings as organisms and as personalities. While psychiatric research on schizophrenia veers again in the organic direction, all the old questions about these conditions, their possible origins, and their treatment are still unanswered, and no one can lay claim to a properly balanced perspective. As long as this remains so, we can expect new generations of dedicated psychiatric missionaries to arise and develop better ways to lead the alienated back, through personal influence and understanding, which for many is and will remain the only hope, to participate more fully in human society. The next generation will have a deeply interesting record of earlier experiences from which to learn. In this field, the early 20th century workers, as well as the more varied and sophisticated therapists who followed, can still provide not only inspiration but useful theories and techniques.

References

1. Jung CG: Memories, Dreams, Reflections. Edited by Jaffe A. New York, Vantage, 1961
2. Brill AA: Lectures on Psychoanalytic Psychiatry. New York, Knopf, 1947
3. Bleuler E: Dementia Praecox, or the Group of Schizophrenias. New York, International Universities Press, 1950
4. Jung CG (ed): Studies in Word Association (1918). London, Routledge & Kegan Paul, 1969
5. Jung CG: The psychology of dementia praecox (1907), in G.G. Jung: The Collected Works, Vol 3. Edited by Read R, Fordham M, Adler G. London, Routledge & Kegan Paul, 1960, pp 1–152
6. Diefendorf AR: Clinical Psychiatry. New York, MacMillan, 1912 (Abstracted from the 1903–1904 7th German edition of Emil Kraepelin's Lehrbuch der Psychiatrie)
7. Kraepelin E: Dementia Praecox and Paraphrenia. Edited by Robertson G. New York, Robert Krieger, 1971 (From the 1909–1913 8th edition of Kraepelin's Lehrbuch, Vol 3, part 2)
8. Freud S: The neuro-psychoses of defence (1894), in The Standard Edition of the Complete Psychological Works of Sigmund Freud, Vol 3. Translated and edited by Strachey J. London, Hogarth Press, 1962, pp 43–61
9. Freud S: Further remarks on the neuro-psychoses of defence (1896), in The Standard Edition of the Complete Psychological Works of Sigmund Freud, Vol 3. Translated and edited by Strachey J. London, Hogarth Press, 1962, pp 159–185
10. Freud S, Breuer J: Studies on hysteria (1895), in The Standard Edition of the Complete Psychological Works of Sigmund Freud, Vol 2. Translated and edited by Strachey J. London, Hogarth Press, 1955
11. Freud S: The interpretation of dreams (1900), in The Standard Edition of the Complete Psychological Works of Sigmund Freud, Vols 4 and 5. Translated and edited by Strachey J. London, Hogarth Press, 1958
12. Freud S: Three essays on the theory of sexuality (1905), in The Standard Edition of the Complete Psychological Works of Sigmund Freud, Vol 7. Translated and edited by Strachey J. London, Hogarth Press, 1953, pp 125–243
13. Freud S: Psycho-analytic notes on an autobiographical account of a case of paranoia (1911), in The Standard Edition of the Complete Psychological Works

of Sigmund Freud, Vol 12. Translated and edited by Strachey J. London, Hogarth Press, 1958, pp 3–79

14. Boyer LB, Giovacchini PL (eds): Psychoanalytic Treatment of Schizophrenic and Characterological Disorders. New York, Science House, 1967
15. Burnham JC: Psychoanalysis and American Medicine, 1894–1918: Medicine, Science, and Culture. New York, International Universities Press, 1967
16. Hale NJ, Jr: Freud and the Americans: The Beginnings of Psychoanalysis in the United States, 1876–1917. New York, Oxford University Press, 1971
17. Brill AA: Freud's Contribution to Psychiatry. New York, WW Norton, 1944
18. Brill AA: Psychological factors in dementia praecox: an analysis. J Abnorm Psychol 3:219–239, 1908
19. Brill AA: A case of schizophrenia. American Journal of Insanity 66:53–70, 1909–1910
20. McGuire W (ed): The Freud/Jung Letters. Princeton, NJ, Princeton University Press, 1974 (Letters 280 F and 282 J, pp 458 and 461)
21. Brill AA: Schizophrenia and psychotherapy. Am J Psychiatry 9:519–542, 1929
22. White WA: Mental Mechanisms (Monograph Series No 8). New York, Journal of Nervous and Mental Disease Publishing, 1911
23. Kempf DC, Burnham JC (eds): Edward J. Kempf: Selected Papers. Bloomington, IN, Indiana University Press, 1974
24. Kempf EJ: The Autonomic Functions and the Personality (Monograph Series No 28). New York, Journal of Nervous and Mental Disease Publishing, 1918
25. Kempf EJ: Psychopathology. St. Louis, MO, CV Mosby, 1920

Index